# THREE PLAYS

# Welsh Writing in English

(General Editors: James A. Davies & Belinda Humfrey)

This volume is published by Seren Books in the above series for the Association for the Study of Welsh Writing in English.

*Already published*

Caradoc Evans, *My People*, ed. John Harris (1987).
Caradoc Evans, *Nothing to Pay*, ed. John Harris (Carcanet, 1988).
Emyr Humphreys, *A Toy Epic*, ed. M. Wynn Thomas (1989).
Dannie Abse, *The View from Row G: Three Plays*, ed. James A. Davies (1990)

*In Preparation*

Idris Davies, *The Longer Poems*.
Glyn Jones, *The Island of Apples*.

# GWYN THOMAS

## THREE PLAYS

**Edited by Michael Parnell**

SEREN BOOKS

SEREN BOOKS is the book imprint of
Poetry Wales Press Ltd
Andmar House, Tondu Road, Bridgend
Mid Glamorgan

**British Library Cataloguing in Publication Data**
Thomas, Gwyn *1913–1981*
    Three plays.
    I. Title    II. Parnell, Michael *1934–*
82.914

ISBN 1–85411–017–9

*The publisher acknowledges the financial support of the
Welsh Arts Council*

Typeset in 10½ point Plantin by Megaron, Cardiff
Printed by Dotesios Printers Ltd, Trowbridge.

# Contents

7 Introduction

23 The Keep

97 Jackie the Jumper

155 Loud Organs

220 Appendices

227 Notes

# Introduction

## 1. The Writer

Although Gwyn Thomas as a schoolmaster in Cardigan in 1941 undertook and enjoyed the responsibilities of producing *The Mikado* as the annual school play, with the musical side looked after by Leslie Wynne Evans, and although all his life he loved to visit the theatre, especially to see an opera on those occasions when his limited purse would run to it, it never occurred to him when he began to be accepted as a writer that he might look to the theatre as a proper outlet for his work. The only evidence that he might have experimented at all in this direction is to be found in a notebook, dating from about 1935, in which a dozen pages or so are occupied by an abortive attempt at a play; at the end of these scribbled pages, losing patience, he wrote: "Rotten. Rotten. There's no shape at all about what I do."

Yet there was about his writing from the first published stories in 1946 a certain elusive dramatic quality, even though he seldom used dialogue as such. Perceptive readers wondered whether films could not be made from his books. Nothing ever came of any of a number of proposals, but options on *The Alone to the Alone* and *All Things Betray Thee* were purchased in Hollywood; the possibilities were there. The first person actively to encourage Thomas to write more dialogue was Glyn Jones, who in 1950 showed his belief in the potential of the schoolteacher then working locally in the Barry Boys' Grammar School by introducing him to Elwyn Evans, a drama producer with the BBC. Encouraged to try his hand at something for radio, Thomas eventually set about adapting a short autobiographical piece he had written for *Coal*, 'Then Came We Singing'. This lyrically recalled the glorious summer of 1926 when, as boys, he and his brothers had revelled in the outburst of creative energy shown by the striking miners when they began to march and counter-march about the valleys of

7

South Wales in rival bands, weirdly and wonderfully got up in carnival gear, and playing their music on any makeshift instruments that came to hand. Finally and successfully turned into a radio play in 1952, the story enjoyed an enthusiastic reception under the new title, 'Gazooka'. Within a short time it was repeated on the BBC's national network. Responding to clamorous repeats for a sequel, Thomas followed 'Gazooka' with several more radio plays during the 1950s, introducing to a public that seemed to delight in it his personal recreation of the Rhondda world of the Thirties, complete with a cast of recurring characters like Mathew Sewell the Sotto, Gomer Gough the Gavel, Milton Nicholas, Edwin Pugh the Pang and Teilo Dew the Doom, who also figured in numerous short stories that began to be published regularly in *Punch* during the decade.

All this activity eventually brought Thomas to the attention of George Devine who, at the Royal Court Theatre, was earnestly anxious to find new writers whose work could be mounted and promoted by his English Stage Company. Devine first wrote to Thomas when founding his new venture in 1956. By this time involved in more work than he could easily cope with (still a schoolmaster, he was also producing a novel a year for Gollancz, radio plays, regular pieces for *Punch*, and beginning a career as a broadcaster with regular appearances on 'The Brains Trust' and 'Tonight'), Thomas found himself willing to experiment in theatrical writing with Devine's supervision but barely able to find time in which to start. In 1958 he published what was to be his last novel, *The Love Man*. With a story based on his highly unusual view of the Don Juan legend, the novel had been preceded by a radio play on the same theme the previous year; so effective was the play, and so relatively satisfying was the monetary reward derived from writing plays for radio rather than from the long and sometimes disappointingly rewarded haul of novel-writing, that Thomas decided to apply himself more seriously to the task suggested by Devine. After two more years and several revisions of his material in consultation with his new mentor, Thomas was able to place a finished version of *The Keep* on the table and a new phase of his career was about to begin.

*The Keep* was first offered to the public for a single performance directed by Graham Crowden on a Sunday in August, 1960. In an anticlimax that was somehow typical of the ill luck which frequently attended Thomas's personal enterprises, a cloudburst descended on London and the Royal Court's auditorium was four feet under water by the time cast and audience assembled. Recalled to give the play a second chance the following Sunday, the audience was immensely enthusiastic, and just over a year later the Royal Court put it on for a season in a new production directed by John Dexter. It received splendid reviews and established for Gwyn Thomas a promising reputation as a playwright. Published both as an individual play and as one of J.C. Trewin's *Plays of the Year* (Volume 24), it later became a repertory favourite, was translated into German and received a rapturous welcome in Hamburg, was broadcast in a version for television, and almost became the basis of a film in which Richard Burton was all set to take a starring role until other matters intervened.

After the warm reception afforded to *The Keep*, Devine was not slow to urge Thomas to provide another script for his company, and this followed in the shape of *Jackie the Jumper* in 1962. Convinced that he had another important play on his hands, Devine set up a production to be directed again by John Dexter for early February, 1963. The critics welcomed the play warmly enough, but the weather was during that month the coldest and most inhospitable for decades; after a few weeks when too few people braved the winter to come and see the play, Devine was forced to withdraw it. Trewin again chose it as one of his *Plays of the Year* (Volume 26) and the theatre magazine *Plays and Players* printed the text, but despite this critical interest the play was considered to have failed and it has never been revived,

Meanwhile another producer had taken a great interest in Thomas's potential after the success of *The Keep*; this was the young and aristocratic entrepreneur, Richard Rhys, wealthy son of Lord Dynevor. Rhys met Thomas and together they sketched out an exciting idea for a play with music to be set in the notorious and neglected docks area of Cardiff. Rhys wanted it to be called 'Tiger Bay' but Thomas, ever one to go his own way, was fascinated with the possibilities which had been drawn to his attention by a television producer friend, John

9

Mead, arising from the use being made in Butetown of a former chapel now being converted into a nightclub. Out of this came the punning title *Loud Organs* for a play that was doomed in 1962 to be no more successful than *Jackie the Jumper* was to be in 1963. *Loud Organs* failed a provincial tryout both in Blackpool and Cardiff for various reasons, among which must be counted the tension which arose between producer and author when the one wanted to turn the piece into a full-scale musical with all the (hideously expensive) trappings of orchestra, dancers, crowd scenes and the conventions of the musical, while the other was primarily concerned with the words and the exploration of a theme. The play did not make it to its planned London venue, nor was the text ever published; the reasons for its being included in this volume are rehearsed below.

One further disappointment affected Thomas's outlook on the theatre at this time. While the creative juices were over-flowing he conceived and worked out with Gerry Rafferty, at the Theatre Royal at Stratford East, an idea for a play with music about the First World War. Contracts were exchanged and Thomas duly delivered his outline and a list of the First World War songs which he thought could be used to punctuate the action. A long silence then ensued, at the end of which, without a word of apology or explanation to Thomas, the Theatre Workshop production of *Oh What a Lovely War*, 'conceived and directed by Joan Littlewood', burst upon a delighted world. Although his wife was outraged and urged that he should take steps to establish his rights in the show, Thomas preferred to put his now-complete script of the play he had been intending to call *Sap* into a drawer, together with other typescripts which had failed to find favour, and forget it.

After this burst of activity, with four stage plays conceived, and three of them written, produced and critically disposed of in as many years, Thomas took stock of his position and decided that despite the happy outcome of *The Keep* (which provided him with a steady income for several years) the theatre was not for him. Instead he allowed his hitherto tentative immersion in yet another new career to become complete. Giving up teaching at last in 1962, he signed an exclusive contract with Television Wales and the West and became a full-time media-man, appearing frequently before the cameras, travelling widely to make film documentaries and consolidating a reputation as a reliable anchor-man with an endless store of words and anecdotes.

The loss to the theatre was not total however. Summarising briefly, he was tempted back several times, producing plays which, though they did not have the impact of *The Keep*, did achieve production, in Wales if not in London, and which may yet be discovered to have real life in them. One play, never yet seen, was written in the mid-60s for Richard Burton, and failed to get into production only because of a series of unfortunate mistimings; entitled *Return and End*, it was an impressionistic fictionalisation of events in the life of a Welsh politician not wholly unlike Aneurin Bevan. Some of the actors and directors who have read it have been so hopeful for the play that it seems possible that its chance may yet come.

In the 1970s there were three further productions. Having allowed *Sap* to lie in the unwanted articles drawer for a decade, Thomas was persuaded to make it available to the Welsh Drama Company, and Michael Geliot's production at the Sherman Theatre in 1974 was highly praised. Two years later *The Breakers*, a new play specially commissioned to celebrate the bicentenary of the United States' Declaration of Independence, was also performed at the Sherman Theatre. Insufficiently edited and under-rehearsed, it was not granted universal acclaim, though Bernard Levin perceived in it a play of potential greatness. Finally, again in Cardiff, a play entitled *Testimonials*, re-worked from a successful broadcast play, received an intelligent and efficient production by Theatr yr Ymylon in early 1979, and there were those who saw it who thought it as good as anything currently playing in London.

When a volume of Gwyn Thomas's dramatic work was first mooted, the idea was to select three or four of what might be argued to be his best plays and leave it at that. Even after the decision was made to include only theatre plays, as opposed to the wealth of radio and television dramatic pieces which might challenge for attention, choosing turned out to be difficult, for all the plays, both those previously published and those existing only in production typescript, read very well on the page. In the event we have preferred to regard this as a first volume in a series and to offer here the first three plays in the order in which they were written. At a later stage a further book will, if the demand appears sufficient, offer *Sap, The Breakers* and *Testimonials*; and a third may in due course appear containing two plays originating in the life and career of Aneurin Bevan: *Return and End* intended for the stage and *A Tongue for a Stammering Time*, commissioned for television, quite different from each other in method and treatment, each a remarkable complement to the other.

Born in Cymmer, Porth, in the Rhondda valley in 1913, Gwyn Thomas was the youngest of the twelve children of a largely unemployed coalminer. His mother dying when he was six years old, he was brought up by his youngest sister Nana, eleven years his senior, in a crowded and under-funded house which contrived somehow through the difficult postwar years to be full of life, laughter, music, song and often highfalutin' talk. A clever pupil at the Rhondda Intermediate School, he was influenced by a charismatic Swiss émigré teacher, Georges Rochat, and followed his brilliant brother Walter into higher education, going to St Edmund Hall, Oxford to read French and Spanish. Ill-suited to the study of languages despite his success, and unable to adapt to the English and wealthy world he found in the university, he was one of the sorriest, saddest undergraduates of his time; he was surpassing glad when he had taken his degree to return to his home in the Rhondda, albeit to a period of unemployment that dragged on for almost six years.

Occasional work as a lecturer for the WEA helped pass the time, as did abortive attempts to become a writer, until at last in 1940 he got a job as a teacher in Cardigan, transferring two years later to Barry. Encouraged by his wife Lyn, whom he married in 1938, he began after the war to submit some of the stories he had been writing to publishers and found success at last. From 1946 until 1958 he published novels at regular intervals, enjoying at least one particular triumph with *All Thing Betray Thee* in 1949. Taken up by *Punch* in 1953, he contributed many short stories over the next fifteen years, some of which were later republished in collected editions. A career in broadcasting became possible after the popularity accorded his radio plays during the 1950s and in the 1960s he made frequent television appearances. His ventures into writing for the theatre have been described above; at the same time he wrote a great deal of journalism and became a popular and provocative columnist.

Suffering from poor health during much of his life, he became seriously ill with diabetes in the late 1960s and was much troubled throughout his remaining years with problems related to the disease. Although his mind remained unaffected, he was physically debilitated by the mid-70s. Even so, his death at the age of 67 in 1981 came as a great shock to many, as he had succeeded in concealing from all but those closest to him both the extent of his illness and the despair he suffered in consequence of it.

Except for brief forays abroad, virtually his whole life was spent in or near the Rhondda Valley, where he conceived all that was significant in his life to lie and whence he could never be with any happiness. Lucrative offers to come to London and make a killing in the entertainment world were always turned down; even when he was out of South Wales just for a few days to make a film or take a holiday, he pined to return, and more than once he inconvenienced a whole film crew by his inability to cope with life away from his native country. It is hardly surprising then to find that, with the exception only of the novel *The Love Man* and two other (unpublished) novels set in Spain, virtually everything he ever wrote has a Welsh setting, or, to be more precise, a setting in or near those valleys of South Wales which he knew and loved beyond all other places in the world. This is as true of his theatre plays as of all the rest of his work, providing one of a number of factors common to the three plays in this volume. Besides the setting, the plays enshrine also Thomas's extraordinary gifts of comic and poetic language, the vitality of his enquiry into the whys and wherefores of an unequal society, the courage of his search for truth about individual and social relationships, the sardonic force of his ironical perceptions about human institutions and interactions, and the sheer, gutsy enjoyment of all the absurd tricks life plays upon its petty players.

# Gwyn Thomas's First Three Plays

Thomas was not as a writer any more than as a man notably self-disciplined. He wrote essentially to please himself, filling exercise book or sheets of paper and tossing them aside for his wife to type up. He claimed that his method was to think things out very thoroughly beforehand, often while going about his normal duties in something of a trance-like state, so that by the time he found an opportunity to write his pieces down all the preliminary work had been done. After that it was simply a matter of getting them onto paper as rapidly as possible. Certainly those who saw him writing testify that the process seemed speedy and to involve no hesitation, no crossings-out, no hurling aside of crumpled and rejected sheets. Having finished, he would leave the rest to his wife, who would type exactly what she saw, leaving, where she could not decipher the writing, gaps for Thomas to fill in later. He made virtually no revisions on reading through the typescript, confining himself to correcting the occasional word mis-read by Lyn or adjusting a mis-spelling where he noticed one.

While this system may have worked well enough, many of Thomas's readers have on occasion wished that he had been fortunate enough to find at his publisher's an editor who, while enjoying the marvellous fluency and individuality of his author's writing, might yet have seen that it would benefit from judicious pruning and tightening, someone like the perceptive and indefatigable Edward Garnett at Cape's in earlier decades of the century. At Gollancz in the 1950s, Hilary Rubenstein was content to deal with Thomas's offerings as immaculate typescripts requiring little or no attention. One of the consequences was that Gwyn Thomas's novels never quite achieved the enduring popularity and importance predicted for them; despite the tremendously enthusiastic welcome extended to his books by a number of reviewers, the public at large found his writings more diffuse and difficult to cope with than it liked.

Even so, by the late 1950s Thomas had begun to learn something of the requirements of dramatic form from two kinds of experience in particular. The regular demand from *Punch* for short stories of no more than 1500 to 2000 words had forced him to be less prodigal of images and to write less tortuous sentences. Secondly, his scripts for radio plays had required a great deal of revision and cutting in order to fit specific time-slots precisely and to achieve the effects sought by the experienced BBC producers with whom he was working. In these processes he learned a great deal about compression and suggestion from Elwyn Evans, to whom a large proportion of the success of 'Gazooka' was due. By 1960, when Thomas was working seriously on a draft of *The Keep*, he was more ready than ever before to acknowledge the need for consultation with those who knew intimately how theatre worked and to undertake revisions and incorporate suggestions when he was convinced they were necessary.

In the great burst of released energy that accompanied his decision to retire from school-teaching in 1962, he wrote three plays which are all, compared with his earlier expansive novels, necessarily and fortunately the product of a relatively disciplined approach. They are nonetheless the product also of the man Paul Ferris called "the greatest talker in the world", and they show unequivocally that, given time and the right kind of constructive criticism, Thomas was able to achieve that balance between talk and action upon which a play depends for its dramatic impact. *The Keep* and *Jackie the Jumper* both have at their hearts critical situations with potentially explosive resolutions; if the crux of *Loud Organs* is less sharply defined, the audience is nevertheless kept interested to the end in wondering about Jim Bumford's function and purposes and how his problems will be solved. In all three plays casts of characters are efficiently and naturally assembled, situations rapidly established and deftly developed, and human dilemmas humorously and poetically explored. Whereas *The Keep* is in many ways conventional, however, set in one room of a typical house in a South Wales valley town and finding its level somewhere between drawing-room comedy and kitchen-sink domestic tragedy, both *Jackie the Jumper* and *Loud Organs* are experimental. In both there is a use of music and of an intriguing mixture of the real and the fantastic which shows a writer anxious to bridge the gap between straight drama and other forms of theatrical expression.

In all three plays there is a sense of the seriousness and

importance of the themes being explored despite the levity of much of the treatment. *The Keep* particularly was hailed as a comic masterpiece and reviewers spoke rapturously of the continuous gales of laughter which rocked the audience. Behind the laughter however there was the pain of bewilderment and dissatisfaction which informed an insistent subtext. For the material of his first play for the theatre, Thomas had perhaps inevitably turned back to his memories of growing up in the bosom of a large family in a South Wales valley. In his introduction to the published version of *The Keep*, he spoke of his interest in the way some families "burst apart like bombs and never again achieve unity" while others "grow circular, deep like old ponds". The Mortons are a united family, so inward looking indeed that they are "creating for themselves a sort of velvet tomb". A father, five brothers and a sister, all adult but unmarried (since the materfamilias or 'Mam' figure has long since died when the play opens), live together in the house that has always been their home; the play examines their responses when briefly an opportunity arises to re-examine and perhaps change radically the way of life they have fallen into.

One can hardly read the text without recalling that the author lived until he was in his late twenties in a terraced house which was also home to his widowed father, to a selection of seven elder brothers who only slowly disappeared to lead their own lives elsewhere, and to several sisters. This is not to suggest that the play is autobiographical, though it undoubtedly throws psychological light of value to those interested in Thomas's life. Whether he felt the family to be a destructive trap in his own case does not matter so much as the use he makes of the concept in *The Keep*, where the family home is an intellectual prison in which the men have half-willingly incarcerated themselves. The keep of a castle may be seen as the inner fortress, the last bastion of defence, but it may also represent a prison — in several of his short stories, Thomas referred to the local gaol as "the County Keep", as if this were a commonly bandied term for such an institution.

While the symbol may have been inspired by some aspects of his recollections of life in a crowded Rhondda house in the 1930s, the Morton family is clearly and inventively different from Thomas's own, and the period of the play is significantly postwar, set quite specifically in 1954. For Thomas, this decade of new opportunity and prosperity, of a return to full employment after the devastating years of decline and desolation, had already begun to turn sour. He understood, as his Introduction acknowledged, that "our community, between mammoth explosions, a unique range of apocalyptic terrors, and a severely trussed sensuality", had taken on some fascinating bruises. His play was, he said, "a May-day parade of our more twitching neuroses". To over-simplify, perhaps, the problem was that, instead of incorporating the splendid philosophical yearnings of the pre-war years of penury, the new, more comfortable society seemed to be forgetting the old ideals of cultural and intellectual improvement and abandoning itself instead to mindless pastimes, sinking through an addiction to soap-opera and bingo. This perception manifests itself in *The Keep* with a certain wry bleakness that is not altogether cancelled out by the joyous comic exploration of the weaknesses of the Mortons, their general ineffectiveness despite their several gifts.

The problems faced by the Mortons however are timeless as well as of the 1950s, for they arise from the very institution of which they are part. It is this which lends the play something of the universality which made it transposable into German: families are little worlds in which there are hierarchies, traditions, regulations, expectations, and assumptions that have to be negotiated by their members, and although the world projected by *The Keep* is distinctively south Welsh, it works according to rules and methods recognisable in many communities around the world. The weak father and the talented but irresolute brothers are ineffective because in thrall, to the authority of their departed mother, to their sense of family and unity against a hostile world, to their fear of the untamed world; they cling to each other and succeed in enslaving their not-unwilling sister not so much because they like the status quo but for fear of finding something worse if they embark on their own lives. After the witty and comical account which the play offers of their little rebellion against the dominant and ambitious but small-minded eldest brother, he too is reduced to a non-threatening figure when, in a splendid coup de théâtre, the news comes that their mother is not dead

17

but fled to a free new life, releasing the sister at last from bondage and leaving the men to sort out some sort of life for themselves, the keep having crumbled at last.

This theme of freedom and responsibility which animates the play is not allowed to dominate it nor to render its development solemn and unpalatable. On the contrary, the dialogue is full of wit and comicality. The anger and despair of the characters is expressed with resignation, the stratagems of Constantine the schemer are ridiculous but also horribly convincing, and the opportunities for Ben and his children to reflect, often aphoristically, on the bewilderments of life are seized with joyous confidence. It is an astonishing thing, a happy and well-made play about life perceived as an inevitably unhappy and destructive absurdity.

In *Jackie the Jumper* Thomas sought a means of dramatising a symbolic story of great importance to the Welsh but again of a wider human significance. He had in his well-received 1949 novel, *All Things Betray Thee*, already explored in one form his fascination with the story of Dic Penderyn, the martyred hero of the Merthyr riots of the 1830s. There he eschewed any suggestion that the meaning could effectively be pointed by presenting a straight historical narrative account of the rebellion. In his play however he goes even further than in the novel to remove his core story from the known historical facts in the case. Derived from the original martyr by way of Thomas's version of him as John Simon Adams in *All Things Betray Thee*, Jackie Rees is a rebel as germane to the 1960s as his original was to the 1830s; ostensibly and loosely set in the nineteenth century, the play embraces both particular and general rebelliousness, seeing the battle essentially as between youth and age, between vitality and entrenched conservatism, and ending on a curious and variously interpreted note of ambiguity.

Far from being a historical narrative play, *Jackie the Jumper* is a fantasy, musically elaborated; its form owes something to fairy tale. In his description of the play in the Introduction to *Plays of the Year*, J.C. Trewin noted its "swirl of language, its sudden lyrical passages, its modulation into balladry" as part of its attractive individuality. Thomas attributed the nature of the play to his youthful predilection for grand opera, whose

18

delicious confections of arrant nonsense fitted in only too well with "a social ambience so emphatically tainted with lunacy as that of a mining area moving into dereliction". The world of Jackie Rees contains, like the world of Dic Penderyn, two great anti-life forces: that of capitalism and exploitation, represented by the iron-masters and property-owners on the one hand, and that of repressive spiritual authority represented by the puritanical Reverend Richie Rees. Jackie takes them both on and, after early reversal and then a near triumph, either comes near to being overcome by them or is actually destroyed at their hands, depending upon how you read the final lines of the play. The songs and musical interludes are integral to the action, expressing and intensifying moods of gentleness and rumbustiousness.

Extremely well constructed, the play offers a remarkable account, playful and touching, challenging and wise, of some basic and baffling human oppositions, and it seems extraordinary that after its withdrawal in the middle of the hard winter of 1963 no one has since perceived its value and attempted a further production.

*Loud Organs* extends the interest Thomas was taking at the time in music as a vital element in drama. Set in a night-club which is based in a former chapel in Cardiff's dockland (not a bizarre idea sprouting from a melodramatic brain, but something which had actually happened), the play seizes the opportunity to exploit the ironies and the oddities of such a conversion, using the action to explore many aspects of contemporary life. There is a reasonably complex story line in which Wffie Morgan, the more or less crooked entrepreneur whose brain-child the club is, is challenged on several fronts by a mysterious stranger who opposes him in matters of love, attitude to society and moral responsibility. Wffie is temporarily defeated, but Jim the challenger is hardly a winner, and the ending is ambivalent. On the way towards it, however, the audience has been offered a splendid roundabout of comic talk, romantic action, philosophical exchanges and provocative social analysis.

No one will be surprised, perhaps, to find that the real subject of the play is not the life of the Cardiff docklands, so much as that of the South Wales valleys. Thus the three rugby boys who come to drink at the club and the three tarts they meet there all hail from the valleys, as do the former boxers and the fallen preacher now acting as waiters, and most of their talk is of the places which have shaped them. Their topics are rugby, mining, rent and boxing, just as they would be if the play were set in Porth or Maerdy. When at the climax of the play the revered featherweight, The Mighty Atom, suddenly and briefly reappears from obscurity, no Rhondda-born watcher could fail to recognise one of his own heroes.

Like *Jackie the Jumper*, *Loud Organs* is about the battle in human society and psyche between puritanism and libido, between repression and freedom. Rumbustious action, punctuated with lively and satirical songs, alternates with moments of touching reminiscence and moods of tenderness and loss, while in two neatly counterpointed acts the play deliberately and penetratingly examines some of the contradictions and difficulties of the human condition. A criticism frequently made of Thomas's dialogue in his novels could be brought against the play, for little if any attempt has been made to differentiate between the way the characters speak; but few actors will complain about their dialogue on the grounds of lack of wit and fire. True to his habit, the author has allowed everyone to speak as well and vividly as possible, and the play is full of memorable lines, jokes and speeches. What seems to have led to the failure of *Loud Organs* in production was not the script but an ill-advised attempt to exploit its 'musical' potential beyond reason, so that the intended unobtrusive club 'combo' of two guitars and a drum-kit became a full-scale orchestra, giving out so much noise and causing the actors to become involved in such frenetic choreographic efforts that they could neither hear their cues nor find breath to speak their lines to advantage. Writing to Thomas on behalf of himself and the other actors a year or two after the production was abandoned, Ronnie Radd begged him to seek a production of the kind originally envisaged, where the music and songs merely complemented the action and were not allowed to dominate it, for they thought the play itself superb and longed for a chance to do it justice.

The play never having been prepared for the press before, the present version has been compiled from several sources, including Thomas's original manuscript (now in the National Library of Wales), a production typescript, much amended, from the period when the play was tried out in Blackpool, and the remains of a revised and again much amended typescript prepared for the run at the Sherman Theatre in Cardiff. Any company thinking it would be good to give it at last the production it merits would do well to bear in mind the hitherto unheard plea from its original actors: let the words work their magic.

All three of the plays give a great deal of pleasure on the page, for those who have the trick of reading drama; but it is seriously hoped that their appearance in print at this juncture will stimulate the theatres of Wales to give them again the life they really need, in production, on the boards. Their discovery will greatly enrich the repertory of British theatre.

# THE KEEP

# Characters

Ben Morton
Constantine Morton
Miriam Morton
Russell Morton
Wallace Morton
Oswald Morton
Alvin Morton
Mr Wilmot
Caradoc Slee

The play is set in the fifties (1954), in South Wales. The scene is the large parlour in the Morton house.

# ACT ONE

*A rather full parlour in the Morton home. The table centre is covered in a cloth of rich red plush. Above the fireplace is a picture of a very beautiful woman in her early thirties taken in the fashion of the 1919 period. At the side of the fireplace is old* Ben Morton, *the father of the clan. He is tidily dressed in a dark suit and seems to be flanking an endless funeral.*

*The door is flung open and in bounds* Con Morton. Con *is the oldest of the Morton boys. He is about forty, powerfully built, and clearly a man who is aiming to swallow the world in two fierce gulps. He is carrying in his hand an open letter which he slaps against his palm with a shout of triumph, before he throws it down triumphantly in front of his father.*

**Con:** I've done it, Dad, I've done it.
**Ben:** (*in a voice that suggests that his experience with* Con *over the years has given him every reason to be edgy and cautious*)

What is it now, Con?

**Con:** My law degree, Dad, I've got it.

**Ben:** Thank God, I was beginning to think . . .

**Con:** And not only you, Dad. Oh I know what they were saying, the lot. I know all the little jokes they were making. There's Con Morton off to London for his annual shot. The only lawyer to see all the laws he was questioned about when he sat for the first time repealed by the time he finally passed. Oh yes. The only lawyer to knit the woolsack into a shroud in lieu of his judicial toga. I know. I've slept with their laughter. And by the time I've made those jokers eat their words, they'll be slapping on an emergency tuppenny rate for magnesia.

**Ben:** No need to be bitter, Con. You'll bring on that rash on your neck again. (*He glances at the picture of his wife.*) We all have our crosses to bear.

**Con:** (*allowing his face to darken with sympathy and patting the old man gently on the shoulder*) I'm with you there, Dad. I've been a pack pony in the cross-bearing business. In all the chambers of that Town Hall to which I've given my life there is no more overworked nerve of social awareness than I.

**Ben:** You've been active, Con, and no mistake.

**Con:** That's a fact. On nineteen committees, secretary of three, treasurer to two and ideas man to the lot. My life's been a meeting, Dad, one long meeting. Even on the few committees I don't yet belong to, the agenda winks to me when I pass.

**Ben:** You've given your life for others, Con, you've been a good boy.

**Con:** I've never put myself first. There have been times when I could have behaved selfishly. You know yourself, Dad. In this very room three girls have sat at my side courting.

**Ben:** That's true. Nearly drove Ossie mad. Couldn't get at the piano. But you've done well, Con, and we're all grateful to you. Me, Miriam and the boys.

**Con:** (*taking his father by the arm, they go and stand in front of Mrs Morton's portrait*) I did it for Mam mostly. She's never been out of my thoughts, any more than she's been out of yours, Dad.

**Ben:** A lovely woman.

**Con:** A thrush.

**Ben:** Organized two soup kitchens for the needy. Banished

26

chilled headbones with her two-ply brand of balaclava helmet in the blizzard of 1919.

**Con:** Runner-up two years running for the contralto solo in the county Eisteddfod. Made three coalowners cry when she sang 'Abide With Me' at the memorial concert to the explosion victims.

**Ben:** A fine woman.

**Con:** Dead now.

**Ben:** Dead for a long time.

**Con:** Except what we do for love of her.

**Ben:** And that's been a lot in your case, Con.

**Con:** (*turns away from the portrait of his mother and picks the letter up from the table with a bitterly reflective look on his face*) I wonder has it been appreciated.

**Ben:** What do you mean, Con? Appreciated?

**Con:** My own brothers. I think they've done as much quiet jeering at me as anybody.

**Ben:** Oh no.

**Con:** Oh yes. When I could have been sitting jocosely at home, getting this degree of mine ten years before I did, or bringing one of those love affairs to a bit of warm fruition, doing myself a bit of real good, what was I doing? Circulating like a wireworm through every articulate group in the county. Drowning in beer at the rugby club when everybody knows that a sipped brandy is the drink of my heart, but with plenty of water, Dad, as you know. If in those groups I could put in a good persuasive word for the Morton boys and the memory of our Mam, that was my reward. Would old Doctor Edmonds have taken our Wallace into partnership if it hadn't been for me? (Ben *nods agreement.*) He would not. When Dr Edmonds had his driving licence suspended for driving backwards through the town faster than he had ever driven forward, who drove him home from the Constitutional Club three times a week during the last two years of Wallace's medical training?

(*Door opens left and* Miriam, *the only Morton sister, mid-thirties, comes in.*)

**Miriam:** You did, Con. You got Wallace the partnership for Mam's sake. Now come on. Your food is getting cold.

**Con:** All right, all right. (Miriam *goes out.*) Who took the manuscript of Russell's novel to London in 1939 and had it published when Russ would have burnt it or buried it?

(*Door opens again.*)

**Miriam:** You did, Con. And if you hadn't been ramming the point home for nearly twenty years Russ might have written another. Your eloquence got Russell a job in the dingiest school this side of the catacombs. And you got Alvin kept on at the Belmont tinplate when a few dozen other poor dabs were getting the push. And you got Oswald the conductor's baton of the Belmont Male Voice and the poor chap's been sipping nerve tonic and giving us the beat at meal times ever since.

**Con:** (*with tremendous dignity*) Miriam . . .

**Miriam:** I know. And I have the feeling that one day you're going to make an oratorio out of all this and have it produced out of the rates. And about that meal, you can dawdle as long as you like. It's gone to coke.

(Miriam *withdraws.*)

**Con:** (*defiantly towards the door*) Right, right. (*Turns to* Ben, *holds up and then solemnly kisses the letter in which the news of his law degree success has been announced. He closes the door behind* Miriam *and makes a huge gesture of relief.*) Now I can say what I want to in peace. Do you know, Dad, that if that news about the law degree hadn't come today I think I would have gone and jumped in the lake, the municipal lake, the lake I led the fight for in 1932.

**Ben:** Oh I don't know, Con. I can't see a boy like you getting wet in public, not in the park.

**Con:** Yes, I would have. Because a man gets weary, Dad. He can put so much into his life's work — expecting the echoes to come together and make some sort of meaning. You expect the world to be blind, but not deaf, not deaf.

**Ben:** You should have stuck to that course of brewer's yeast that Miriam was giving you. You're on edge.

**Con:** I'm all right now. (*He slaps his hand on the envelope.*) This makes everything plain, everything good. I know exactly where I'm going now and it'll take the municipal steam roller guided by my enemies to stop me. I know where I'm going and my brothers are coming with me. (*He shivers and sits down.*) God, when I think what might have happened if the news in that envelope had been different.

**Ben:** It'll be a big thing for you, Con. A robe and a big wig and

28

putting the fear of hell into the sinful. You'll be a fine judge, Con. You're many-sided in your mind. You'll walk all round a thing, staring at it until it gives up its truth, just not to have you walking around it and staring. You're like your grandfather, Con. Prospero Morton, Prospero Sine Die they called him because he was always standing up in those debates down at the Institute asking the extremists to defer judgment on life indefinitely until all the facts were in. But I wouldn't like you to be a hanging judge.

**Con:** I don't want to be a judge. Everything I want is here in Belmont, in this town. Mr Leighton Lewis, the Town Clerk, is retiring in December. And I'm going to be his successor.

**Ben:** You, Con?

**Con:** Me. I've said that to a lot of people in the Town Hall and they've sniggered. (*Pats envelope.*) They knew I had to have *that* in my pocket before I could even apply. Now I've got it. That's why I've slaved as I have done. That's why I've lit the lamp in my room after coming in at ten or eleven from a round of committee meetings. I've done so much studying of the law in my bedroom between dawn and midnight even the mice are literate and slip writs into the mousetraps.

**Ben:** I know, boy, I've often heard you thumbing the thick books and groaning.

**Con:** That letter was delivered to the Town Hall. I thought that that address would give a feeling of mercy, of urgency to the examiners. It was delivered at half past eleven this morning.

**Ben:** Second post.

**Con:** I'd just come out of a session about refuse disposal with Mr Leighton Lewis. Right at the end he slipped out that he was finishing in December and he seemed to be smiling his delight that I'd never have the proper qualifications to apply. I just held the letter for about ten minutes, staring at it.

**Ben:** Doubt about the outcome. Terrible thing, doubt.

**Con:** The only other person in the room was Rose Rees. You know Rose, the typist.

**Ben:** Nice girl. Sings 'I Know That My Redeemer Liveth' at the quarterly meeting in Moab. Real conviction but a bit flat.

**Con:** That's it. I trust Rose. But I wouldn't have trusted even Mam to be with me when I opened that letter from the University. (*Indicates his middle.*) I was ice cold all around

29

there. I had to stare at the painting of Alderman Percy Gribble on the wall to keep me from fainting.

**Ben:** Very stern and restorative, the Alderman.

**Con:** Then I told Rose Rees, very quietly, "I'd like to be alone, Rose." And she went. That's it. There was the news. The news I'd waited fifteen years for. What do you think I did then? What would you have done, Dad?

**Ben:** I'd have fetched in Rose Rees to take the edge off my excitement. Years ago, of course.

**Con:** I went down on my knees to thank God that the envelope had come to me as it did, saving my dreams from that last terrible crumble. I got down on my knees.

**Ben:** Quite right. Be on the safe side.

**Con:** I found myself thanking Alderman Percy Gribble.

**Ben:** A bit like God in his last years, the Alderman. I'm glad for you, Con.

**Con:** Oh, the fight's not over yet. There's a whole world to be remade. Starting with that very squalid little mid-Victorian convenience, the one that looks like an iron maiden and gives the voters the sense of being trapped, down in Omdurman Row, right up to the Constitution of the Aldermanic Bench.

**Miriam:** (*from door*) I'm putting on a second lot of chips, if you're interested. (*She closes the door with a touch of petulance.*)

**Con:** Isn't that typical. I stand ready to tread the last few yards that separate me from Sinai and somebody asks a question about chips.

**Ben:** Throughout the modern age potatoes have clearly hindered the Celt.

**Con:** Not a word about this yet to the boys. (*Pointing to envelope which he puts into an inside pocket.*) They stand each and every one of them on the brink of their greatest moment.

**Ben:** They need cheering up. They've all been pretty miserable lately.

**Con:** We'll put a stop to that. At this moment I need them all happy and smiling and confident behind me. For Mam's sake the Mortons are going to close their ranks. (*Shouts through the door*) I'll be in for a quick bite after I shave. (*To Ben*) I've got three or four smartish calls to make tonight. Every one of them will make a big thunder in this front room if my luck holds. Keep your fingers crossed, Dad.

(*His brother* Russell *appears just as he approaches the threshold.* Russell *is about thirty-eight, fairly handsome and expressing in all features a mounting fatigue and impatience. He throws some books down on the table. He sinks into a chair.* Con *studies him anxiously.*)

**Con:** Hello Russ, see you later, boy. (*He goes out.*)

**Miriam:** (*from door*) You eating, Russ?

**Russ:** A couple of biscuits and a cup of tea, Mir. No hurry.

**Ben:** Some chips and chops there. Sustain yourself, boy.

**Russ:** (*strokes stomach*) Got to think of this, I'm pushing the Burnham Committee for a new lining. (*Nods at door.*) What's Con so chirpy about?

**Ben:** Oh, you know Con.

**Russ:** (*sombrely*) I know Con. And Con knows us. That's the trouble.

**Ben:** Full of dreams and schemes as usual.

**Russ:** When he talks, fall flat on the floor at the count of three.

**Ben:** Oh, buck up, Russ. Con has never had a thought that wasn't for the town and his brothers. (*Outer door opens.*) That'll be Wallace back from the surgery.

(Wallace *comes in. He is about thirty-two, slackly dressed and having about him the same hints of tension as* Russell.)

**Ben:** Hello, Wallace.

**Russ:** How's it going, Wall?

(Wallace *throws a light top coat on to the settee.*)

**Wallace:** That surgery. A spring broke loose from the couch. For two years I've asked him to provide a new one. He says the Welfare State has pampered enough people into decadence without putting in his own oar.

**Russ:** I've heard him make that speech about the Health Service. He's good. If the Music Halls weren't dying, he could do a double act with Malthus.

**Ben:** You can give people too much. You know that, Wallace. (*Defensively*) People are getting a lot too much, I know. When I was a kid of twelve I was down under, in the pit. At twelve. Door boy in the old steam coal. Hear the tram, open the door. Afraid to open my food parcel, because the rats would be up on my lap, bold as brass. Terrors for bacon. In the winter never saw the light of day.

**Russ:** There are still some Eskimos in the same fix.

31

**Ben:** You're laughing at me.

**Russ:** I don't laugh at anybody.

**Ben:** Some people get too much for nothing. You ask Con.

**Wallace:** Some people have been getting too much for nothing for centuries. They've done all right on it.

(Miriam *comes in with a tray bearing tea and two piles of sandwiches.*)

**Miriam:** Now then, you two. These are yours, Wallace. And here's your fancy, Russ. Tongue and tomato.

(Wallace *draws up a chair by the fire.*)

**Wallace:** Now then, Miriam. Get off your legs for a couple of minutes and sit here.

**Ben:** (*with delighted complacency*) Just like her Mam. Always in a bustle, always waiting to serve. She never gets tired, do you, Miriam?

**Miriam:** (*flopping into a chair*) No, never. Just feel as if my back is breaking at times, but Con says that's due to a lack of calcium in the tap water. He's been urging the council to do something about it. They are going to pour some stuff into the reservoir. He'll have us rigid as guardsmen in no time at all.

(Russell *pours the tea and* Wallace *hands it round.*)

**Wallace:** Here you are, Dad. Just as you like it. Dark as your father's philosophy. I bet there was some quality of joy in that phase of utter gloom that Granch reached when he couldn't get about much any more.

**Russ:** Joy? (*Takes a sandwich and just touches his lips with it.*) He must have had it hidden away like a smuggled pearl. If there had been a divining rod for gaiety it would have split up the middle at the sight of Granch.

**Ben:** He came from a hard time. He needed a simple faith.

**Wallace:** He overdid it. He wore his black serge like a second skeleton.

**Russ:** He used to drag me upstairs to watch funerals from the front window. They used to sing as they marched in those days. The full treatment.

**Ben:** Took the sting and the shame from death, those hymns. The dead would not have felt alone as they must do now.

**Russ:** It was terrifying. He used to sit there at the front bedroom window. He could gauge exactly the status of a funeral by the quality of the hats and suits. He could foretell the quality of the funeral tea that would follow, the exact amount of cold ham that would be served. "This will be a two-slicer" he would say, "or a three-slicer, a four-slicer". It brought death into the same friendly sort of ambience as pigeon fancying.

**Miriam:** (*very quietly*) I bet Mam hated him.

(*A deep silence.* Russell and Wallace *look curiously at* Ben, *who has dropped the spoon with which he was stirring his tea and is staring at* Miriam.)

**Ben:** What did you say?

**Miriam:** I said I bet Mam hated him. He would have depressed a corgi.

**Ben:** Do you know who you are talking about? (Miriam *takes a sandwich and makes no reply. The father gets up and walks slowly towards* Miriam. *He stands accusingly in front of her.*) You are talking about my father, one of the three survivors of the explosion of 1896. The man who dug the foundations of Moab chapel with his own two hands in gratitude for his deliverance. Moab, the chapel you've worshipped and sung in since you were a child. (*He fumbles about in an inside pocket.*) I've got an article that Con wrote about him in the *Gazette*.

**Miriam:** I've read it.

**Russ:** Miriam's tired, Dad. Wash-day.

**Wallace:** Miriam's always a bit tired after a heavy wash.

**Miriam:** Not since you got me the electric washer. My thoughts are as fresh as daisies.

**Ben:** I never thought to hear a child of mine say a spiteful word against her own grandfather.

**Wallace:** Sit down, Dad, and don't take it so much in earnest. You can't expect us all to see things in exactly the same light as you or Con for that matter. Psychologically Granch stayed stuck in that explosion. There was a strong whiff of methane about most of his concepts. And that religious fervour of his went over the top a little too often. He helped build Moab at a time when the town had at least five chapels more than it needed for its spiritual exercises.

**Russ:** And then marched us there like Frederick the Great.

**Miriam:** If he could have found a bible big enough he would have had us inside drying like rose leaves.

**Ben:** He felt it was his duty to be like that. That was the time when I failed you as a father. The time when I was wild and dissolute, when I was a travelling agent for Morgan the monumental mason. Flashing out catalogues of headstones at the voters and taking to the drink through sadness every time I made a sale. It was Granch who was your strong arm in trouble at that time.

**Miriam:** And didn't he let Mam know it. He'd have us all sitting around the kitchen and he'd stare at us with eyes of dark cloth.

**Ben:** He was bitter and sad. It was all my fault.

not? Anybody selling monumental masonry in some of the towns that were on your beat, where the only concession to gaiety is a striped shroud, deserves a bath in drambuie, no less.

**Ben:** (*agonizedly*) That wasn't all, Wallace, that wasn't all.

(*He paces up and down the room, evincing every symptom of guilt popular in the nineteenth century.*)

**Russ:** What else was there? What else could there be in West Wales? Women?

**Ben:** Lust, my dear boy, was never a trouble with me. If ever anything of that nature stirred me at the bottom of my mind one look at my catalogues was enough to send me back to January. Not since I heard the Reverend Morley Morris, the Missionary, explain what happens to the more incontinent lechers in Borneo, has sex been a serious nuisance to me.

**Russ:** What happens to them?

**Wallace:** Never mind about Borneo. What happened to you, Dad? Tell us. I've always wanted to know what went to make you as you are now. Let's have the partitions down. Con's out, so you can speak freely.

**Ben:** It's for Con's sake and my Dad's sake that I am going to say this. (*Very solemnly*) No one will ever know how near I came to perdition.

**Wallace:** Too vague, Dad. Just give us the hub of the dossier.

**Ben:** I was in a town in West Wales. There had been a revival. The place was humming with the joy of salvation. Even lovers on the hillside at the very peak of their carnal passion would signal their urges to one another with lines from the hymnal.

**Russ:** That could find a place on TV when they break away from the family audience.

(Ben's *face has lost its melancholy.*)

34

**Ben:** The revivalist had a stroke, in the pulpit itself, and he died. He was riding some terrible metaphor of doom bareback and he had this stroke. It was late autumn. The town was sad and flat. It lost its resistance to the 'flu epidemic that was raging at the time and hundreds died. There was a boom in headstones of every shape. I filled three order books and wore out two catalogues in a month. The favourite line was the marble with a single angel, wings folded, and the plain words 'Waft him, or Waft her, Angel, to the sky'. It was a tremendous period for Morgan the Mason. He took on extra men and put two quarries on double time. He promoted more stonework than one of the pharaohs in Egypt. It nearly ruined him.

**Wallace:** What did? (*making gesture of a man tapping hammer on chisel*) The stone dust or that line about 'Waft him'?

**Ben:** (*voice hollow as a drum and fingers clutching at collar in the horror of totally recalled embarrassment*) No. I spent all the deposits. It was a kind of madness that struck me. I had been home just before. Your dear Mam had been fierce with me. I hadn't been sending money home. She had to crawl to Granch to get money for your bread. You were small then. It was terrible, the way I made the money fly. It was a tidal wave of ale. I put a thickness of foam on the estuaries of the Towy and the Teifi.

**Wallace:** What was the end of all that?

**Ben:** Mr Morgan the Mason found out about the deposits. He was terrible in his wrath. He had carved so many angels he thought he had them at his command like a bomber squadron. First he wanted to plant me under one of his larger models. Then he threatened to put the law in motion unless he got his money back. I caused more confusion in graveyards west of Neath than death itself. Con and your grandfather were my saviours.

**Wallace:** Con?

**Ben:** Yes, he had the same thrust then as now. He was only young. He persuaded your grandfather to sell five houses to settle with Morgan. He got me a job collecting the rates and my lips have never known the taste of malt since. A sip of whisky taken on a cold spoon when my bronchitis frowns and that has been all. So never let me hear you sneer at Con or your grandfather. When he came here to live it was to give me a new

35

life.

**Miriam:** I wasn't sneering. All I'm saying is that he wore his hair shirt so long he almost tickled the lot of us to death. Especially Mam. He hawked that lovely voice of hers around too many vestries singing songs praising death and running down drink and sex. And one night when her patience with him was worn right down to the canvas she turned to me in this very room and said she wished that he or she was dead.

**Ben:** No, no. You must have misheard her, Miriam. There was great love between them. Let me tell you something. (*He goes to stand near the portrait of his wife. He looks sidlingly at it as he talks to his children.*) I can see it now. Mam had got the telegram that said her sister was dying in Wilksbarre, in America. They were twins, very devoted. We decided Mam must go alone. When she was leaving this house for the last time, when she was leaving for America to see her dying sister on the journey that was to end in her death in that rail crash near Philadelphia, she took my hands as she leaned out of the window of the train, gave me her loveliest smile and she said: Ben, she said, I'll never be able to thank your father enough. First for keeping the children alive and now this ticket all the way to Wilksbarre to see Gweno on her death bed. (*Goes and stands directly in front of the picture, his head bowed.*) Poor Dinah May. One of the ten unidentified bodies. Buried there. So silent and so far away.

**Russ:** What happened to the sister?

**Ben:** Got better like a flash, when she heard the news about Dinah May. Right as rain to this very day. Now I must go to the kitchen to take my nightly cup of Epsom salts in luke warm water. The queen of harsh laxatives, as Doctor Edmonds, your partner, always tells me, Wallace. It is his own final draught of the day and what a picture of a man he is . . . it is a solace to me, the purgative harshness of that mixture. It terrifies the system and banishes the memory of those loud sinful nights of long ago.

**Wallace:** Good luck, Dad. After that, you deserve Luther Long as a bonus. Tell Luther to cheer up. The last time I called in he was reading the Book of Job with a migraine, in a poor light.

**Ben:** Wallace, you'll have to develop a much more sombre

tongue if you are to measure up to the greatness of Doctor Edmonds.

(Ben *goes out*.)

**Wallace:** The greatness of Dr Edmonds. What a myth that old boy has woven around himself. I just left the old wreck in the Constitutional Club crouched over the snooker table wondering whether to pot or operate.

**Miriam:** He getting on your nerves?

**Wallace:** He *is* my nerves and he's shaking.

**Russ:** What's to do? Five brothers, one sister. Not stupid, not repellent. All whirling about with their own feelings. But held together like a dumb constellation in the sky. Not one of us married. Why should that be?

**Wallace:** Apathy, indolence, a slightly sub-normal sexual beat, the quality of Miriam's cooking, sheer accident.

**Russ:** That's not all. A big part of it is the kind of shinto that Con has developed around that picture of Mam. Con is a vortex. And he sees to it that none of us will ever stray too far away from this little group. There's his own crazy dream of getting to be the Town Clerk and becoming a sort of municipal Peter the Great. When you were playing with the idea of following Willie Erskine to Canada he set you alight with the idea of becoming the medical officer of health and showing the last stigma of inherited poverty in this borough to the door.

**Wallace:** That was a bright notion. It must have left powder burns inside my skull.

**Russ:** And when I wanted to get out of that school and settle down as a resident termite in the County Library he lit that beacon about starting a residential school in that derelict mansion up in the hills for kids from the slummier parts of Belmont.

**Wallace:** Pity you hadn't got out of it years ago.

**Russ:** Where to? Canada? Oliver Marsden on our staff went out there. Right in the middle of the prairie. Sort of handyman. Drives the school bus. Paints the school, looks after the school chickens and gets two guide dogs to lead him to the blackboard when the snow blinds him.

**Wallace:** I wasn't thinking of teaching at all. That book you wrote way back in the thirties. It was nice. Got a lot of good notices. A few gall-stones shaking around inside it but it was a lovely book none the less. Then not a word. How can a man just shut up like that? Come out with such a song and then fall back into silence.

**Miriam:** (*putting her hand on* Russell's *knee*) I know. I couldn't explain but I know.

**Russ:** Mostly I've told myself that was all I wanted to say, that those years I wrote about had some excitement we'd never know again. Time since then has been a kind of spinning tedium. You can finger it into different shapes if you like, but the stuff at the core of it is dark and unlovely. Do you remember how my novel ended?

**Miriam:** Mam going to America. Where she left the house. The last time we saw her.

**Wallace:** And you described it exactly, exactly as it was. It was late in the morning, must have been about eleven. Her train out of Belmont was at twelve. Her bags were waiting in the kitchen. Con was dancing about. He wanted to make a start because he was sure there'd be a crowd at the station to see Mam off.

**Miriam:** She gave Con a slice of custard pie to keep him quiet.

**Wallace:** That's it. Then she said: We'll all go into the front room and sing together for the last time. Ossie was at the piano. We sang that old American revivalist song 'Flee as a Bird to Your Fountain'. (Miriam *and* Russell *hum this tune as* Wallace *proceeds passionately to recreate this scene.*) I stood here. Miriam was there. You Russ, were here. Then Alvin, Dad and Granch were in a corner somewhere, but singing hard — and Granch was crying because the song had vague religious affiliations. Then we stopped singing. Mam went to the door. We were going to follow her. I remember thinking: "It'll be a fine thing for all us boys to be in a procession behind her, her looking so smart in her new clothes, all the way to the station." But she turned at the door.

**Russ:** And she said: "Don't move. Stay just like that. I want to take away the sight and sound of you, just like that." The moment must have done something to stun my mind because I find it hard to get beyond that point. She looked lovely. Ossie kept playing because he was crazy about some new thing he had learnt to do with his left hand on the lower register. So he never saw her go. And Con has worked up such a mystique about the whole thing that Ossie's left hand has never been the same

38

since. All I recall is that she looked lovely. What was she wearing?

**Miriam:** A black, broad-brimmed hat. And a black coat trimmed with astrakhan. Bought it in Cardiff. Sale. Bit tight but fetching. She wanted light blue but Granch said black. He thought Mam's sister might have a bit of money to leave and he didn't want Mam to look flippant at her death bed.

**Wallace:** That's Granch.

**Miriam:** Do you think she knew?

**Wallace:** Who?

**Miriam:** Mam.

**Wallace:** Knew what?

**Miriam:** That she was never going to see us again, that that was the last time.

**Wallace:** No, thank God. We never know. Ignorance is the only true and reliable skin.

**Russ:** And a wall came down at that moment. I tried to drag my pen over it but it was no use. Something ended there and I've lived in the most agreeable silence since. Or maybe I was more stupid than I thought and had nothing more to say. Perhaps that was the way it was meant.

**Miriam:** (*almost angrily*) No, it wasn't meant to be like that at all. It was a fine book. It was just meant as a beginning. It was warm and tender like a perfect steak. You've got the whole world in you to say. (*She jerks her head up petulantly at her mother.*) But somebody's put a spell on the lot of us and we walk around in a grey quiet gaol.

**Russ:** You can't argue about a thing like this. Death operates even more oddly in art than in the National Health Service.

**Wallace:** And what do you feel now, Russell?

**Russ:** Something is stirring. Something is changing. We've made a handy little compost of absurdity here and out of it something really rare and outrageous is going to flower.

**Wallace:** We are the compost, and Con will be the only flower.

**Russ:** I don't know.

(*The telephone rings in the next room.*)

**Wallace:** That'll be the first instalment. It'll be that woman evangelist, Mrs Moxon, wanting a bromide for that vinous husband of hers. He's already got flat feet walking around the landing while she composes her thoughts for a pre-sermon sleep.

**Miriam:** I'll take it, Wallace. You stay where you are.

(Miriam *goes out; her voice can be heard answering the telephone.* Russell *walks to the piano and picks out the melody of 'Flee as a Bird'. He sings softly.* Wallace *speaks the words with an ironical simplicity.*)

**Russ:** (*putting the piano lid down*) Oh, the great ugly pathos of men's dreams.

**Wallace:** Amen. (*The telephone conversation stops and* Miriam *comes back.*) Who was it?

**Miriam:** An amateur magician burned doing a flame act in the Go as you Please in the Bannerman Club.

**Wallace:** I warned the Committee about that. My bag on the hall table?

**Miriam:** It's there.

**Wallace:** Won't be long. Feel like coming down to the Club for a slow pint, Russ? Do you good.

**Miriam:** Go on, Russ. You're becoming a proper hermit, a ghost. You've spent every night for the last three months in this front room. It's almost as if you were waiting for something.

**Russ:** That's it. It would be silly to miss it when it came.

**Wallace:** So long both.

**Miriam:** So long, Wall. See you.

(*As* Wallace *is going through the door the youngest but one of the brothers,* Oswald, *is coming in. He is slighter in build than* Wallace *and* Russell. *He is rather stooped and unhappy.*)

**Oswald:** Oh, Wall, have you got any of those nerve powders you gave me last week?

**Wallace:** Head still bad?

**Oswald:** Head, hands, feet. I've got the shakes.

**Wallace:** I'll get you a fresh load. Keep you numb till Christmas.

(Wallace *goes out and the front door slams.*)

**Oswald:** (*shuddering and taking a seat*) It's affecting my work. Me. Two years ago awarded the Trevethick medal for the coolest ticket collector in the region. Now I take minutes and I'm so much on edge. Only this morning I accused two travellers of inventing place names just to torment me.

**Russ:** You overdid pride. You shuffled those tickets like a card sharp. You were bound to start foxing yourself sooner or later.

(Russell *goes to the cupboard and decants a drink*.) Have two fingers of this tonic wine.

(Oswald *gulps it down.*)

**Oswald:** Oh, that's better than the parsnip wine we had last Christmas. (*Then his face, from a climax of light, gutters down to an almost total darkness.*) That Con has done for me. He's got me on the run, honest he has.

**Russ:** Stop running and parade the facts.

**Oswald:** I was there, the worst second tenor in the Belmont male voice choir. I was happy putting in my little note from time to time. Then Con comes along. Gets admitted to help with the audit. He takes over the committee. He rigs the meeting where they are choosing the new conductor. The obvious choice is Caradoc Slee. Seen Caradoc? A treat. Stroke iike Beecham.

**Russ:** Top notch. Conducts himself as he talks.

**Oswald:** But the baton goes to me and Slee goes back to my old place in the second tenors. I'll say that for Caradoc. No pride. The proper modesty of a true chorister. He could have left the party flat, but he's stuck on.

**Miriam:** Don't abase yourself, Ossie. Honest, there are times when you are like a slug.

**Russ:** Miriam's right, Os. We've got to learn to sneer right back at life. We anoint the feet of the damn thing with so much unguent it's slipping about in front of us. (*He leans over and snatches up a copy of a newspaper that has been resting on a pouffe.*) You read what the *Gazette* said about you when it gave you a write-up last week on the carol concert in the memorial hall?

**Oswald:** I didn't see it. I didn't dare to look. It was my first concert as conductor. When I picked the paper up my right eye started to water and all that tonic from the pills started to clank. I don't know how I got through that concert. My baton seemed to be shaking about in my hand like the rod of Moses.

**Russ:** It went off fine, Os. Listen to what it says here. (*He begins reading from the newspaper.*) "The carols were as sweet and tender as the night that inspires them. There was a genuine glitter of starlight on some of the sfumatura effects".

**Oswald:** That wasn't sfumatura, that was the baritones shutting up in a kind of phased withdrawal to spite me and put

41

me off. But read some more. It's a kind of oxygen to me, Russ, that stuff from the paper.

**Russ:** (*reading*) "Your correspondent could not help noting, as the concert proceeded, that these traditional concerts, in years past, have sometimes been marred by the excessive bravura of Mr Milo Ashton, the late conductor, a well-loved man, but as a conductor prone to bawl and to coax his choristers into the posture and tone of a herd of miuras".

**Oswald:** Of what?

**Russ:** That's a type of bull. The writer of this is Vulcan Philpott. Vulcan won a ten day bus trip to Pamplona in Spain in the Easter raffle at the Bannerman Club and he throws in these Spanish words to show he was on the bus.

**Oswald:** Oh, aye. Let's hear some more from Vulcan.

**Russ:** (*reading*) "With Mr Oswald Morton, the new conductor, we have returned to the mood of quietness and sincerity that belongs to the heart of a carol. With Mr Morton we were witnessing the first authentic miracle. With Mr Milo Ashton, on the other hand, we had a volume of sound that would have defeated the three wise men and swept the manger bare."

**Miriam:** They should have given that Vulcan more than ten days on that bus.

**Oswald:** (*his temporary gaiety quite gone again and back to his old wariness*) Vulcan is a friend of Con. Con put Vulcan up to writing all that stuff about the authentic miracle, and the starlight.

**Russ:** Could be. Vulcan will use any stick to beat Milo Ashton. Milo threw Vulcan out of the glee-men three years ago.

**Oswald:** I was there. It was a dramatic scene. Vulcan was coming at the notes from every angle but the right one. Milo tapped for silence. (Oswald *acts the incidents of this tale with solemn concentration*) He was staring at Vulcan. "Gentlemen," he said, "let us check. Are we using the same piece of sheet music?" That was the end of Vulcan. And now here he is putting me on this pedestal. (*He holds out his glass for another helping of the tonic wine and Miriam fills it for him.*) I know what his game is too.

**Russ:** What is it?

**Oswald:** There is some person or persons wishing to drive me off the hinge, somebody who's got a grudge against this family or against the clerical staff of British Railways. Take Caradoc Slee.

**Miriam:** How is Caradoc these days?

**Oswald:** Very strange.

**Miriam:** He always was . . .

**Oswald:** He was all right until he broke off his engagement to you.

**Miriam:** Let's forget about that. That little affair broke up about the same time as Caerphilly Castle.

**Oswald:** He was all right until then. A nice sweet forthcoming little bloke. Then Con gets talking to him, persuades him that it would break Caradoc's mother's heart if Caradoc gets married.

**Miriam:** Con? Did he do that?

**Oswald:** I bet he did. That Con. He's at it all the time. Shaping life. Giving it orders, adjusting its buttons every whipstitch. Now Caradoc, he just stands there among the tenors, carrying these two griefs.

**Miriam:** How's Caradoc's hair on top now?

**Oswald:** It's got about three months to go.

**Russ:** Carrying on about Con. If you don't work off this persecution mania about him you'll be ordering a mental truss.

**Oswald:** I'm wondering.

**Russ:** Wondering what?

**Oswald:** I can get promotion if I'm willing to move to Swindon. It'll make a difference to my pension and it might keep me sane for a year or two longer. By God, doesn't that make the grave sound awfully near, that stuff about the pension.

**Russ:** Why not? A mobile thing, the grave.

**Miriam:** Do what you think is best, Os. Don't walk against the wind. Any chance you get to do yourself a bit of good, take it. Don't hang on here against your will.

**Oswald:** I'll ask Alvin when he comes in. I'd always take Alvin's word on anything. You know, Russ, I think Alvin's the best of us, counting out Miriam. All the ups and downs he's had in that damned tinplate works and the sunshine is always on his face.

(Alvin *comes in, he is the oldest of the brothers. He is a little older than* Con, *say about forty-one. He is wearing a dark suit of not very brilliant cut.* Oswald *looks at him with astonishment, for* Alvin's *expression, far from being sunlit as* Oswald *has just said, is one of dourly passive misery.)*

**Oswald:** What's up, Alvin?

**Alvin:** Been to the area meeting of the union at Birchtown.

**Miriam:** I'll get you a cup of stew.

**Alvin:** Thanks, Miriam. (Miriam *leaves the room.* Alvin *sits down and rubs his head.)* God, don't people talk when there's a bit of trouble about.

**Oswald:** What people? What are they talking about?

**Alvin:** Those boys in Birchtown. They'll say one thing to you as you're walking into a meeting. But when they stick their hands up on a vote, it's for something different.

**Russ:** What's the double talk been about this time?

**Alvin:** You know how we've been fighting for the last two years to keep our tinplate works open?

**Oswald:** Nobody's fought harder than you, Alvin.

**Alvin:** And a lot of good it's done, too. (Miriam *comes in with the soup.* Alvin *takes it and blows noisily at the mixture.)* A lot of good. We heard the news today. The company are putting forty people off next week and we'll go on a four day week after Christmas. (*He takes a sip at the soup and smiles up at* Miriam *who is looking at him concernedly.)* Thanks, Miriam. It's beautiful. And I wanted it. I walked most of the way back and with cold news inside the body it's not good. I'll have to tell them tomorrow in the works.

**Russ:** It's tough.

**Alvin:** A lot of them will have to leave the place. There's nothing for them here.

**Oswald:** Most of the baritones in the choir are in the tinplate.

**Russ:** It's the same old tale. A shift in investment and the same poor devils start the trek again.

(Alvin *puts the soup down in almost one fierce gulp. He winces and groans as the hot liquid burns the back of his mouth, but he seems intent upon punishing himself.)*

**Alvin:** You lose people. You lose people. When the dark comes down and the enemies are stirring in the shadows in front of you you shout "Charge" and you stumble flat on your face, alone like a clown. Your friends are a hundred miles away laughing. And in the quietness a whole side of life in Belmont will be taken to bits and buried. Oh, I'm sick. The speeches I've made. On the site of the Belmont tinplate works the monks of Belmont set up their rudimentary forces six hundred years ago. You dug up that fact for me, Russ. It was the opening sentence that nearly got me a scholarship to Ruskin College.

**Russ:** I remember. We were doing a monk project at school.

**Alvin:** The Belmont monks. Puh. One of the smart alecs at the meeting today said that the only difference technically between us and the holy brothers is that our trousers show and our hours of prayer are less fixed. All I can say is that I hope I'm one of the forty to get the push.

**Russ:** Don't talk like that, Alvin. Just look after yourself.

**Alvin:** We'll all try that. Then we'll be in real trouble.

(*Their father comes bustling in. He has heard the last word 'trouble' and wants instantly to restore blitheness.*)

**Ben:** What's this? What's this? (Alvin *gives him for reply just one long disgruntled look.*) Come on, buck up, Alvin. What's this?

**Russ:** Alvin's been to a meeting at Birchtown. The world wants less tin. Some people are going to be put off at the tinplate works.

**Ben:** (*complacently*) Oh, is that all?

**Alvin:** (*savagely*) What do you mean? Is that all? Isn't that enough? Who are you supposed to be? Herod or George Schwartz?

**Ben:** You should hear Con about this tinplate. He says that when he gets a bit of real power in this town, and that won't be long, you can take it from me . . .

**Alvin:** Con ought to buy you a bell, Dad. You're the best crier he's got. You and Con are the best duet since 'Il Trovatore'.

**Ben:** That was no way to talk to your father, Alvin.

**Alvin:** I was talking to myself. I was upset. Don't mind me.

**Ben:** Don't feel down in the dumps about the tinplate. I heard Con talking about it in the Chamber of Trade. They invited me because Con was the guest speaker. I was proud of Con, watching him there, talking to all those toffs, as if he were their boss. He said he wants to see Belmont cleansed.

**Russ:** In what sense cleansed? What sort of dirt did Con have in mind?

**Ben:** He says it's a disgrace to have a thing like that tinplate works slap in the middle of the town.

**Alvin:** We'll try wearing flowers in our hair, just to please Con.

**Ben:** He wants new clean industries like plastics. He said to those gentlemen in the Belmont Arms that since we've given security to everybody, religion, enterprise, honesty and good manners have all gone down the drain.

**Russ:** Big drain.

**Alvin:** Con said that?

**Ben:** He did and the gentlemen clapped for a whole minute.

**Russ:** They should. That was a fine statement. We were worried about where all those things had gone to.

**Ben:** Con is a fine man. He's well in with Mrs Loomer-Barkway who owns the works. Did you know that he had been up to her house seven times for tea, up in the mansion? I think she fancies our Con, Mrs Loomer-Barkway.

(Alvin *hands his soup cup to* Miriam)

**Alvin:** Could you fill this for me, Miriam? I need strength.

**Miriam:** Pleasure, boy.

(Miriam *leaves the room.*)

**Ben:** Con will see you all right, Alvin. Con is well in where it counts.

**Alvin:** I don't want him to see me all right. And I don't want people like that Mrs Loomer-Barkway to have the final say in how well and how often we eat.

**Oswald:** Con, a lover and all, in that mansion? Cheeeee.

**Alvin:** I suppose Con would like all the sacked to be the old chaps who'll shuffle off to the grave, happy to be helping the national economy to a healthier pulse-beat and singing "Jesus wants me for a deflator". Well, there'll be a few younger hands among them and they'll all be ready to set up a hell of a yell, just for old sanity's sake.

**Ben:** (*horrified*) A yell? Oh, no, Alvin. You wouldn't want to do a thing like that. Not with us set up so tidy, so decent.

(Alvin *looks at his father in laughable stupefaction.*)

**Alvin:** Why not, for God's sake? Yelling is the real trade for man. Creeping along, taking the boot, in the dark behind a wall, singing hallelujahs every time the cat in the adjoining room is too tired to find you or bite you, that's for mice.

**Ben:** What talk is this? Mice? Hallelujahs? (Miriam *comes in with the soup*) Don't give him any more of that. He's raving now. What are you on about?

**Alvin:** That damned Con. He invented the lot of us. We are all

46

lodging in the back of his cunning ambitious bloody head. This is the end of the road. This is where we explode this settled happy home like a bomb.

**Ben:** No, you're ill, Alvin. Wait till Wallace comes in. He'll get you one of those compresses for round the head that give you instant relief.

**Alvin:** (*with quiet grim authority*) Con has said his last word. He's my trouble. Every time that boy talks my frontal lobes do a fandango.

**Ben:** Easy now, Alvin, easy boy. We've built up this little peace we know from little pieces of luck and patience. One hard breath and bang it goes. Easy boy.

**Russ:** Sorry, Dad. Alvin's right. It's evening. We're all like dogs before a storm, fed up to the scalp and beyond.

**Alvin:** We could stay here another twenty years, the raw material of some corny dream of Con's about the family group being the golden corselet of society. We've all got other places to be. Is that right about the promotion I heard they were offering you at Swindon, Os?

**Oswald:** That's right. But Swindon . . .

**Alvin:** Never mind about Swindon. Promotion is a city in itself. And that conducting in the choir is making you a nervous wreck anyway. Keep at it and you'll be the only conductor wearing a hair shirt with his black bow tie. What about you, Russ? How are you fixed up, boy?

**Russ:** All right. Johnnie Hargreaves, three doors down. He's got a headship in London now. I'll try there, I think. It'll be a nice change dealing with the really finished type of juvenile savage after the experimental types we breed in the shadow of the steel works here. What about you, Alvin? Will you hang about here for a bit?

**Alvin:** No. From now on, one tinplate works after another will close down. I don't want to see it. I'll slip out of this place as quiet as a mouse. I'll do a last essay for the trustees of Ruskin College on the need for politeness among doomed artisans. Then I'm off to Birmingham. You remember Hughie Pugh, son of that chemist, Pugh the Purge. Hughie's got a welding plant in Birmingham. He wants me to join him. Clean job too.

**Russ:** London, Birmingham, Swindon. It sounds like the beginning of a poem on dissolution. What about you, Miriam?

(Miriam *does not make an instant reply. She moves slowly around the room, studying her brothers and the furniture alternately. There is a half-smile on her face.*)

**Miriam:** Now let me see. I've got me a new electric washer. I've got my new radiogram. I've got my new television set. I've got my new rimless specs to slip on in the dark to watch it and cheap aspirin from Wallace to bear it. I've got my new dark dress to wear when I next sing 'I know that My Redeemer Liveth' at the next quarterly meeting in Moab. That's about all. Unless you've got some new lines in dreams and coffins you'd like to show me.

**Russ:** Anything you want, Miriam, we'll get for you. Whether we are here or elsewhere.

**Miriam:** Thanks, Russ. No. I suppose I'll just stay here, cooking meals and making beds, until there's nobody left to do these things for. Then I'll lie down and sleep. I feel horribly strong. I've never wasted my strength upon love or ambition. I've never even sung with all my pipes. I'm cautious. I'll last a long time. I'll see you all off.

**Oswald:** Don't talk like that, Miriam. You're making me shake; you're making Dad shake.

**Russ:** You think we're right?

**Miriam:** In what?

**Russ:** In wanting to leave Con with his dreams down, in thinking this place is stifling us all.

**Miriam:** Russ, I don't think it matters. It may be the result of too much cooking but I don't think anything really begins or ends. Stifling never really comes from outside, does it? Anywhere you go, you'll find something daft or stale. Con's dreams are not the worst dreams on this earth, and Hughie Pugh's welding plant will go the same way as the tinplate.

**Alvin:** Not before I've had the use of it long enough to get the smell of this place off me. The moss has got into you, Miriam. You've got vestry poisoning like Dad. (*He looks fiercely around the room.*) And this room is poison too.

**Ben:** (*his arm upraised in preposterously overpitched rage*) How dare you say that?

**Alvin:** Keep it for the pensioners' Eisteddfod, Dad.

(Miriam *makes for the door, opens it, then turns.*)

**Miriam:** Go, you. You'll have the shock of your lives. You're

48

worse hypocrites than Con. At least he shows a light when he shuffles around so you can duck. But you are a lot of cunning cripples, you lot. You've stayed in the old home, because of Mam, because of Con, because of me. Let me tell you why you've stayed. Because you wouldn't have had it so easy anywhere else. You'd have needed guide dogs to find wives who cook like me. Not one of you has cleaned his shoes since I broke my arm on the ice in 1927. You've been free to grumble into my ear until my mastoid bone started to flake. God, what a lot of moaners you've been. You, Russ, about that school and your lost genius. You, Ossie, about that ticket office and your choir. You, Alvin, about the tinplate works, signalling the red dawn every time some clumsy clown in that ramshackle dump drops something on himself and breaks a toe. If any one of you had grumbled like that over the years to a wife she'd have been sprinkling weed-killer into your porridge and good luck to her too. If Con had ever ordered weed-killer in bulk I'd have been tempted to slip you a dose myself. You are on to too good a thing. You'll never leave here. You're part of the walls, like me. You've got nowhere else to go. Oh, I know, you'd pack your bags. You'd get as far as the station. You'd have the male voice party to give you a round of anthems to blow you the last few yards into the train. Then you'd think of the old front room, the singing round the piano, this nice cotton-wool shell of a world, the best rehearsal for death there is. You'd think of how all other women but me frighten you to the devil. Con is the only one of you who has taken up steadily with another woman and that's that Mrs Loomer what do you call, who's fifteen years older than he is and cosy as the town hall. And you'll notice that he sent her his first posy only on the day when she was made a County Alderman and the spearhead of all the big committees. Then last, you'd think about my steak and kidney pies, my chips, my broth, and my unbeaten twenty-four hour service and back you'd come faster than greyhounds.

**Russ:** You're wrong, Miriam. This moment was bound to come. We've just been shrugging off the decision from year to year. A man catches a glimpse of what he's shrunk into and he tries to get back to his full height. That's what most of the Sunday papers are about.

**Ben:** Miriam's right, boys. You can't go. You mustn't go. Not now. Not now.

**Alvin:** What's so special about now, Dad?

**Russ:** What?

**Ben:** Guess.

**Alvin:** This morning . . . somebody decided to sack forty people from the works and I argued blue hell with a Jehovah's Witness on the way into Birchtown. We were both put off the bus.

**Ben:** No.

**Oswald:** I gave a woman a shilling too much change on a day return to Abersychan. I told Mr Meeker, the station master about it. I must have been delirious to tell Mr Meeker. He gave me a look and told me that before nationalization I would have been lashed to a buffer.

**Ben:** No, something important, about the most important thing that's ever happened to us as a family. (*to* Russ) You tell us what you think happened this morning.

**Russ:** We instituted a new type of patrol through the school toilets, throwing the doors open brusquely and calling upon the occupants to stop and repent. At least three boys will go through life with a stoop and two with a stammer. I give you my word, Miriam. We'll go. This shrine . . . (*he points to the picture of his mother*) this shrine will crumble. This side of death every man must perform some act of liberation.

**Miriam:** What was that?

**Russ:** I said that this side of death a man must perform some act of liberation.

**Miriam:** I thought so. Look, Russ. I'm no philosopher. I just prepare food, and I have a feeling that sentence wouldn't rise in the oven. These big rolling sentences about a man having to do this and man having to do that give me a pain in the pinny. Any clown who starts shooting them off should be sentenced to a year's housekeeping. They mince things up finer and simpler in that Sunday school class that Con foisted off on me when he ran short of scripture. (Miriam *turns to her father*.) Tell them what happened this morning.

**Ben:** Con got a letter.

**Alvin:** Every morning he gets hundreds of letters. He's the most written-to official in Belmont. He tells everybody in town, if you've a trouble, write to Con Morton. He's a kind of municipal high priest. The Town Clerk warned him that if he didn't give up operating as the town's conscience he'd have him reduced to a junior clerkship.

**Ben:** The Town Clerk is jealous of our Con and always has been. He sees that in local government Con's got the touch of genius. The heart of your brother Constantine is the heart of Belmont.

**Alvin:** Put that back in the hymnal where you found it. He's a meddler, a petty crook of the emotions. The things he's promoted. You remember that time when he started that fund to provide caged birds for the aged and lonely.

**Ben:** A beautiful thought. My Uncle Laban hasn't been the same since he got his four canaries.

**Russ:** That's true. He never had a limp until he tried to get into one of those cages.

**Oswald:** Oh, aye. Con got a shoal of letters from bird-lovers. There was that old lady in Inkerman Place. A parrot owner and a lover of temperance. She had taught the parrot to sing the whole of that temperance song "Lips that touch liquor will never touch mine". She consulted me about pitch and tempo. Then she tried to teach it the first six bars of the Hallelujah Chorus. Bird's tail feathers started to smoulder. I had warned her against Handel but she would have it.

**Alvin:** And don't forget Mrs Wigmore five doors up. The budgie queen with a line in delusions that wouldn't disgrace a major prophet. She told Con she had a budgie with three heads that only sang with two. Could she be giving it the wrong seed?

**Ben:** (*very quietly*) All right. Spread your libels, break my heart, and have your bit of callous fun. Now I'll tell you what happened. What has Con wanted for a long long time?

**Russ:** To run us and run Belmont. He's done it.

**Alvin:** To court a wealthy widow who is also an alderman. He's done it.

**Ben:** (*in desperation to* Oswald) *You* know. Tell them.

**Oswald:** Yes. I know, Dad. Con has wanted to be Town Clerk. He's wanted to see his name in big letters at the bottom of those notices about elections and foot and mouth disease and so on.

**Ben:** And why hasn't he been able to put in for the job of Town Clerk?

**Oswald:** Because he couldn't pass enough exams. He kept

51

failing.

**Russ:** Certain aspects of the law always foxed him. He told me that his nature was too essentially liberal for him to see a tort in its proper dim light.

**Ben:** That's no longer so. Exams will madden his brain no more. The news came through this morning. He's a lawyer now. Passed flying.

**Alvin:** That so?

**Ben:** That is so. (*The three brothers look at each other with a mixed expression on their faces.*) Aren't you glad about it?

**Russ:** Yes, we are, Dad. We are very glad. For Con's sake. For the examiner's sake. For the law's sake. It will save a lot of ulcers all round.

**Ben:** You won't leave now, now that you know.

**Russ:** Why not?

**Ben:** This is the last mile of the road for Con, the thing he's been fighting for for years, the chance to make flesh of his dreams and your dreams.

**Alvin:** That's a word that should be outlawed. Dreams. A dream edited by Con would be anyone else's nightmare. Con can reach the summit alone like Moses. We'll send him wires of congratulation from London, Birmingham and Swindon respectively.

**Ben:** (*with tremendous dignity*) I'll never forgive you for this. (*The brothers look at him quite unmoved.*) That doesn't move you, does it? (*Tragically.*)

**Russ** and **Alvin:** No.

**Ben:** I've led a foolish life. And this is the last instalment of the price I have to pay. I've lost your respect.

**Alvin:** Don't make a tract of it, Dad.

**Ben:** (*pointing to the photo of his wife*) If I can't appeal to you, can't she?

**Russ:** That's a black and white picture, Dad. We want colour. Don't try to argue. This is autumn. The tree is stripping off. For years under the cover of sheer laziness we've crouched here out of the wind. We've warmed our bellies against Miriam's stove and become bits of ivy on Con's lusty oak. We've done our duty. We've kept the family name before the public steadily enough for Con to use it as a kind of singing commercial. I wrote a book and the stuff of the second unwritten one is stuck in me like a gall-stone. Left to myself I wouldn't have written one at all. Con stood over me. "Tell the world about us Mortons," he'd say, "about Mam and the sonata of tenderness she was and how a mysterious shudder ran through this house at the very moment when she was killed in that train crash in America. Tell how the house throbbed with music and love." That stuff. Now he's urging the putting forward of my name as a candidate for the presidency of the Local National Union of Teachers Branch, knowing that I get a rash under the armpits at the mention of committee work. And Alvin here. He's been a little trade union Prometheus, having his vitals gnawed away by the anxiety of all those poor dabs who smell doom over in those rolling sheds. And Ossie, the only conductor to arrange an eight line harmony for his own anxiety neurosis. Now is pay day. At this very moment when Con is standing most confidently on the mound of our collective achievement, boredom and agony, we shall slip from beneath him.

**Ben:** That's mean, Russell, mean.

**Russ:** Of course it's mean. (Miriam *returns from kitchen with plate.*) A man owes it to himself to do at least one astonishingly mean thing before he hits the box, so that he'll have an accurate idea of the total flavour of this gambit.

**Miriam:** You're at it again, Russ. Beating your teeth and making a real anthem out of the rattle. A man owes it to himself to be fed and to breathe. You're fed, you breathe. You're here for keeps. So we'll strike a bargain. I'll ration you to four big black statements about life a week and you'll make a point of praising my coconut dainties.

(*She extends the plate to him and they smile at each other as he helps himself to a dainty.*)

**Alvin:** It's settled then. The Exodus is under weigh. We've got some letters to write. Let's get busy. (*He claps his hands with joy.*) This is marvellous. It's like what old Cadmon Moore used to tell us in those lectures on historical determinism down at the Institute. "Great gales of change will blow . . . " (Alvin *lifts his arms in imitation of the late* Cadmon Moore, *an attitude of evangelical fervour.*) "Great gales of change will blow and you will be as helpless to resist them as the dust on the desert's floor."

**Miriam:** From one part of the desert to another. That's an even better trip than we used to do with the Sunday School. Apply to me for tea when you want to wash the grit out of your mouths. And that Cadmon Moore, the prophet of gales, he couldn't even raise a puff. He died pecked to death by his wife. I was with him when he died. He wanted to lay some kind of gipsy's curse on her. But he had read too many books on the dialectic to be able to remember the formula.

**Russ:** A gifted teacher, Cadmon. Lived too soon or too long. Should never have hung on in this place. We won't make the same mistake, Miriam. (*He jumps up.*) Now then, Os. Let's get down to those letters.

(*The front door is heard opening and into the room comes* Wallace.)

**Wallace:** What's all this? (*He studies in particular the bewilderment on his father's face.*) There's electricity in the air. Explain.

**Alvin:** We've made up our minds, Wallace. The family is breaking up. Russ is going to teach in London, Ossie's taking a promotion in Swindon, and is breaking his baton over Con's head. And I'm dodging out of the tinplate before the roof falls in. I'm off to Birmingham.

**Wallace:** Now isn't that queer?

**Alvin:** What's queer about it? We couldn't have stuck it out like this for the rest of our lives.

**Walllace:** I know that. What's queer is that in the Bannerman Club a quarter of an hour ago I had a phone call from London. It was from Jackie Bennett.

**Miriam:** Jackie Bennet the doctor? He's in South Africa.

**Walllace:** He's back on a short holiday. He's in London now. He's got a practice in Pretoria. Getting too big for him. He wants me to go up to South Africa House tomorrow and arrange to join him.

**Miriam:** You going?

**Wallace:** Something all at once is pushing us. I've got no wish to stay loyal to this place and wind up as a subordinate figure in old Doc Edmonds' last delirium.

**Russ:** As Granch would have said: "The Lord hath spoken".

**Oswald:** Seems like it.

(Wallace *goes to the cupboard and brings out a bottle and glasses. He pours out and hands round.*)

**Wallace:** I had been planning to keep this for Miriam's birthday, but let's drink to the exodus, the great dispersal, to the blessed tendency of human beings to burst apart out of their own mousetraps.

(*As they are lifting their glasses the front door is burst open and is banged shut with startling suddenness. They all look a little surprised. They let their glasses drop a few inches.* Miriam *has left the room after shaking her head at them sardonically.*)

**Russ:** Whoever's there, the toast shall be drunk.

(*They lift their glasses again as* Con *bursts into the room.*)

Curtain

# ACT TWO

## Scene One

*Same as Act One.*

**Con:** What's the matter?
**Wallace:** We've been drinking a toast.
**Con:** (*his face lighting up and with mock bashfulness*) Oh, to me. Dad told you about the law degree. He shouldn't have told you. (*He points to the glasses.*) But thanks all the same for making such a fuss. A toast from my brothers. That's all I need to make this the biggest night of my life.
  (Russell *tilts his wine glass to drain the last few drops.*)
**Russ:** It wasn't to you, Con. If you came into the toast at all, it was very obliquely.
**Ben:** They are going away, Con. These fools want to leave their home.
**Con:** Leave home. Now, of all times. Now. This is a joke. This is one of Alvin's daft little practical jokes.
**Alvin:** I gave those up when I started doing committee work for the Union. You can't do that and laugh.
**Ben:** They are going. (*points to* Wallace) Africa for him. He's leaving old Dr Edmonds in the lurch. (*points to* Russell) London, leaving those boys down in the Steelworks Road who worship him. (*points to* Oswald) Swindon, leaving just when he's bringing the tone of the Belmont Orpheans to the quality of velvet. (*points to* Alvin) Worst of the lot. Birmingham. He started the rain falling tonight. He's going to work in a welding shop run by Hughie Pugh, leaving all those people in the tinplate works to face a dark future alone.
**Oswald:** (*embarrassed*) More room for you now, Con, you can branch out. And when you go to London on big important business I'll wave to you at Swindon. It helps there. A wave.

56

**Con:** Go on, put the cherry on the trifle. Say that rates have been abolished and I'll know that my mind has been off on some peculiar holiday chime of its own.

**Oswald:** No, Con. I think rates have got a very steady future. And war.

(Miriam *comes in.*)

**Miriam**: So they have a date with light and life.

**Oswald**: That's right, Con. Light and life.

**Miriam:** Let them go. My bet is that they won't get as far as the door of Belmont Station. (*looks at* Alvin) Oh, I remember what I came in here for. How do you like your chips these days, Al? Your tastes have been chopping and changing ever since you started thinking about redundancy.

**Alvin:** Chips: pale and soft, like always —

**Miriam:** Right. That'll take a bit longer. This is going to be a very late supper. I've thought a lot about chips. Here's one for your book of axioms, Russ. I think man would sit more easily on the earth if he always had exactly the sort of chips he fancies. Man's soul needs an anchor of potato.

**Con:** (*shooting his head up from his bitter reverie*) What was that?

**Russ:** That was Miriam. She and I are making up a poultice of philosophic plasters for all contemporary manias.

**Wallace:** Now we'll drink to you, Con, and to the day when you acquire enough power to stop yourself twitching.

**Con:** All right. Have your joke. I'm used to it. I've got broad shoulders. (*His father pats him assuringly on the broad shoulders.*) Anyone who goes out and gets things done is used to it. He's judged always from the point of view of the people in the graveyard. (*Looks cunningly around the group. He laughs and speaks in a voice almost cracked with the desire to be gay and confident.*) Now let's stop these nursery games. But I was shaken there for a minute when I heard Dad saying those things. Do you know it's a kind of nightmare I've often had. Not in sleep, but sometimes at late evening. Tired, coming back from some long session at the Town Hall. Not a sound anywhere. Then the gladness would start slipping away from me. I'd start sweating with fear. Must have something to do with that particular stretch of road. Remember I was chased along there when I was about nine by that sex maniac when I was wearing that velvet suit I had used for my recitation in the Eisteddfod that day.

**Oswald:** He had his eye on you right through the Eisteddfod. That was a fine bit of running you both did and that suit was very tight on you. (*to* Russell) Is there any sense to the ways and purpose of love?

**Con:** Always on that stretch of the road that spurt of dread that would make me break into a run until I got to the door, the front door of our castle, our fortress.

**Ben:** That's right, Con. Our castle, our fortress. (*To* Russell) You hear that?

**Russ:** I hear it.

**Con:** And do you know what it was I was always afraid of?

**Wallace:** I could name a thousand things.

**Con:** Not that I'd find Miriam or one of you dead. But that you'd all be waiting to tell me that you were going, or even that you were already gone. The house empty and Mam betrayed, just like you did tonight to give me a real fright, to have a bit of a laugh at me. Now let's drink that toast, a real one. To the united Mortons, strong, crafty, undefeatable. Let's drink to them. (*He and* Ben *are the only ones to lift the glasses which* Con *has gone charging around the table to fill. The rest stand around quite still watching them curiously.*) Well? (*The brothers leave their glasses on the table untouched. To* Oswald *who stands nearest to him*) You got cramp?

**Oswald:** (*moving his arm*) No, no. Quite sprightly.

**Russ:** What we said wasn't a joke, Con. We're on our way.

**Wallace:** Pretoria.

**Oswald:** Swindon.

**Alvin:** Birmingham.

**Russ:** London.

**Con:** No, you're talking nonsense. And you tell me this tonight, of all nights. The most tremendous and fertile evening of my life. I've been talking my tongue right down to the canvas, for you, for you.

**Russ:** And we've done our whack for you. To get you into the Town Clerk's chair. All right. Have it, fill it, keep it. Now let's have one discussion in this room that will be free of sentimental claptrap about Mam.

**Alvin:** This is it, Con. Midnight. The tinplate works is falling to bits and I don't want to be part of the ruin.

**Oswald:** I never want to see another chorister. In Swindon I'll take up knitting. Very soothing, that.

**Ben:** Knitting? Did that first glass of tonic wine madden you, Oswald?

**Oswald:** No, no. I don't want to knit anything in particular. I just want to knit and knit until I've got enough stuff to muffle all life. It gives out some funny sounds when it bangs against me.

**Russ:** And I'm going to a part of London where I won't have to see the slummy look on the faces of those kids I teach with just a thin wall between me and the noisiest steelworks in Britain.

**Con:** No, no. You've got to hear what I have to say, what I've done tonight.

**Wallace:** I vote that we all go back down to the Bannerman Club, before Con gets into his oratorical stride.

**Alvin:** It'll be nice to have you at a safe distance, Con.

**Ben:** And you say that to the boy who was a father to you during the years when I betrayed my trust.

**Alvin:** Dad, it would have been better all round if you had kept your end up and your trust betrayed. You find me anything more dismal than a happy reveller who returns to moan to the tents of the pious and I'll say a good word for the tinplate industry. (Ben *sinks desperately into a chair and covers his face with his hands.*)

**Oswald:** Never mind, Dad, I think everybody's got a touch of this three day 'flu that keeps on. You know that Willie Wedlock the farrier, two doors up?

**Wallace:** (*delighted by the diversion that might possibly get them from under the tension that* Con *is wishing to bring down on them*) Short man, incipient D.T.s and a guilt complex as thick as a wall. What's up with him?

**Oswald:** Drank three pints of the Jerusalem wine, that wine with the bits of stuff that goes up and down, up and down.

    (Oswald *does a graphic description of this wine.* Ben *glances at* Con *wondering whether he will anger him by taking a saving interest in* Oswald's *story.*)

**Ben:** I know, I know. It ferments and goes up and down. Wedlock keeps a jar of it in his front room window and I've often felt like calling in and telling him it looks a bit sinister.

**Oswald:** It's out of sight. Wedlock scoffed the lot. Stripped off and ran up and down the tip stark naked and shouting "I am the living God."

**Ben:** What was he shouting?

**Oswald:** "I am the living God." Naked and saying it loud and clear. A powerful bass-baritone, Wedlock, but always one for using his voice wastefully.

**Con:** (*in an outraged voice*) Do you mind?

**Oswald:** Mind what, Con?

**Con:** Mind if I make one of the most important statements of my life.

**Oswald:** Oh, you go ahead, boy.

**Con:** (*pointing to* Russell, Wallace *and* Alvin) I mean this for you three particularly. I think Ossie has been in some way deafened by the male voice choir, and he's beyond the reach of normal argument. In any case, I've got confidence in Ossie to do the right thing. He likes me. I have the feeling that you three don't like me, do you?

**Russ:** Don't ask questions like that, for God's sake. You're not a kid any more. What do you want to be liked for?

**Con:** All right. Forgive me for asking. It's not my fault that I dream of a life where there will be more tenderness and security than there is now.

**Russ:** When a man can make a statement like that in cold blood, that man's skull truly understands why his skull is made of bone.

**Con:** (*very quietly*) Very well, Russ. Had I been vulnerable to jibes, I'd have dropped in my tracks a long time ago.

**Russ:** Instead of which, you've lined your tracks with other people. It's easier.

**Con:** I want to tell you about today. (*He goes and stands in front of his mother's picture.*) I want to talk like we did when we were kids. Without barriers, without distrust.

**Russ:** Watch the forks.

**Con:** I've been selfish. But today, tonight, let me tell you something. For the last couple of hours I've talked, connived, bullied, without a single thought for myself. I suppose you know that I passed my final law exams.

**Wallace:** We were glad about that, Con. Genuinely glad. (Con *shakes hands solemnly with* Wallace.) Now tell us about this moment of illumination, this saintliness.

**Con:** I want no illumination. I want no illumination. I want the conviction and the warmth of this home. I want this cloak of brothers around my body. As for saintliness, the only halo I'm after is a small photo and a short tribute in the *Gazette* of the Association of Local Government Officers.

**Ben:** It'll be a long tribute, Con, and a big photo.

**Con:** Perhaps, perhaps. But I'll be satisfied at the moment just to drop my voice and be listened to.

**Alvin:** Right, right. You've softened us up. Now unveil the tablets.

**Con:** I'll start with you, Alvin.

**Alvin:** Good.

**Con:** You feel desperate about the tinplate works, don't you?

**Alvin:** I do.

**Con:** I was on the telephone to the chairman of your regional committee five minutes after the meeting ended.

**Alvin:** That was sharp of you.

**Con:** I'm the Secretary of the Belmont Development Council. I've got to keep my finger on the pulse.

**Alvin:** Well, you can take it off. The tinplate has had its lot. Forty get their cards next week and I'll be among them. If I stayed on I'd have to watch and feel the thing die in bits and pieces and that would make me very angry, Con, very wild.

**Con:** I spoke with Mrs Loomer-Barkway tonight.

**Russ:** That's a fragrant remark. We're proud of you, Con.

**Con:** You know who she is.

**Alvin:** Yes, I know. She's rich, she's stupid, and a snob. She's had her picture in *Vogue* once as a fancy dresser and two hundred times in the *Western Mail* as a torpid thinker.

**Con:** She is also my friend.

**Ben:** Oh, Con, you're doing well.

**Con:** She listens to me.

**Russ:** What kind of new courting routine is that, listening?

**Con:** You know very well what I mean. She's leaned heavily on me since the Colonel's death.

**Ben:** And a better shoulder she couldn't have found.

**Alvin:** That colonel. A cold fish. He was the one steel magnate who could cool one of his own furnaces with a glance. God's answer to Cort's retort.

**Con:** Without the Loomer-Barkways this county would have stayed a cabbage patch. Coal, iron, steel, ships, at the helm of each one you will find a Loomer-Barkway.

**Russ:** There was also a brand of rickets named after them during the slump.

**Con:** A slander.

**Oswald:** (*bemused*) Those furs she wears. Have you seen that black one? (*He addresses the question vaguely to his father.*)

**Ben:** Since I turned over my new leaf I try not to be sensuous. You do the same, Oswald.

**Oswald:** Once on a freezing day she was standing in the Town Square. It was the time Alvin was on the Ban the Bomb Committee and he talked me into marching around the square with a sandwich board. It said: 'Humanity's Last Chance' back and front. Mrs Loomer-Barkway came up and wanted a policeman to trundle me off to the County Keep for sedition.

**Con:** A brother of mine, in a position like that.

**Oswald:** The policeman was a chorister and he wouldn't take action. So I sidled up to Mrs Loomer-Barkway and I started to explain to her in a low voice all the things Alvin had told me about what was happening to those kids in those Japanese cities. She said: "Keep your distance, sandwich man." They were her very words. "Keep your distance, sandwich man."

**Con:** (*groaning and shuddering with embarrassment*) My brother. (*to* Alvin) All your doing. No wonder our Os is just a single exposed nerve, dragging him into antics like those.

**Oswald:** She offered me a coin and repeated her words. She's got a loud rich voice.

**Ben:** A rich contralto. Once I heard her sing 'Land of Hope and Glory' at a Coronation tea. In the open air, but she still made the cups rattle and the jellies shake. A good voice but too autocratic for oratorio.

**Oswald:** Then I found my head getting closer to that fur she was wearing. I couldn't help it. I rubbed my cheek into it. Something to do with being starved of love, I suppose, or never seeing a fur like that so close up before. It was beautiful. She gave a snort and pushed me hard. She sent me reeling down the steps of the public convenience.

**Con:** (*horrified*) That happened to a brother of mine?

**Oswald:** Fact. On a Saturday afternoon with this slogan about humanity's last chance all around me. That experience gave me a new law for living.

**Russ:** What was that, Os?

**Wallace:** Never rub your face into a woman's fur coat while she's still wearing it.

**Oswald:** No. Never fall down the steps of a public convenience wearing sandwich boards; you get into a terrible tangle. That caretaker there, Mortimer Marsden, he stood over me and said: "Oswald" he said, "I have seen many men coming down those steps at speed and with many needs. What is your need, Oswald?"

**Con:** I'll have the Town Square and the toilets banned to the more whimsical type of sectary and agitator.

**Wallace:** What started this affair between you and her? I can imagine you working up to a fair heat over an agenda, but not the widow of a tycoon.

**Con:** Heat, as you call it, doesn't enter into it. The colonel always discouraged sex. He always considered it an improvident bolshevik sort of thing. Mrs Loomer-Barkway agreed with him and our relationship has always been cool and socially minded. I met her first when I was organizing the memorial service for the colonel. I got him two more hymns than any other dead man in the Celtic fringe. I gave her the idea of a printed history of the Loomer-Barkways. She invited me up to the Hall.

**Oswald:** The where?

**Con:** The Hall. They call the house the Hall. It's a mansion. I wanted Russell to do the writing of the book. It would have made him.

**Russ:** Made me what? You dragged me up to that mausoleum just once. What a family. One lot of correspondence was about one Loomer-Barkway contesting an affiliation warrant. He suborned fifteen of his steel workers to swear that they had had full access to the plaintiff. She was given a pension and a medal by the Welsh Tourist Board for shocking the wits out of Calvin. And that Mrs Loomer-Barkway. Coo.

**Con:** You'll change your mind about her before the night is out, my boy.

**Russ:** Not without shock treatment I won't.

**Alvin:** Change my mind about her.

**Con:** I will. We talked about you tonight, Alvin. She wants to show her appreciation of the way you've worked on behalf of the older workers.

**Alvin:** You mean she's going to suspend the sackings?

**Con:** Forget the sackings. That's policy, her policy, the Government's policy, God's policy. What we're talking about is you, Alvin, you, my brother, not about a covey of codgers and dodgers who'll have finished on age grounds in a few years anyway. She's going to make you Assistant Manager.

**Alvin:** Me?

**Con:** You. Eighteen pounds a week and a lot of nice clean office work to keep you out of the rolling mill. And you can give up your union work as well. You've been moaning enough about it. You've complained enough about the unions being the only vehicles with square wheels ever to try to take the workers to paradise. Now you can board your own little wagon and stay nice and quiet. (*He looks delightedly around the room.*)

**Alvin:** And what kind of perfume does that sprinkle me with?

**Con:** Perfume? What are you talking about?

**Alvin:** Let's get out of the shawl. You are asking me to take the job of Assistant Manager so that I'll stand aside and watch a whole platoon of my comrades walk industrially into the grave without as much as a stroke of the drum from me.

**Con:** Oh, stop mucking about with words. If humanity had choked most of its drummers at birth we'd have walked more neatly in step.

**Alvin:** Nothing doing. Tell Mrs Loomer-Barkway that we made a few principles in those works as well as tinplate.

**Con:** All right, Alvin. You've got full marks for a rousing speech. Now listen. That's a new art, just listening. Nothing can stop these people getting the sack next week. The best economic brains of the land have decided that a little controlled unemployment is the only magnesia that will relieve our current flatulence.

**Wallace:** I'm writing in to the *Lancet* suggesting a quick lobechtomy as the only remedy to all who apply medical metaphors to social matters. Human beings are not corrupt and operable flesh. Nor are their groans and sighs symptomatic burbs.

**Con:** Typical. Typical. You talk pity and threaten to clip my cortex. I'd rather be trepanned in a good cause than in no cause at all.

**Oswald:** If it doesn't interfere with local values, fair enough.

**Con:** And on top of government directives, Mrs Loomer-Barkway is the Moses on this Sinai and she wants the tinplate works to shrink. But we're going to be smart, Alvin, we're going to be cunning.

**Russ:** Slip on your second pair of braces, Alvin. Somebody's after your buttons.

**Con:** Ignore these poets, Alvin. I've got an answer to them too, before we go into supper. You want to see the works saved, don't you?

**Alvin:** I want to see change geared to the needs of the people. No more masses of people to be turned to stone to make a bit of rockery for some damned administrative genius in London.

**Con:** I'm with you there, boy, all the way. The past has got to be taken off cautiously, but never, never let it be a shroud.

**Ben:** Good axiom.

**Con:** There are two things to be done. There's got to be someone left at the tinplate works with enough faith in its future to see that it keeps in being. We've got to triple the *local* demand for tinplate. To hell with exports. Do you know, I even tried to interest old Lemuel Sugden, the undertaker, in tinplate caskets. We've got to hold the line, keep the works breathing even if it means a complete reversal of the old trade union notions. Principles should be like skirts; up or down according to the moral atmosphere, with what a man wants at a particular moment.

**Alvin:** I'll think about it.

**Con:** That's the spirit, boy. Creative doubt. Nibble a chip and slide slowly towards self-interest.

**Alvin:** Don't say any more. I'm trying to persuade myself. It's hard.

**Con:** Of course it is. But you can forget about that train to Birmingham.

(Alvin *leaves the room.*)

**Russ:** And no doubt you are coming down the chimney with packages for us too.

**Con:** For each of you the package of his dreams. I told you. This has been a night of opening doors. You, Wallace, I know have been going crazy with Dr Edmonds. In my plans I had him reckoned a corpse five years ago with you free to improve and expand the practice. But you over-did the kindliness. The trouble that causes. You doubled his income and halved his work. You gave him the free time to preserve his mind in snooker and his body in scotch. And that notion of going to Africa is a poor one too.

**Wallace:** I'd prefer to be disgusted in a temperate zone. But I've travelled the full distance here. I can't take any more of it.

**Con:** Most of us have lived against the grain, Wallace. But we always get at least a part of what we dream of.

**Russ:** Con, you are the only man who could write a report on municipal sewage and a Christmas cracker motto simultaneously.

**Wallace:** What have I dreamed of?

**Con:** You know as well as I do. You know how you've chafed at having to go along to that surgery every morning and evening, plagued by an incoming tide of individual complaints, staunching a cough here, easing a hernia there, the regulars, you call them, the stalactites that drip into a pattern of enduring horror.

**Wallace:** They're good people. I'm sorry to have thought and talked about them with occasional contempt.

**Con:** Good people. Spoilt bodies, spoilt lives. But you've got vision, Wallace.

**Wallace:** I've also got asthma brought on by working in a surgery with all the earmarks of an old grotto. Age and death will cure both.

**Con:** Think of the way you used to talk to us in the kitchen.

**Wallace:** That was in the days when I was suffering from ingrowing pamphlets.

**Con:** Given a chance your dreams might blaze again.

**Wallace:** Leave them in peace.

**Con:** I won't leave anything in peace. That's my function. To set things on edge, a sharp edge. Yesterday Mrs Loomer-Barkway was elected chairman of the County Health Committee.

**Russ:** That's a big step forward. Her first big economic drive will be to replace X-ray by hearsay.

**Con:** She's more enlightened than you think. She's already settled in her mind who the next County Medical Officer will be.

**Wallace:** Me?

**Con:** You. And without much delay. You can start doing all the things that you and Russ have thought about and talked about for years; start from the social bottom. Get rid of all the old sores and imbecilities. To give a new dignity and eloquence to all the people of this region.

**Russ:** From Bessemer Road Modern Secondary School. Put out your pipe, Con. Opium won't help.

**Con:** This isn't opium. This is solid fact. You won't be at Bessemer Road Modern Secondary School for long, Russ.

**Russ:** I know that. I'll either be in London or I may decide to stop my traffic with the young altogether and go and sell candyfloss in Porthcawl.

**Con:** You won't be in either place. Remember your old idea of giving every child in this part of Belmont at least a month a year of residential schooling in lovely clean surroundings away from all the conditioning squalor of home life.

**Russ:** Is the wine all gone?

**Wallace:** There's another bottle left.

**Russ:** Let's have it. When Con is in this mood my despair becomes as tangible as dandruff.

(Wallace *produces a bottle and pours from it.*)

**Con:** I never thought to hear a word like despair in *this* room. I've got something better than wine. I don't want to sound like Moses . . .

**Russ:** You will, don't worry.

**Con:** . . . but I'm leading you two boys on to the hilltop from which your promised land will be for the first time visible. You remember, Russ, one Sunday afternoon you and I went for a walk over Belmont Mountain. We stopped to look at the Loomer-Barkway mansion. Do you remember what I said?

**Russ:** You said that Edward the Seventh slept there twice.

**Con:** Yes, that's significant. But what you should have remembered me as saying was that I thought that house would be ideal as a school for those kids who can't think for fumes in that school you teach in now.

**Russ:** You might well have said that. You said a lot.

**Con:** Mrs Loomer-Barkway gave that mansion to the County Council yesterday. It is going to become just the kind of school you visualized. And you are going to be the first headmaster.

**Russ:** (*to* Wallace) Do you hear someone stitching a web?

**Con:** No web. Just glory and liberation for you all. What becomes of me is of no moment.

(Oswald *comes ambling in from the kitchen, chewing.*)

**Ben:** And what have you got for Ossie?

**Con:** For Ossie, too, I have my gift.

**Oswald:** Oh, no. Please Con. Leave me alone. I don't want anything. I'll just shuffle off to Swindon and I'll hand the baton of the choir to Caradoc Slee.

**Con:** Nonsense, You've got to be saved from yourself. Toscanini, Sargent, Roscoe Rees of Trecysgod, I bet all the greats of the baton have had these moments of failed confidence and recession.

**Oswald:** That Roscoe Rees had a face of brass.

**Con:** That's what the world saw. The brass. But I have seen Rees before a concert sweating and panting in his front room whipping his sheet music with his baton and cursing his own mother who was trying to feed him with beef tea.

**Oswald:** Well, well. Roscoe Rees, beef tea.

**Russ:** That's the state you'll get Ossie in if you keep on. Berserk in the front room.

**Oswald:** What was that gift you were speaking of, Con? But make it small, Con, make it humble, make it private.

**Con:** It's a gift of a triumph, Ossie.

**Oswald:** Oh, God.

**Con:** The gift of a triumph. Something that will lift you clear out of the rut of your own self-contempt.

**Wallace:** There's no winch big enough for that.

**Con:** Have you heard of Cosmo Joslin?

**Wallace:** Cosmo, the T.V? The boy who did brilliantly at Oxford?

**Con:** A genius. And rapidly emerging as Britain's premier television producer. And a Belmont boy.

**Russ:** What's the link? Have you bought him for Ossie?

**Con:** Cosmo has been asked to produce the first live telecast from this country to Canada. A programme to reflect the whole heart of Britain.

**Russ:** Good. Canada's had this coming ever since they sent us the Rocky Mountain singers.

**Con:** Cosmo came to see me. He wanted to know the item that would best convey the soul of his region.

**Wallace:** A face reflecting the combined ravage of chapel religion and pit labour.

**Russ:** Part of the roof of the school's main hall shaken loose by subsidence at the very moment when the Head was reading a piece from the Bible about avenging bolts and Jehovah's wrath. The kids gave him the biggest clap of their lives.

**Oswald:** Those people waiting for the last train on Saturday night, against those railings outside Belmont station and clasped in a last embrace. And the way they snarl when I say to them such things as: "Stop it" or "There's always tomorrow."

**Con:** Leave squalor out of this please. A body of men united in song. That's what I suggested. The Belmont Orpheans. We were at your rehearsal last Wednesday night, Os, but you didn't see us. He was fascinated by Ossie. Fascinated, that was Cosmo Joslin's own word. The humble artist, the unpretentious dreamer, a man of sweetness and modesty. It will be a five minute spot. And the emphasis will not be on the singing but on the face and body of Ossie.

**Ben:** It'll be your moment, Os.

**Oswald:** But I'd die. I haven't got the sort of gestures.

**Con:** Don't listen to this lot, Ossie. This is going to be the experience of your lifetime. And at the end of it you'll have grown six entire feet.

**Wallace:** If a man doesn't like what he is already he doesn't need a single inch more of it.

**Con:** Size is all.

**Wallace:** Boy, what a Town Clerk you are going to make. The mayor will need the strength of a bull to lift his chain.

**Con:** If my brothers are not with me I don't want to be Town Clerk or anything else.

**Oswald:** Honest, Con, forget about me. When those cameras start flashing at me I'll go out in a dead faint.

**Russ:** That's what he's after. Cosmo Joslin wants to be the first T.V. producer to show an all male party with an utterly senseless conductor in front of them.

**Con:** There will be no fainting.

(Miriam *comes in and takes a seat. She has some bulky bit of knitting in her hand.*)

**Russ:** Who's the cardigan for, Miriam?

**Miriam:** It's not a cardigan. (*glances at* Con) It's just something I want to make big enough to muffle life.

**Con:** (*pettishly*) I was saying that there will be no fainting. Canada will see Ossie's gentle saintly face plain and smiling on the home screen. Because between now and the T.V. date Ossie is going to have one of the richest and most ennobling experiences he's ever known.

**Miriam:** He's found you a woman, Os.

**Wallace:** If he has, take it easy, boy, take it slow, I've seen a lot of you late developers burn themselves out.

**Ben:** I don't like this bold talk about women, not in here, not in the front room.

**Oswald:** (*embarrassedly*) Oh, Con wouldn't be thinking anything like that. I know sex has got its place, and it's inspired many a fine choir piece, but I don't fancy it much myself.

**Miriam:** You'd prefer a nice cutlet of hake, wouldn't you, Os?

**Oswald:** I fancy warm fish. It's my fancy any time.

**Con:** Could I call on you lot for a bit of piety, a sense of fitness? Haven't you got the gumption to realize that I'm on the verge of saying something grave and loaded with significance?

**Russ:** You've been rolling out these messages for the last twenty-five years. We can stand another one.

(*Knock on door.*)

**Con:** That will be Mr Wilmot now.

**Russ:** Wilmot? The Chief Deacon down at Tabernacle. He's a right one. Clear the floor for a rolling clown.

**Con:** You'll regret that when you hear what Mr Wilmot's errand is about. (*Goes to the door of the parlour.*) Come in, Mr Wilmot.

(*Mr Wilmot comes in. He is a short ponderous man. He carries a large parcel under his arm. He shakes hands gravely with Ben and then nods at Miriam and the brothers. His eyes become less cordial as they land on Russell and Wallace. Just as Mr Wilmot starts fiddling with the paper around the parcel, Alvin comes in and stands chewing by the door, watching Wilmot with the closest interest.*)

**Alvin:** (*pointing to Wilmot*) What's he up to?

**Wallace:** He and Con are planning something.

**Alvin:** The last time Wilmot was in here was to say that God is not mocked and put up the rent of the little hut where we hold our lodge meetings.

(*Wilmot produces from paper a plaque of about three feet bearing letters of silver paint.*)

**Con:** Look at that. Isn't it beautiful? Isn't it absolutely lovely?

**Russ:** What does it say?

**Con:** Read it to them, Os.

**Oswald:** It says: To a Mother of Sons, erected on the Wall of the Chapel she attended through her life by Alvin, Constantine, Russell, Oswald and Wallace Morton.

70

**Miriam:** No daughter? What do I do? Leave on the next plaque?

**Con:** Your monument is us, Miriam.

**Miriam:** Fair enough. Find me a stretch of wall and I'll hang you up on it.

**Alvin:** What's this for?

**Con:** It's a plaque, a memorial plaque.

**Alvin:** I know that. But what's the point of it? Why drag this up? This sort of gesture should be in the mind, not hung up on walls.

**Con:** Alvin, my boy, your heart has been on the chilly side ever since you went over to the Rationalists.

**Ben:** Fact. Put me on edge at many a meal. Catching me in the middle of a mouthful and urging me to face up to the coming darkness without God, hope or anything. Got my stomach in many a tangle I can tell you.

**Con:** Love operates at many different levels of heat.

    (*He utters that sentence with great pomp as if it is the first sentence of a public report of great importance. A great quietness follows.*)

**Wallace:** That's one for the Borough Surveyor.

**Miriam:** It's that that makes people look so strange.

**Ben:** (*quoting from a temperance hymn*) And many a loving heart doth sink, In the dusk of gambling and drink . . .

**Wilmot:** A lovely thought.

    (Wilmot *raises his right arm and with* Ben *is going to launch into another couplet.*

**Wilmot** and **Ben:** And many a . . .

    (Con *interrupts them.*)

**Con:** Some loves can be contained. Some can be expressed in an occasional cool thought. Others cannot. Mine cannot. My love for Mam and you cannot be confined here. (*Taps head.*) It's got to be expressed in acts. The memory of that wonderful woman is as alive to me today as when she left this house fifteen years ago.

**Russ:** All right. We remember. Ghosts walk and we keep them company. (*Points to plaque.*) But remembrance that needs as barbarous a token as that should go the whole hog and get buried alongside the subject.

**Wallace:** It's certainly a token.

**Wilmot:** (*proudly*) Best teak. Top price. Luminous paint. Shows in the dark. Just right for you.

**Wallace:** Too true. I always look at plaques in the dark.

**Russ:** Honest, Con, with your lack of taste you could have been a leader of nations.

**Alvin:** And will this thing be hung up somewhere?

**Con:** Of course.

**Alvin:** Where?

**Wilmot:** Where it says. (*Holds up plaque to read*) In the Chapel she attended through her life. Then come your names as the erectors and donors . . . it reads like music.

**Con:** You can't be furtive about a thing like this, Alvin.

**Russ:** You could be. But you won't be.

**Alvin:** (*marvelling*) And it'll be unveiled, like a cenotaph?

**Russ:** (*in exactly the same tone as* Alvin): Curtains, cord, the lot?

**Wilmot:** Purple curtain, satin cord.

**Con:** No point in spoiling the ship for a pennorth of tar. There's no beauty without a bit of ceremonial.

**Wallace:** Trumpets?

**Wilmot:** Not in a place of worship. Too blaring.

**Ben:** Very harsh, the trumpet.

**Alvin:** And who'll do the unveiling?

**Con:** Our mayor, Mr Wyndham Smillie.

**Alvin:** Him? He is Mam's second round of doom.

**Con:** He's a member of the Chapel and just the man for the job.

**Wilmot:** A prince of the prayer meeting. A voice of gold, and, on a line of genuine communication with God, a tongue of love.

**Alvin:** And how he's licked around. He'd have sold his mother if his father hadn't beaten him to it.

(Mr Wilmot *and* Ben *hold up their hands at each other in horror, and make as if they are waiting for a signal to faint.*)

**Russ:** And he will also have the casting vote in the appointment of the next Town Clerk.

**Con:** (*very angrily*) Look. I've given you warning of that. Have your own malicious thoughts. Traduce me in any shape or form you think fit. But let no one dare, *no one* I say, let no one dare suggest that I would ever use my love for Mam as a tactic, a device. The plaque will be unveiled four weeks tomorrow. The dignitaries who'll want to be there won't be all together in Belmont until then. I wouldn't want anybody who cares, who really cares, to be away from this. The night before the unveiling we are going to have a little celebration here to mark the occasion. The family and a few friends.

**Miriam:** Let's get in training. Cold meat and hard-boiled eggs out in the kitchen.

(Alvin, Russell, Wallace *and* Miriam *leave*. Oswald *makes to follow them but* Con *fixes his eye and one arm on him and* Oswald *reluctantly lingers*.)

**Con:** And there'll be a special place for you at the ceremony, Os.

**Oswald:** Me again?

**Con:** You are going to conduct the Belmont Orpheans in a special version of that lovely old hymn that meant so much to Mam. 'Flee as a Bird to your Fountain, Ye who are Weary of Sin'.

**Wilmot:** Sin. It's everywhere.

**Ben:** From end to end. All over. Always busy, sin.

**Con:** Could you rig up some plangent harmonies for the bass in particular? You know how Mam liked the great rumbling of the bass.

**Ben:** That was funny with me a bit on the tenor side.

**Wilmot:** She heard you deep, no doubt.

(Oswald *goes to the piano and picks out the melody of 'Flee as a Bird'. He enriches the bass line*.)

**Con:** (*softly to* Ben) It's going to be all right, Dad.

**Ben:** Is it, Con? Is it?

**Con:** They'll have their doubts, their bit of sourness. But they'll think of what I've said tonight and they'll see that we in this house have got to depend on each other, that they can't do much without me, that I can't do much without them. And when we stand together around that unveiled plaque a month from now we'll know a unity we never knew before. (*He puts his hands almost passionately around the thick gilt frame of his mother's photograph*.)

**Oswald:** I think I've got it now. That thick line on the bass. Like syrup. (*He stops playing*.)

**Con:** She's never ceased to be with us. Her love will never let us down. Watch that picture when all the dreams we've talked about tonight come true. Wallace, Medical Officer, Russ, his own school, and writing books again. Ossie, conductor of note and possibly a station master if he can learn to look arrogant under one of those peaked caps.

**Ben:** And you the Town Clerk.

**Con:** Watch that picture and watch that plaque. You will see Mam's face on it, plain, beautiful, beaming and weeping, like she

73

was whenever we did anything that made her glad.

**Wilmot:** I can see her now. I'm glad we stuck out for teak. Belmont will take this monument to its heart.

Curtain

# Scene Two

*Hint of time lapse, then back to the same room.* Ben, *clothed as before, with the sole difference of a wing collar, is sitting down. The memorial plaque has been put to stand just beneath the picture of Mrs Morton.* Miriam *comes in with every sign of exhaustion.*

**Miriam:** Well the banquet is ready. The biggest thing since Babylon.

**Ben:** The middle room's looking a treat. This evening will wipe out the last memory of a slump. All that meat. All those trifles. And those bottles of wine. I suppose they *are* all tonic wines, are they, Miriam?

**Miriam:** They're cheap and weak, if that's what you mean . . . They won't set off any flares. You won't see Mr Wilmot jump across the table at Mrs Loomer-Barkway.

**Ben:** She is coming then?

**Miriam:** Last I heard.

(Oswald *comes in. He is wearing a black bow tie with a soft white shirt. His step is light and he is ostensibly quite blithe. He is chewing.*)

**Oswald:** Took a bit of that chicken. I think that with more white meat the Celts would have been a steadier lot.

**Miriam:** How are you feeling, Os?

**Oswald:** Fine. (*He glances at himself in the mirror.*) That Cosmo Joslin the T.V. has given me a lot of confidence. He showed me a little clip of film he made of me. I look really nice.

**Ben:** No vanity now, Oswald. Nurse your nerves. And cure yourself of trembling every whipstitch. But no vanity. It will lead you to wanton boldness.

**Oswald:** I hope so, I just stand in front of the choir now, eyes

74

closed, hands hardly moving, just inviting them to follow the throb of my spirit, as Mr Cosmo Joslin says.

**Miriam:** Do they follow?

**Oswald:** Softly, but they are there.

(*Knock on outer door.*)

**Miriam:** I'll see. (*Sounds of voices and laughter. Door closes and* Miriam *comes back.*) Mrs Richards the Bon Ton sent the box of coffee cups over. The ones I ordered only came in this afternoon. Come on, Os, help me to get them unwrapped and washed. You'll find an apron behind the kitchen door.

(*While* Miriam *has been speaking* Oswald *has been standing in front of the mirror, performing the gestures and making the grimaces of a conductor who is coaxing a great body of voices into the most delicate of sfumatura.*)

**Oswald:** That'll have Canada on tiptoe, when I bring the whole choir down to that pinpoint of sound in 'David of the White Rock'.

(*He sings the last four notes of the song to demonstrate this particular bit of diminuendo, conducting himself with a pencil he has taken with a flourish from his breast pocket.*)

**Ben:** Honest to God, I think I prefer you the way you were before, Os. Tender, listening to every sound on earth in case it was a cry for help.

**Oswald:** Don't deny me this, Dad. I was sick of being a jelly. Do you know what Cosmo Joslin says I'd be ideal at?

**Ben:** No.

**Oswald:** Handling the baton in front of a large girls' choir. He says my voice has got the kind of subdued maturity, a kind of waiting passion that would provide a perfect visual balance to about eighty singing virgins.

**Ben:** Did Joslin say that?

**Oswald:** His very words.

**Ben:** He's some sort of joker, that Joslin. You are being drawn into something, Oswald. You were better off as a nervous wreck. Eighty singing virgins. And you in front of them. Proud and wanton and the lessons of the Sunday School just a faint echo on the howling wind. This Joslin will be the death of you, Os.

**Oswald:** Oh, no. It said about him in the *Radio Times*: "indubitably a golden talent, possibly a genius." And he's a local boy besides.

**Miriam:** (*just showing her head round the door*) Os, if you'd take your crown off and slip on an apron, you could give me a hand with these coffee cups.

**Ben:** That's right, boy. Help Miriam. There's nothing like slipping on a pinny to restore a man to modesty and reason. (Ben *suddenly looks distracted and terrified.*) Miriam, do you have the feeling that something is going to happen?

**Miriam:** Yes, shortly. Twenty people are going to walk into this house.

**Ben:** No. Something bad. (*He runs his hand over the top of his head.*) Whenever this part of my scalp itches . . . I had it just before Mr Morgan the monumental mason found out about those deposits. I had it just before your Mam died. I've got it now.

**Miriam:** You've just got an itching scalp. Everything's fine. Con's at the wheel. Our chimney is being cleaned by an all-season Claus. We are on the hallelujah train.

(Oswald *follows* Miriam *out of the room. The kitchen door is heard being shut. The front door opens and* Con *noiselessly comes up the passage, slips into the parlour and stands before* Ben, *first in a posture of sagging deflation which graduates in seconds into an almost lunatic despair. He is wearing a long black overcoat. He takes a bottle from each pocket of his coat and places them on the table.*)

**Ben:** What's this, Con?

**Con:** Brandy. For the last toast to Mam.

(Con *lets out what he, as a trained reciter of poems, thinks to be a high-grade peal of maniac laughter. It sends* Ben *dodging behind the table.*)

**Ben:** Anything wrong, Con?

(Con *paces fiercely up and down the room. He stops in front of the plaque, snorts and turns it to face the wall.*)

**Con:** Everything. Everything. The fools, the perfidious fools. Tricked, tripped, trapped, sent headlong. Whose paid clown have I turned out to be? Sent headlong. Is there dirt on my face? Do you see dirt on my face?

**Ben:** (*peering*) No, Con, you're middling clean. You want your evening shave but no dirt that I can see.

**Con:** Sorry Dad. There's not supposed to be any dirt. I can't even use a metaphor any more and have it make sense.

**Ben:** Sit down, Con, and tell me.

**Con:** If I sat down in any of these chairs I'd burst.

**Ben:** Take your coat off then.

**Con:** I'll never feel secure enough to take the thing off again. (*He tears the wrapping off one of the bottles and stares entranced at the amber glow of the glass. Very softly*) They'll skin me when I tell them. They've been waiting years for this, this one chance to catch me hanging from a limb, dangling helpless.

**Ben:** Who? Tell who? Tell who what?

**Con:** Wallace, Russell, Os. Not Alvin. He's a savage. He's brought this on himself. (Ben *leans forward and shapes his lips in an urgent 'what?' but* Con *cuts him off by pointing at the bottle.*) There'll be no toasts drunk here tonight. Get some glasses from the cupboard, Dad. We'll have a little tot apiece to keep our minds from falling apart.

(Ben *handles the bottle as if it were a hissing snake.*)

**Ben:** Best Brandy. Bad stuff, Con. I haven't had a drop since I left that job with the gravestones down West.

**Con:** (*sternly*) Get the glasses. (Ben *gets up, fumbles in cupboard and comes back with glasses. He begins nervously and inexpertly to decant.*) You should have stayed down there in the West with the singing and the drinking and the enjoying of death. (*He sips his drink and looks around the close plushly muted room.*) I'm sorry for what's happened to you, Dad. But there'll be nobody in the whole world to be sorry for what's happened to me. I'm the monkey. I really believed in scratching and climbing. Then somebody takes away my hands, then the trees.

**Ben:** You're no monkey, Con. That's what I say to Alvin when he's on about that Darwin. We're not monkeys.

(*He throws the whole glass of brandy down his throat defiantly.* Con *has his glass nuzzled against his lower lip.*)

**Con:** I can see their faces now. That Wallace. That Russell. I can see their faces now. A hard pair, those two. Knowledge doesn't make people nicer, does it? They withdraw into a shadow and watch and watch. Watch me doing somersaults on their behalf and they'll skin me alive. Russell's been working like an ox getting together a programme for the new residential school. Wallace has been taking up all the research he did in preventive medicine so that he can blind the council with science when he gets the interview for the M.O.'s job.

**Ben:** And Ossie putting on a side and a stroke I never saw in the boy before. Conducting himself in the mirror and talking openly

77

of virgins.

(Con *lifts his hands and stares at them.*)

**Con:** Oh, we were climbing fine: and then somebody took away my hands and then the tree.

**Ben:** Who did that? Who dared to do that to you?

**Con:** That Mrs Loomer-Barkway. The grandiose bitch. Oh, the willing pointer dog I've been for her. The only huntress ever to use the same tool for shooting and retrieving. Who showed her the side alleys and the short cuts that would get her to the top of the pyramid in record time?

**Ben:** Con Morton.

**Con:** Myself. Every single net of mine has fouled on her.

**Ben:** (*frantically disturbed*) What have you been up to, Con?

**Con:** A fishing reference, Dad. Don't follow my words too closely, Dad. Just watch out for the implications.

**Ben:** All right, Con.

**Con:** That mansion she was going to donate as a school. Decided at the last moment to hang on to it as a private reserve.

**Ben:** So there goes Russell's school.

**Con:** There it goes. And as for the Medical Officer's job . . . she decided to get into the mayor's good books. She found that the mayor has a nephew who's been practising medicine in Kenya. He's coming home in a month or two.

**Ben:** We thought the Spanish 'flu was bad but this woman will have us sneezing worse than that. But she must have left Os alone. She couldn't have done anything to torpedo poor Os's chances with the T.V.

**Con:** Oh, yes, she could. She got hold of Cosmo Joslin and told him that the idea of a male voice party is flat-footed and a bore. She said: "The sight and sound of men bawling are the expressions of this region's traditional cavemanship."

**Ben:** She said that to Cosmo Joslin?

**Con:** Right in his ear. Cosmo was impressed. He's cancelled Os's choir and he is going to have the band of girl pipers from Birchtown.

**Ben:** A noisy lot, those pipers.

**Con:** Beyond noisy. The fruits of some utterly mixed marriage. Welsh costume. Scottish pipes. Canada will think we've shaken our last screw loose when they see that lot.

**Ben:** Joslin is out to down the Celt. What Edward the First started, Joslin will finish.

**Con:** And while I was beginning to find an answer to these things, that Alvin has to break loose.

**Ben:** Oh, it's a pity about Alvin. There he was for the first few weeks of his job as Assistant Manager of the tinplate, depressed and pensive, quiet as a lamb and wonderfully sad and hopeless about mankind, just as a man ought to be if he wants to get on.

**Con:** Then Wallace has to fetch him some of those hallelujah pills, those super tonic tablets that have been known to bring people hopping back from the tomb.

**Ben:** He hopped all right.

**Con:** He did and all. When Mrs Loomer-Barkway told him to sack those ten chaps for working the old go-slow tactic I talked him into seeing that she was right, that such trouble-makers would destroy what little there was left of the works. He didn't argue back much. He didn't seem to care and I thanked God for that. Then Wallace slipped him those pills. He associated his own grievances with that pay dispute over at the big steelworks and every metal worker in that place will be downing tools on Monday of next week. He even supported that little strike of council grave diggers who wanted a ten per cent rise when they struck rock in the Black Meadow. And there was that Alvin whipping up their greed and praising the quality of the graveyard rock. He made a speech in the Institute urging all voters who have no natural bias towards living to hurry up and die quickly to as to embarrass the council.

**Ben:** He's at the root of it all, that Alvin. Urging those diggers to leave the dead about. That's the last straw. That's what radicalism has been leading us to all these years. First you close the gates of heaven, then you find you can't get into the Black Meadow. No wonder Mrs Loomer-Barkway turned nasty.

(Con *gets up and starts beating one hand passionately against the other.*)

**Con:** No, it wasn't Alvin. Not altogether, not altogether. It was me too. You don't know yet what I did. Oh, yes, it was me too. Have another brandy, Dad.

**Ben:** Oh, no, thank you, Con. That was a fine big one I had before. If it wasn't for the sadness you are casting about I'd be real warm. (*Pushes the bottle away from him.*) Oh, no. I couldn't have any more.

**Con:** Be mad, Dad. This is liquidation Tuesday. Let's give it a two-delirium salute. (*Pours himself and* Ben *a moderate measure.*) Dad, there are two types of people that defile the human race.

(Ben *pops the liquor into his mouth as if eager not to have the stuff touch his lips or teeth.*)

**Ben:** Two types. Defilers all. Name them. Denounce them. Drive them into the open, Con.

**Con:** People who default in the payment of their rates and sneer at local government, that's one lot.

**Ben:** Harry them, Con. Give them no peace. And who are the other lot?

**Con:** People who are intemperate in their sexual feelings, people who suddenly betray our cherished standards of decency.

**Ben:** Worse than the defaulters those. Quieter, more private, but every bit as much of a nuisance. Get after them, Con. Jail them, doctor them if need be, but let us have a clean solvent world. My boys have nothing to fear. Cash on the nail and chaste as snow. Even I have been a bit of an example to you there. The only debt I ever owed was the deposit on one hundred and fifty-one gravestones to the monumental mason Morgan. And I've never been a goat on the flank of carnality. I'm not sure whether it was good moral stamina or too much beer but I always seem to have had a solid Sunday School bench where my love fever should have been. And you are the same, Con. You'll never be troubled. You'll go straight to the top with not a button out of place.

(Ben *pours himself out another drink. His delight is waxing but* Con *is pacing again to an ever faster rhythm of embarrassment and even anguish.*)

**Con:** You're wrong, Dad.

**Ben:** (*only half hearing*) I'll just sip this.

**Con:** (*louder*) You're wrong, Dad.

**Ben:** What's this? (*Stares at* Con *with an almost candent pleasure.*) I like this showing of darkness in people I thought floodlit from stem to stern. Well, well. Put that back, and speak out, Con.

**Con:** I thought ambition had burned all that nonsense out of me. No town wants a lecher in charge of the rates yield. Then a fortnight ago, I was up there in the mansion with Mrs Loomer-Barkway. It was a long lovely room we were in. Big fire. Pictures of the late Colonel Loomer-Barkway around the walls. Very stern, his eyes everywhere, keeping our minds on the highest things.

**Ben:** (*wagging his finger almost roguishly at the picture of* Mrs Morton) A splendid thing, pictures of the dead, for keeping tidiness all around.

**Con:** We were drinking sherry. A well known brand. Very dear. Between that and the fire it was warm. We were happy, laughing. I watched her mouth as she spoke. It grew big and warm.

**Ben:** You should have kept your eyes on the glass, Con, or the colonel. Anything but the mouths of women.

**Con:** Then we spoke of the plans she had for me when I got the Town Clerk's office. She was wearing a gown of crimson velvet. She looked fine.

**Ben:** She would too. She's got the broad contralto form to carry off a gown of that order. A bit like Mam, Mrs Loomer-Barkway, come to think of it.

**Con:** (*in a sudden rage*) Don't think of it. That velvet was wrong for me. And the fire and the wine. Must be those velvet suits I wore when I used to recite as a kid. The sight of the stuff sets gongs throbbing inside my head. We should never come across anything so smooth on so basically rough an earth.

**Ben:** Plush is a terrible trap to men whose fingers are torn and want the feel of peace.

**Con:** I was drawn into daring. It was a rich cordial moment. I felt I had the world on my shoulder, snug, like a fiddle tuned and ready to play.

**Ben:** It's then you've got to watch.

**Con:** It was the clumsiest bit of bowing in the history of the urge. I bent over her in what I thought to be the real Valentino style.

**Ben:** A bad model. He wasn't hindered by the chapels. We make love with a chapel hanging from each wrist.

**Con:** She had something on her wrists. She gave me a clip that sent me spinning right across the room. She's strong. She jerked me half-way out of my collar.

**Ben:** She would. A broad contralto is the equal of any man, especially when enraged.

**Con:** She said she'd ruin me. The next day she announced she would not be coming to the unveiling of the plaque. And the rest of the council were in a hurry to follow suit. The whole hive of bees is after me, Dad. I'm going to be stung to death. (*He gives a laugh of noble desperation.*) I planned this night as the first big round in my battle for the Town Clerk's wig. Now I'll be lucky to keep my scalp. That's all I'm left with. An armful of ashes and the memory of Mam. Russell, Wallace and Alvin will have my top hair from keeping them away from those places they wanted to go to.

(Oswald *comes in wiping his hand with his handkerchief.*)

**Oswald:** I think I'll have a drop of that.

**Ben:** No, no. Keep away from it, Oswald. You remember how you were after five glasses of parsnip wine last Christmas? Laughing fit, then around the middle of the room shouting that God is not mocked.

**Oswald:** I've got to learn to live with a flourish.

**Con:** (*almost in a whisper*) You are not going to be on the home screen, Oswald.

**Oswald:** A flourish. Miriam was just saying in there that I've got some sort of cramp of the spirit that I'll have to get rid of.

**Con:** (*just a little louder, but still* Os *does not hear*): You are not going on the television, Os.

**Ben:** He's deaf with pride.

**Oswald:** I'll probably turn out to be like that Gogwin.

**Ben:** What choir did he have?

**Oswald:** He was a French painter. Left his family after years of quiet respectability. A mouse. Then he flared up. Went to live in the South Seas. Painting right and left and bold as brass with women.

**Ben:** Oswald, it puts me on edge to hear you talk like this. When you were nine in the Sunday School you won the Williams Pantycelyn award for the best essay against drink and carnality. I sometimes think you should have died in that moment of piety and happiness.

**Con:** (*loudly*) Os, there's not going to be any fame. Cosmo Joslin has changed his mind about you. He's opted for the band of girl pipers in Birchtown.

(As Oswald *is going to make reply there is a knock on the front door.* Oswald, *bemused, asks* Con, *in mime, if what he has just said is true.* Con *shakes his head: yes.* Ben *has gone down the passage to see who is knocking. He comes back with the air of one who feels that the total of trouble has been increased.*)

**Ben:** It's Caradoc Slee, to see Oswald.

(Caradoc *comes in behind* Ben. *He is dressed in dark grey, even*

82

*to his hair, and his face is round and gentle.*)
**Con** and **Os:** Hullo, Crad.
**Caradoc:** Hullo, Os, hullo, Con.
**Ben:** You're a bit early for the banquet, Crad. You want to sharpen yourself up with a look at the dainties, no doubt.
**Caradoc:** No. No thought of food in my mind, Mr Morton.
**Ben:** Oh, aye. I remember from the time you used to come here after Miriam. All your hunger in the mind for the music.
**Caradoc:** Something like that, Mr Morton. (*Caradoc* taps Oswald *on the shoulder. Oswald is still in something of a daze and* Caradoc *has to tap him again before he turns round.*) Os, we held a meeting.
**Oswald:** What you say?
**Caradoc:** We held a meeting, Os.
**Oswald:** Meeting?
**Caradoc:** The boys in the choir held a meeting.
**Ben:** How could they hold a meeting without Os? He's the leader.
**Caradoc:** The meeting was about Os. That's why he wasn't there. They've tipped you the black spot, Os. You're out.
**Oswald:** You mean I'm not even the conductor any more?
**Caradoc:** No. They've forced the baton back on me. They said that with the new style of conducting foisted on you by that Cosmo Joslin, with you just standing there pointing at them, they didn't know whether they were being conducted or accused. (*He* taps Oswald *once again on the shoulder.*) No hard feelings, Os?
**Oswald:** At the moment there's no feeling at all.
**Caradoc:** But you are still welcome to your old place in the second row of the second tenors.
**Oswald:** Thank you, Crad. (*He suddenly relaxes and begins to smile.*) I mean that, Crad. I'll feel safe back there among the boys. I tried to put a gay face on it, talking about being dissolute and so on. But (*he pats his chest*) my pipes were trussed up like turkeys all the time. I haven't got the bone structure or the build for anything but quietness really. Do you know out there in the kitchen I suddenly started thinking about those eighty virgins.
**Caradoc:** (*very solicitously*) What's this now, boy?
**Oswald:** A type of young female choir that Cosmo Joslin fancied, and wanted me to conduct. I thought hard about them, about those young girls, close to me after a fine performance, warming

83

to me, and wanting to kiss the hem of my sheet music. Just thinking about it I dropped two cups. Ask Miriam. She'll tell you. Two cups. If I'd come anywhere near the real thing I'd have worked my way through fifteen whole sets of crockery. And I'm going to forget about that Swindon thing, too. Very harsh and truculent towards ticket clerks east of Chepstow, they tell me. I'll just pat the earth of this place a little more cosily and tidily around me.

**Ben:** That's right, Os. A tidy grave, that's the most we can hope for.

(Caradoc *gets up and looks at the plaque.*)

**Caradoc:** Is this the plaque? (*He turns it round and reads the inscription.*) She was a fine woman. Fancy her dying so far away.

**Ben:** She went to see her sister, her dying sister. And the sister's still alive, fit as a fiddle.

**Caradoc:** Seems daft, don't it?

**Ben:** The Lord giveth and the Lord snatcheth away.

**Caradoc:** It's nice to have a slogan to cover all such things. They'd look terrible, left too bare. (*He touches the plaque again.*) She was a fine woman. A great rich contralto. If she hadn't looked so sad she'd have been a real Carmen. A fine woman. Like Miriam. Miriam in?

**Ben:** Aye, she's in.

**Caradoc:** Can I see her?

**Ben:** You're a mature man, Crad, and you know where the kitchen is.

**Oswald:** I'll come with you, Crad. I want to tell Miriam the news about the choir and to say how sorry I am about those cups.

(Caradoc *makes for the door but when he speaks he addresses no one in particular.*)

**Caradoc:** It's a funny thing, but every time I feel an impulse away from the choir work and towards a bit of private affection I get shadowed like a convict. After you, Os. It would be a shock to Miriam to have her see me coming so suddenly into the kitchen after all this time.

(*During all this exchange* Con *has been sitting at the table, his hands stretched flat on the plush table cloth, staring ahead and taking no interest in the conversation save occasionally to shake his head pointlessly in the manner of a battle fatigued victim. When the door closes behind* Oswald *and* Caradoc, Ben *gets the brandy and the glasses and again puts them on the table.*)

**Ben:** You need some more of this, Con. You never looked so far away. Come back to us, Con.

(Con *bolts the drink his father sets before him and his gesture could not be more richly desperate. When he speaks his voice has a maximum bitterness.*)

**Con:** The tramps, the beach combers, the vagrants, the meth drinkers, the sleepless rakes with vapour trails of affiliation warrants and attachment orders streaming behind them, they are the lucky ones.

**Ben:** Oh, I don't know. Plenty of risks there, too, you know. I've seen that old meth give many a man the shakes.

**Con:** Never try to give life a lead. It's a venereal old mule. To be whipped for fun but never goaded into a brisker trot. And I'd go before the Belmont Business Men's Club and repeat that.

**Ben:** No, you wouldn't, Con. You'd be sorry and change tack back to hope as soon as that terrible word venereal left your lips.

**Con:** I'd tell them where their initiative and optimism land a man. The closet. The double bolted closet.

**Ben:** Don't worry, Con. You saw how Oswald took it. Mild and soft as butter.

**Con:** Ossie is his own churn. He's just a butter ball . . . but you wait till Wallace, Russ, Alvin . . .

(*Front door opens. There is a burst of laughter,* Russell *is heard singing without the words of the first bars of 'Flee as a Bird' and they both guffaw after the first note.* Wallace *appears first. He seems surprised as he looks around the room.*)

**Wallace:** I expected a multitude, a crowd of plaque worshippers.

**Ben:** There was a hitch, Wallace, a bit of a hitch.

(Con *pours himself a glass of brandy.*)

**Con:** A hitch? An earthquake, you mean. Life is a smoking ruin.

**Russ:** Ruin? (*He stares hard at* Con.) Who set the fuse?

**Con:** So many people, so many people. For years this place has had its eye on this family, envying us, wanting to slap us down, to make us look fools. They've done it. You may not have heard the trap open, but we're hanging. The flag is up over the gaol.

**Russ:** You'd better water that brandy, boy. This is no talk for a Town Clerk.

**Con:** (*with a great ring of bitter amusement*) Town Clerk, ah.

**Wallace:** (*to his father*) What's up? Is this his sinus trouble again

85

or plain schizophrenia?

**Ben:** This is the night of the long knives and they all landed on Con. That Mrs Loomer-Barkway, dressed in plush, Con, full of wine and warmth and riding a hopeful crest up there in the mansion. Trapped into lust. I'd told him, warned him. Stick to intrigue, I said. Stick to betrayal, even drink. But leave the lust alone. He tried to fondle her, she sent him reeling.

**Con:** (*very softly*) There'll be no headship for you, Russell.

**Russ:** That was a nice drop of ale down at the Bannerman Club tonight, Wallace. I'm glad I came down with you.

**Con:** (*still softly*) There'll be no medical officer's job for you, Wallace.

**Wallace:** I told you about the new steward. Too ignorant to fiddle.

**Con:** All right. Turn on me. Stop playing with me. This is your chance. You've waited long enough for it. I'm nailed in front of you. Put the boot in.

**Wallace:** (*going over to the cupboard*) What sort of wine would you like, Russ?

**Con:** Didn't you hear what I said?

**Russ:** That sweet white I think. That'll put me in the mood to meet the mayor.

**Con:** (*to Ben*) They don't hear me. Can you hear me?

**Ben:** Like a bell.

**Con:** It's the beer. They're full of it. But it'll wear off. Then they'll butcher me.

**Ben:** (*softly to Wallace and Russell*) Boys, don't you understand? They've pulled the mat clean from under our Con. We've been left holding the plaque. They are making a mockery of Mam.

**Wallace:** If they find that sort of thing nourishing, good luck to them.

**Con:** You mean you're not upset? You're not angry?

**Wallace:** No. All streams don't flow in the same direction. Things haven't been so bad for us today, have they Russ?

**Russ:** Not bad.

**Ben:** What's up?

**Wallace:** Early this morning old Dr Edmonds was playing snooker in the Club. He'd been at me all the afternoon. Spending too much time with the panel patients and the chronics. So I gave him a piece of my mind. I told him that when I became Medical

Officer of Health . . . (Con *shudders and groans.*) . . . the first thing I'd do was quarantine his mind. He kept playing snooker. Didn't say a word. Then he got the full flavour of what I said. It was too much for him. He had a stroke. The practice is mine.

**Ben:** Well, potting the last colour, you say? Tchew. And who had a seizure on your behalf, Russ?

**Russ:** Not a seizure, exactly. Doom was a little blander in my case. The Education Committee pondered the risk of an evangelical headmaster and they've appointed me deputy head to keep the balance on behalf of cool indifference. And they found that as a result of his daily appeals to the more godless pupils to return to the chapels, there was a record number of collection boxes being looted. And there was another funny thing. The number of kids who have come on to me since the news got around that I might be moving. Kids who have been looking at me for years past with their brows just an inch from the ground. I'd have said that all they wanted was to let me have it in the back with a sharpened easel-peg. And there they were sidling on to me and asking me to stay. They might just have been wanting to get me in the right position for that peg, but it was touching all the same. In any case, after teaching for twelve years in the reek of those foundries I don't think I could ever get used to really fresh clean air. I'd see the pupils too plain.

**Ben:** Home is best. Staleness and all.

(*The front door opens.* Alvin *comes in with a rush. He shoots a glance at* Con *who is lifting a glass of brandy to his lips with the expression of a man who is wondering when best to start scooping out the small fragments of his heart.*)

**Alvin:** Sorry, Con. I mean that. I heard about the bust-up of the banquet here. I know you blame me. (*He laughs at the look of black bitter revulsion that has come over* Con's *face.*) My position was simple. If the high-ups want a pool of unemployment we were not going to be the first bloody ducks. We walk and we're not waterproof. We've made our point now. We'll not be coming out on Monday.

**Russ:** That's a pity. I was hoping that if you eased up on the smelting for a day or two I might be able to get my first clear view of the back row of Form IV B. What happened?

**Alvin:** We had a meeting tonight. Colonel Rogerston, head of the big steel works, he was there. Very stubborn man. Wedded to the past. Still fighting Magna Carta. But he was like a lamb tonight. He said the strike of the Belmont gravediggers made him see the hub of industrial relations for the first time. He's sentimental about death and the dead and this was the one nerve that could jolt him into the foothills of compassion. And I kept humming snatches of Blake's 'Jerusalem' in his ear as the negotiations went on. I think that helped to break him down a bit too.

**Wallace:** It would.

(Wallace *hands* Alvin *a fair ration of wine.*)

**Alvin:** He took quite a fancy to me. Do you know what he did?

**Russ:** Asked you to switch off 'Jerusalem' for a start.

**Alvin:** No. He wanted to know if I'd like the job of Assistant Welfare Officer at the big works.

**Ben:** Oh, that was shrewd of the colonel. That'll shut you up, Alvin.

**Alvin:** I suppose it will and all. I'd like to be cheerfully corrupt for a change. To fuss about the tea and the towels instead of the political awareness of man. That would be nice.

(Con *gets to his feet with as much dignity as he can muster.*)

**Con:** I'm glad for you. You've all come in here trailing your bits of glory. I'm glad for you. Glory's something. But for me this is the night of deprivation, of anticipated death. You go on your bright chattering ways and prosper. I am left with only one of the many things that buttressed me through the years. (*He points to his mother's picture.*) Nothing will alter that. Nothing. Tomorrow I shall be myself again. This will be my only, my last moment of squalid sorrow.

**Ben:** That's the hammer, Con. Bad thing, that squalid sorrow.

**Con:** The sight of this plaque hung on the wall of Mam's chapel will be the deathless guarantee that this family cannot and will not be destroyed. (*His voice becomes very quiet.*) You'll come with me?

**Wallace:** Surely, Con. With pleasure.

**Con:** And the day after tomorrow I shall start again. I'll be bruised a little, my fingers trampled. I'll stoop a bit. I'll scurry where I walked before but I shall be ready once again to dedicate my talents to pay tribute to the nobility and sweetness of that woman, our mother. Nothing will alter that. Nothing. (*He utters the last word loudly. At the very moment of utterance three slow knocks are heard on the front door. Con almost jumps on to the* *table.*) That'll be the mayor. That'll be Mrs Loomer-Barkway. They've changed their minds. They can't do without me. Or it may be the Town Clerk. Or alderman . . . get me some of that mint for my breath and hide the drink in the cupboard.

**Ben:** (*very dubiously*) It'll be somebody for the banquet, no doubt.

**Alvin:** Doesn't sound like a reveller to me. A very thoughtful knocker, that one.

**Russ:** I'll go and see.

(*The kitchen door opens.* Miriam *goes hurriedly down the passage.*)

**Miriam:** It's all right, Russ. I'll go. (*Front door opens. Voices.* Miriam *comes back in very slowly, looking at a letter in her hand.*) It was delivered to the wrong address. It's for me.

(Con *returns to the table holding the bottle which he has been on the point of hiding in the cupboard. His confidence is coming back to peak. He marches around decanting brandy for one and all.*)

**Con:** And what if they don't come? That slimy mayor. That broad imperial bitch. Those creeping deacons.

**Alvin:** You're on target, Con, but take it easy.

(Miriam *is sitting on the sofa. She reads the letter quickly, looks shocked, and helplessly moved. She reads it again and looks up at the picture of her mother.*)

**Con:** We don't need them. We'll stand together, fight together. (Miriam *puts the letter in a pocket of her dress as if she has decided to say nothing about it.*) We don't want any outsiders. Miriam couldn't leave us if she wanted to. Can you see her living with a dab like Caradoc Slee after all those years of us, the real thing, the top notch Mortons? Tell that Slee to go. Get him out of that kitchen. And give him his marching orders. The Mortons need no dilution of Slees. Go and tell him. Get him out. What do you want with a barbarity like marriage after all those years with us? (Miriam *smiles in a rather sinister derisive way at* Con. *She pulls the letter from her pocket.* Con *goes up to the plaque and fingers it.*) From this coping stone we shall rebuild and conquer.

**Miriam:** (*softly*) You won't, you know.

(Con *has not heard her.* Ben *has joined him at the plaque.*)

**Ben:** I'm glad we picked the wooden one. Best teak, very warm to the hand.

(Russell *bends over* Miriam.)

**Russ:** What did you say, Miriam?

**Miriam:** He won't, you know.

**Russ:** Won't what?

**Miriam:** He won't use that plaque for anything but kindling.

**Russ:** Why not?

**Miriam:** Because Mam didn't die in that wreck.

(Wallace *has come to sit on the sofa with* Miriam.)

**Wallace:** What did you say?

**Miriam:** He won't use that plaque because Mam didn't die in that wreck in America . . . (Con *has now come to stand right in front of* Miriam *and is pointing his hand at her as if to make it easier to believe that she is really there and saying these things*.) Because the body they found Mam's handbag on wasn't hers. She walked away from the accident.

(Con *is absolutely horrified, bereft of air. He stands in the middle of the stage gaping; his jaw seeming to fall away from his face*.)

**Russ:** (*tapping* Con) You heard that?

(Con *continues to gape and gasp and shake his head about like a stuck bull*.)

**Miriam:** (*loudly and vindictively*) Mam didn't die in that accident. She got out of it and kept heading West.

**Con:** (*furiously*) What's that? What's that you say? You dare to say that, you dare even to *think* that in this room. (*He gropes in his inside pocket*.) I've got the cutting here from the *Belmont Bulletin*. Black and white. Pictures of the train. Inset of Mam.

**Wallace:** Be quiet, Con. Go on, Miriam.

**Russ:** Yes, go on. If she walked away from that wreck, why didn't she . . .

**Miriam:** Come back? Because she didn't want to. She went on to California. She joined a man she had been in love with before she got married.

**Ben:** (*speaking from about three fathoms of stupefying grief*) No, no.

**Con:** She's off the hinge. She's mad. That Caradoc Slee has driven her up the wall. Get the ammonia. Strap her down.

**Russ:** Have some brandy, Con. (*He walks around the picture and the plaque*.) Well, well. No wonder I woke up so often with the feeling that this thing was still around, creeping behind the walls blocking my mind.

**Wallace:** Why didn't she come back at all, Miriam?

**Miriam:** Because there were certain things of which she had had enough.

**Ben:** No, no. (*His voice is hardly audible and his hands are feebly upraised, as if to resist the oncoming of a ghost.*)

**Russ:** Don't whisper against the wall, Dad. It won't budge. The thing has been hardening in the pod for years. It's tear-proof. When Con started in on this plaque project he was tempting someone to say something. It's been said.

**Wallace:** What things, Miriam? What things didn't she want to come back to?

**Miriam:** Granch, Dad, his memorial stones and sad benders. But it was Con who broke her back. He had taken over the whole family, she said, and in nightmares she could hear him talking, talking. So she got up and kept walking. I'm glad. Doesn't it make you feel good that the odd death isn't a death at all. Just a change. That someone sees an open door and walks right through it. In a damned locked up smouldering place like this one sees a door and uses it.

**Wallace:** Yes. Glad.

**Russ:** Yes, glad.

**Ben:** *No*, no.

**Con:** Was all this in that letter?

**Miriam:** The letter contained only a tiny part of the story. Most of it I knew a year ago. I got the letter from Auntie Gwen. By God, the news needed some keeping to myself.

**Russ:** Why? Why did you do it? Why didn't you tell us?

**Miriam:** Because a person as bottled up as I am does good work on the cork; I was waiting for the moment, the absolutely ripe moment. It would have been the hanging of that plaque. Then I'd have let the horses gallop. It would have blown you selfish mushrooms through the roof.

**Con:** (*taking a desperate pull at the grog*) She'd have given us away with the preacher's blessing still fresh on the plaque.

**Ben:** His words still misting the teak.

**Russ:** Stop buzzing, you two. What sort of life did Mam have, Miriam? It's a daft question, but I'd like to know. Was she happy?

**Miriam:** Very. The man was a singer. They formed a double act. They worked in cabaret. Folk songs and ballads. You remember how good Mam was with those things. They became quite famous and they were happy. She saw a door and walked through it.

**Con:** I'll raise the rates on those bloody doors if it's the last thing I do. (*He is struck by a chilling thought.*) Is she still alive? She's not coming back to Belmont, is she? She wouldn't dare to come back to the home she defamed, would she?

**Russ:** He's reading captions again.

**Miriam:** No she isn't, and she wouldn't. She served us well to the end. She died a fortnight ago. It says so here. (*She touches the letter.*) It's from the man. He says he's grateful for the chance of having been able to share Dinah with us.

**Ben:** Share Dinah. That's a thought. That's a terrible thought.

**Con:** Do you see what this means, this dreadful story? Fraud. Adultery. Singing to drunkards for money. And us with the plaque ready for hanging. They'll pull us through the mud.

**Miriam:** As far as I'm concerned the story finished when I read this letter.

(*Caradoc and* Ossie *come in from the kitchen.* Ossie *goes straight to the piano.*)

**Oswald:** We've worked out a wonderful new bass line for the 'Flee as a Bird' version we're going to sing around the plaque. (*He begins to play.*)

**Miriam:** And by the way, Caradoc and I are going to get married three weeks Monday.

**Russ:** That's fine, Miriam. That'll be something nice to lay on the new grave.

**Caradoc:** I've just remembered, Mir. That's the day of the big concert in the Memorial Hall.

**Miriam:** It's only a little thing. We can work it in just before the last chorus. Come on, Caradoc. Let's go out.

(*Caradoc goes over to the piano. He listens attentively and puts in an extra note at the foot of the bass line.* Ossie *hums and smiles delightedly.* Miriam *stands by the door waiting.*)

**Wallace:** (*standing in front of the picture*) That's it. That's the way it should have been. Another year or two in front of the bath tub and the stove and that would have been the shabby end of her. That's it. The bold bid for fulfilment. To dodge away from under the falling dark. That's the therapy to preach and teach.

**Russ:** This is just how we were that noon on the day that Mam left. Con there, Dad there, Wallace here. Ossie at the piano.

(Miriam *leaves the room, opens the front door and shouts.*)

**Miriam:** The air is good out here. The air is brand new. Come on, Caradoc.

**Russ:** And I thought how good it would be if we formed a procession behind her to the station, to follow her to the end of wherever she wanted to go.

**Miriam:** (*loudly*) Come on. The air's coming down from the mountain just for us.

(Caradoc *shakes his head sadly.*)

**Caradoc:** I think there's a bit of wildness in Miriam, you know.

(Caradoc *points out a last harmonic adjustment to* Ossie. Wallace *and* Russell *look across at each other and give a nod of agreement.*)

**Wallace:** Let's go. I've got to see a man about some new furniture for the surgery.

**Russ:** And I might catch the tail end of the Youth Employment Committee.

**Wallace:** That's the stuff. Do a little good on earth, then sit down to a nice long pint.

(Caradoc *leaves the room and finds* Wallace *and* Russell *immediately behind him. He pauses at the door and looks at them.*)

**Caradoc:** Always the same. Whenever I take a step towards love, a queue forms.

**Russ:** Carry on, Crad. We've got our own ways to go.

(Ossie *sings the line 'Ye who are weary of sin'.* Ben *gives a kind of howl.*)

**Ben:** Who had the cheek to take me away from sin? The warm old lovely sin. Who was the stupid bastard who talked me away from sin? I'm cold.

**Con:** They left the door open. (*Raises voice.*) Ossie. The door's still open.

**Ben:** Am I dreaming this? Is this the full effect of brandy on a Sunday School stomach?

**Oswald:** Better switch to cocoa, Dad. Your brain is smoking. (*He turns around.*) Why is the room so empty? Where are they gone?

**Ben:** They left the door open. It's getting cold.

(Con *stands by* Oswald *at the piano.*)

**Con:** We'll close the door, Os, behind us. (*He looks at the picture.*

*The light on the stage begins to fail.*) We are lost, Os. For the moment, we are lost. In the light of our burning we shall show each other the way.

**Oswald:** (*bemused*) Burn what? What are you hinting at now, Con? Way to do what? Get a grip on yourself now, Con. Why did they all go away? Didn't they like my arrangement? Are they holding the banquet somewhere else? (*Looks at* Ben.) Why do the whole world's teeth seem to be chattering? I don't get much luck. Not even in my own front room I don't get much luck.

**Ben:** Your mother didn't die in that accident. She was living with some chap until the very spring of this year.

**Oswald:** Spring? (Oswald *continues to play. Then he stops suddenly and shoots his head up.*) Well, well. (Oswald *turns and just points silently at the picture of his mother.*) Dear, dear. (Oswald *resumes his playing.*)

**Con:** Come on, Os. We are going out and we are going to insult somebody. We are going to be fractious and hostile for the first time.

**Oswald:** I don't think so, Con.

(*They leave the room. The light fades and one beam only plays on the face of Dinah May. A chair is knocked over by* Ben *on his way to the door. We see his figure outlined in the lamplit opening of the doorway.*)

**Ben:** And all along the banks of that river, that spring, that summer, the women were warm and lovely and good, and business was buzzing like bees and there was money in my pocket. It was a golden year for light ale. And there was a velvet sky. Where is the road to renewal? Where is the path of return?

(*The light on Dinah May becomes more brilliant. In the darkened part of the stage where* Ben *is once again moving and groping another chair goes over.*)

There *is* no road. (*Another chair goes for a dive.*) There is no path. There is no renewal. There is no return. I am on the floor, Dinah May, flat on my perishing butts, my love. I'll be with you for ever, Dinah May. God help me, God help us.

(*The banquet in the middle room becomes visible.*)

There it is, the banquet. To where there is food and light people will come. I can hear them now. The people. The M.P. The Moderator General of the Methodist Circuit. The Mayor. The Alderman. Mrs Loomer what you call. Ivor Novello. Oh, he's dead, poor dab. The Chamber of Commerce. The Buffs. The Hearts of Oak, the bloody lot. My boys, my girls. They are coming. I can hear their feet on all the pavements of the earth, coming to my food and light. I can hear them . . .

(*He pauses and shakes his head.*)

I can't, you know. But I've got to say so. I've got to think so. How are we doing in the ghost line, Dinah May?

(*The light on Dinah May dims ands the full light returns slowly to the stage. Ben is discovered crouching immediately beneath Dinah May's portrait.*)

Who gives the beat for this caper? (*Rises with intense difficulty and speaks right into the picture.*)

What drove you forth? What drove me inward? (*He cups his ear.*) Silence. We are dead, Dinah May. (*He puts his arm round an imaginary lady.*) Come with me to the banquet, Dinah May. We musn't waste, see. Miriam slaved over that grub, I can tell you. Nice girl.

(*He goes around into the middle room and we see him approach the banquet with a look of nearly insane delight. We see him offering titbits to the shade at his side, smiling seraphically.*)

Silence. Silence.

(*And at that moment sounds of footsteps on pavement and great laughter are heard.*)

Curtain

# JACKIE THE JUMPER

# Characters

Miriam Morgan
Jim James
Iestyn Best
George Chislett
Janet
Jackie Rees
Reverend Richie Rees
1st Crow
2nd Crow
Aaron Mead
Mr Luxton
Colonel of Militia
County Sheriff
Mona Luxton
Eirlys Luxton
Arianwen Luxton
Soldiers
Village Girls
Foundry Workers

# ACT ONE

*In the background the reflected glare of great furnaces. A sad, sweet dirge to which the workers dance. Two musical themes commingle here. One, a lament of great plangency, the other a serenade. The two, mounting each other, could give a good picture of grief knocking its stupid old head against hope.*

**Janet:** For how far did we follow him?
**Chislett:** Until we grew hungry and the road was as hard as hell

99

beneath our feet.

**Janet:** For how long did we follow him?

**Chislett:** For a lifetime multiplied by as many of us as were there.

**Janet:** When he bade us follow him no more, did he look back?

**Chislett:** Twice.

**Janet:** Did he wave at us?

**Chislett:** Once.

**Janet:** What was the time of day?

**Chislett:** The sun was falling hot and straight upon our heads.

**All:** The Jumper, Jackie the Jumper. Where is he now, the Jumper?

**Janet:** Where was he leading us?

**Chislett:** To a place of calm, clean peace, whatever that means.

**Janet:** Was there such a place?

**Chislett:** We'll never know. Such men have a way of creating a whole new sky of promise. A sky that makes the earth and us look different. Then they vanish.

**Janet:** What was the very last glimpse you had of him?

**Chislett:** He was jumping across the stream that borders the forest.

**All:** The Jumper, Jackie the Jumper.

(*The music makes a leap.* Jackie Rees *appears at the top of the mound, radiant, smiling. He raises both his arms in a fervent gesture of greeting.*)

**Janet:** Jackie's back!

(Jackie *is broad, curly-haired and bright-eyed. The rhythm of the dance becomes swift and joyful.* Jackie *takes girl after girl into his arms. He stops suddenly and points at the flames.*)

**Jackie:** Oh what a lovely flavour of hell it has.

(*The dancers launch into a thumping song.*)

**Chorus:**

Iron, iron, all new iron,
We make the stuff in molten streams,
No time for love, no time for dreams;
Hours before the masters yawn
We shuffle to the mills through the still of dawn.
Tap the ovens, tap the sky,
We'll work and shrivel until we die;
Let's dance and whirl till we lose the light;

Let the flesh give welcome to the night.
Till every girl and every boy
Steps into the heart of a molten joy.

**Jackie:** That's it. Let's wipe away this pox of smoke and toil and get back to the laughter that must once have been the King-thing on this earth.

**Chorus:**
Till every girl and every boy
Steps into the heart of a molten joy.

**Chislett:** That's it, Jackie. A molten joy. Oh! I wish this day would go on for ever.

**Janet:** We're glad you came back, Jackie. We missed you. Where've you been?

(Jackie *vaguely waves in a direction away from the flames.*)

**Jackie:** Over a lot of mountains, down a lot of valleys, asking people why they were knitting inch-thick shrouds for themselves, giving up the art of loving.

**Chislett:** What answers did they give, Jackie?

**Jackie:** They didn't give any answers. They looked right past me and kept on knitting.

**Chislett:** They would. Mad for shrouds since the preachers and the iron hit them. If they don't get you with a hot doctrine, they get you with a hot ingot.

**Jackie:** And who swings the hottest doctrine?

**Group:** Your uncle, Richie Resurrection Rees.

**Jackie:** You're right. May his God disquiet him. And who swings the hottest ingot?

**Group:** John Ironhead Luxton.

**Jackie:** And his iron is hardening over all the land like an old dark vein.

**Chislett:** Are they after you still, Jackie?

**Jackie:** Like hounds. In the last year they've blamed four strikes, one cattle pox, ten deaths and nine rapes on me. I'd need to be a man-sized grasshopper and a shire-stallion to get around the way they say I do.

**Janet:** Mr Resurrection Rees preached a tremendous sermon against you last Sunday. Scorched the woodwork, terrified the women, cured the deacons of the screws and made the windows rattle.

**Jackie:** He would. I'm the best raw material! On the sermons he's preached against me he's come to be the Mahomet of the chapels. If he had paid me to be a vagrant and a goat I couldn't have served him better. And my father, his brother, he got such a hell of a time between the two of us he was glad to go.

**Chislett:** The furnace door burst and he took it in the face. I saw it. I was there. It was the early morning and Ironhead had been piling on the heat all through the night to meet some special order. From the French or the Russians. Some lot that want a harder grasp on life. It came out like a cork from the bottle, the door. Your father was there, right in front.

**Jackie:** He was glad to go.

**Chislett:** He didn't know if he was glad or no.

**Jackie:** He was. He had a way of planting himself in front of little explosions and taking the lot. Ironhead and Resurrection need willing victims to keep the iron pure and the species blushing. My old man was one of them. If ever he went to hear a really strong preacher, and he had a knack of knowing where the hell-fire boys would be banging the pulpit, he'd come home with no control over his bowels or his limbs. They'd have him running around like a kid in the dark.

**Chislett:** Very good with terror, the hellfire boys.

**Jackie:** Then his brother would come around urging him to have me chained, gelded, branded, deported, and God knows what. And with every suggestion the old man nodded and said he'd see to it right away. Every time he came shuffling near my bed, I kept my back to the wall and my hands ready and my eyes sharp.

**Chislett:** That's a terrible situation in a bedroom, Jackie. Back to the wall, tense and expectant, not knowing what tool your old man has got sharpened for use.

**Jackie:** He had no luck. The one time he tried to ease his widower's life with a bit of backlane jobbery he ran into the one woman in Ferncleft who liked to have her passion seamed with violence. She beat him half to death.

**Jim James:** Uncertainty is all around. You go up a back lane with the best of bad intentions and you tangle with Jem Mace's sister. Have you ever made a mistake like that, Jackie?

**Jackie:** No, Jim. I don't want to boast, but I know the way. I have good sensitive feet and my throat usually manages to find the right sort of song, the right shape of welcoming door. Nothing explodes in front of me. Nothing has fettered me. Nothing has yet degraded me. And it never will.

**Chislett:** They're closing in, Jackie, Resurrection Rees said last week that you'd reached the end of your course. He said you'd seduced your last girl, corrupted your last honest working-man, and insulted your last God.

**Janet:** Oh! he was in top form. I was glad I'd bought a new shawl to go. When he spoke about the girls his eyes were just like moons and he looked just like you. He's working out a new benediction to make us proof against you.

**Jim James:** He said you are turning this place into a Sodom and Gomorrah.

**Jackie:** Where's that?

**Jim James:** Two noted centres of laxity in the long ago. Sodom and Gomorrah.

**Jackie:** They talked about them in the theological college my uncle sent me to. But I always sat in corners where the sound wouldn't penetrate.

**Jim James:** . . . And he says you'll have us all queueing up for tickets in the next whale. He's asking God never to take his eyes off you.

**Jackie:** That'll be a comfort in the mountains, in the nights. Oh! well, let's forget Resurrection Rees and Ironhead Luxton and their burning manias. Let's have a few hours of affection before you crawl back to your cottages and your stink-holes. And when the first daylight stirs I'll start walking west to tickle me a trout on the banks of the Teify, and spread a little dismay and curiosity among the pious.

(*A thoughtful quietness hits the group. They stare at the leaping furnace lights. The men start whistling a soft counter-melody to some such folk tune as 'Aderyn Pur' and they lead their girls on to a kind of grass bank. They lie down in postures of frank passion. The top couple are* Jackie *and* Janet. George Chislett *and his friend* Miriam Morgan *are the bottom couple. Their bodies sink more cosily into the earth and their crooned song touches silence.*

*Then there is a black, discordant crash of wind and brass. In comes* Richie Resurrection Rees, *followed by two attendants, small men with all the stigmata of timid piety upon them. Regardless of context they have their hands half-raised to express horror.* Richie Rees *is a big, handsome, passionate man, with a voice full of Old Testament bugles, and long fingers nailed with anathemas and ready at all times to project accusations. He points at the silent clumps of lovers. He stares at them incredulously and turns to his companions. They hide their faces and their whole expression is that of men who have now seen humanity cover the last yard of its depraved course and are now giving up the ghost.*)

**Rev Rees:** No! (*His companions shake their heads to back him up but do not try to compete with his voice.*) No! No! (*There is no stirring from the lovers.*) Locked in carnality in full view of the world. Deaf with it!

**Companions:** Their ears are stopped with it.

**Rev Rees:** Lechery is death!

**Chislett:** It isn't, you know.

**Rev Rees:** Lust is ruin.

**Jim James:** Lust is all right.

**Rev Rees:** Stand and be named. Stand and be shamed, physically wanton, morally lamed. Stand and be named. (*The couples are intimidated and one by one they descend the hillock to stand before the evangelist. Only* Jackie *and* Janet *remain undisturbed. They give an enormous groan of pleasure that makes* Rev Rees *clench and raise his fists.*) You two, stand and be named.

**Jackie:** (*without lifting his head*) My earache is back. (*Raises voice.*) Stop bawling there.

(Janet *peeps from beneath* Jackie.)

**Janet:** It's your uncle, Mr Resurrection Rees.

(Jackie *rises slowly and faces* Rees.)

**Jackie:** I thought so. Still keeping the urge on the hop, uncle? How are you, sir?

**Rev Rees:** I shall be a lot better when I see a set of iron bars around you, you disgraceful vagrant. And you others, to your homes. It's little wonder that Mr Luxton finds you incapable of doing a fair, decent day's work. Shuffling about the foundries like a gaggle of torpid ghosts. Little wonder, gallivanting here like goats with nightfall just a finger or two away. Last Sunday you were in the place of God, listening to my cries for a cool cleanliness. Tonight you gallivant like stoats at the behest of this demented whore-master. He has only to appear for the pest of promiscuity to break out again, the pest that once threatened to break the back of our people beneath the weariness of depletion and the multiple complications of a teeming bastardy.

**Jackie:** You're certainly blowing on your chips tonight, uncle.

Your tongue's a gelding-knife and no mistake.

**Rev Rees:** Go, you others. I have things to say to this man, family things.

**Jackie:** Stay where you are. He's just one of a whole legion peddling brands of death. He drains your hearts of heat to make a true gift of it to that ironmongering scamp on that hillside yonder. You are making a hobby of being cowed and dispersed every time these dervishes start to howl their case for submission and toil. Let us break the theological teeth of this chipmunk, then let's restart our revels.

(*The lovers resume their crooning tune and turn once more to their little Venusberg on the hillock.*)

**Rev Rees:** Consider, you people. This man is a phantom. He was not here yesterday; he will not be here tomorrow. He'll be on his way, shattering fresh maidens, subverting honest artisans. But you'll be here. And I'll be here. Mr Luxton, the ironmaster, will be here, and the furnaces in which you work will be here. His sort of laughter and his sort of freedom are death.

(*In the Top Right of the stage a darkness forms, and into it* Jackie's *friends back.* Jackie *turns to them and tries to beckon them to come back.*)

**Jackie:** You've got them, uncle. You and Luxton have found the words, the mood, that put the snuffer on their dreams.

**Rev Rees:** No dream was ever snuffed by lifting men and women above the level of cats and dogs. (*He steps nearer* Jackie.) I told you never to return to this place.

**Jackie:** I came back here by error. I travel in circles.

**Rev Rees:** Narrowing and vicious circles. You've had your chances. Twice I sent you to the theological colleges. In the first you inveigled the Principal's wife into mortal sin on a vestry bench. In the second you exploited a summer full of sunstrokes and converted three of the students to Mithraism, and sent two of the others hurtling into the Towey in an ecstasy of disbelief. You have avoided work and chastity as if they were deadly venoms. When you are free and footloose I have a vision of holy wedlock bent with strain and going black and blue with severe bruising. I found you a job in the furnaces that could have made you a captain of industry in twenty years. How long did you stick it? One day.

**Jackie:** It was a day in late spring. I went to the works down a lane flanked with bushes of laburnum. Have you ever smelled that flower when it is coming fresh out of the night? I went into the foundry. All the laburnums in the land wept with the betrayal. My nostrils ached and bled.

**Rev Rees:** And you went on another of your tomcat errands. Poaching the fish of the masters, poach the wives of your friends, if you have any. Eighty-nine seductions charged to you in Carmarthenshire alone.

**1st Crow:** Ninety, Mr Rees. The girl with the stammer came back later with a full statement.

**Jackie:** I bet she did. You moths would see to that. Uncle, you make it sound too easy. You see me a prowling badger, sniffing out of the thicket to try the nearest bedrooom door. We are in the same business, you and I. To assuage loneliness, to take the sting out of indignity. You do it with a great poultice of faith and words. I with a controlled burst of small affections.

**Rev Rees:** How dare you compare yourself with me? Look, nephew, I have come far. I am the leader of my denomination. My voice is reaching into corners of the land where enthusiasm of the soul had been dead for two hundred years. I am going to lead our people into a new cult of diligence, earnestness and restraint. There will be no place for the old outlawries, the old indecencies. They will be confined in a belt of freshly made iron.

**Jackie:** That will mean a set of completely new postures. But we grow on challenges.

**Rev Rees:** We will rise from the bog of our old improvidence.

**Jackie:** Then we'll really feel the cold.

**Rev Rees:** That's enough. You are an illness, a fever, a nuisance. You will leave this place tonight.

**Jackie:** Tonight?

**Rev Rees:** By dawn you will be twenty miles away from here and still moving as fast as your depraved legs can carry you.

**Jackie:** I could sleep here until morning. I've got lots of friends here.

**Rev Rees:** Any cottages in which you lodged would by morning have a smouldering thatch.

**Jackie:** And if I stay?

**Rev Rees:** You'll be destroyed.

**Jackie:** By some miracle of yours?

**Rev Rees:** Tidily, by law.

**Jackie:** What crime have I done except kindle a fire in a few cold grates?

**Rev Rees:** The new morality creates new definitions of crime, each one elastic, each one a noose.

**Jackie:** You mean that for the few harmless follies in which I've engaged you'd see me hang.

**Rev Rees:** You're as harmless as foxglove, as hemlock. You're deadly. You operate like the sort of strange smell that maddens animals. You landed back here about fourteen hours ago. Right?

**Jackie:** About that. I stopped just outside the town to help an old man prune a tree. A bell was chiming ten. I throw that detail in to show I'm not a monomaniac. A chaste antic, pruning.

**Rev Rees:** Fourteen hours and a ferment spreads. Hundreds of men have stayed from work, have sat in taverns till they curled in stupor, gibbering of some wild utopia of sensual ease and joy. Women have peered furtively into back-lanes in search of lost lovers. And the men who went to work mutter of strikes because a few of their number have been laid off, because a few pence have been whittled off a wage here and there, because a loaf costs a little more. And what image is in the minds of these people when they commit these follies? Yours. What good is it for Mr Luxton to tell them about shrinking orders from the Government, the swelling costs of imported wheat? What good is it for me to preach to them in times of danger that the first demand of God is a cool compromise on all matters that might end in death or deprivation?

**Jackie:** What's all this got to do with me? Just an innocent goat, going his way. Ever since I can remember the price of bread has been rising like a lark and wages have ruptured themselves trying to catch its tail. Ever since I can remember, eating has been as sensual as grouse-shooting, and I know houses where evictions have been so frequent, it's been genuinely difficult to get in for people coming out. Ever since I can remember I've known people get the poke from Mr Luxton's works because they passed your chapel with a frown and exchanged a few pints of ale while talking about the fitness of providence. But I've never talked much about these things. I've tried never even to think about them.

**Rev Rees:** You have ways of moving and looking that would spread disaffection among sheep. (*He turns to his companions.*) You may go now. Wait for me at the bottom of the lane. We have

to see Mr Luxton before the night is done. (*Exeunt the two crows.*)
Now Jackie. (*His voice is lower, even more urgent.*) If not for your
soul's sake, for your family's, for my sake and for the sake of your
father who beat his heart to fragments on the stony thought of
your limitless iniquities. Jackie, I am walking to a great end. I
don't expect you to see this for you have been walking sightless in
Sodom for many a year. Proceeding by touch but striking hard.
Upon life, Jackie, there is much dirt and some of us are destined
to be primarily cleaners. The bristle on which you will finally be
impaled is already in the making. Since my first mission of revival
seven years ago I have done much. I have reduced the number of
children born out of wedlock yearly from one hundred and thirty
to fifteen. I have reduced the number of women beaten black and
blue by drunken husbands from three hundred to seventy, a
welcome change of heart and colour. I have driven ten idle and
blasphemous tavern keepers into the foundries and two of them
into the diaconate. Girls who twelve months ago flaunted a
drooling carnality now wear a sheath of turgid modesty. I have
taken the wild horses of sin by the bridle and slowed them to a
gentle trot. If they do kick my flock in the head now it will be an
injury, not a decapitation.

**Jackie:** I'd say you'd slowed sin to a half-paralyzed sidle.
Morally, you're a stroke. You've certainly put the roof back on
wedlock. If it rains now it doesn't leak. And one might hear
things more clearly in life for the decreased rush of ale which can
be a great deafener. But I still don't see what this has got to do
with me.

**Rev Rees:** I don't want the things I've done undone, or gainsaid.
Next week I am addressing a congregation in London among
whom will be members of Her Majesty's government. My theme:
Christian humility in master and man as a healing unguent in
industrial relations. It will take my name far beyond these hills,
plant the banner of my zeal well to the east of Cheltenham. I want
no hindrance from you. I don't want it thrown in my face that I
am the uncle of Jackie the Jumper Rees, the most insolent defiler
of shrines and trampler of virginities since the opening of
Transgression Road. If you were to stand trial for multiple
subversion there would be showers of shame from Milford to
Shrewsbury.

**Jackie:** Trial? Uncle Richie, this time I really think you've blown your hymnal. Even in a court of mutes they'd laugh you out of it.

**Rev Rees:** You are the sacramental victim, the expendable pagan. You have no root here. Your passing would provoke tears but no fists. Go! Tonight. Twenty-four hours from now I may be able to do nothing to help you save quicken your passage to hell. Start walking westward until you reach the sea and you will not pause then. You will continue on foot to Ireland until you confirm your manifest lack of faith in miracles.

(*Exit* Rev Rees. Jackie *does a sort of slow hopping dance about the stage. The furnace flickers have started again. He holds out his arms to them, then rejects them.*)

**Jackie:** We are rarely more than a light flickering between two identities. I could have spoken all the words he spoke. And he, I suppose, could have doubled for me. We inhabit a procession of wombs that grow darker, and we avoid the one authentic birth by acts of clownish mischance. Straighten your legs, Jackie, and get out of this.

(*He heads left, away from the furnace flares. He leaves the stage. Music is heard, a great, swinging, sad song. Comes back and starts softly to sing*)

**Jackie:** Through the full light of a noisy day
     I am someone else with a horse's neigh,
     Swinging in joy from heart to heart,
     Singing "Darling, darling, till men do us part."
     But when music trembles or the sun has set,
     I am not at ease, I cannot forget.
     My mind breaks silence, I am ill beset
     In a yawning gulf of numb regret
     For all the beauty I have not met
     And which may never come my way.

(Janet *comes back. She stretches out her arms to* Jackie. *Behind through the shadows come Jackie's friends, and in the richest possible harmony they sing the song that* Jackie *has just sung, changing the singular to plural.*)

**Jackie:** And Richie Rees says, "Come what may, You'll never get lost if you work and pray."

**Chislett:** (*to* Jackie) Sand in your bread, cuts in your pay, Staunch your wound with work and pray.

**Janet:** What did he say to you, Jackie?

**Jackie:** He said a skyful. It would have taken a whippet to follow it all. Seems Luxton and he have me tabbed as the second instalment of the Black Death. He wants me clear of this place before morning. He talked something about arresting me. Why should they arrest me? What is this iron-smelting doing to the brains of men?

**Janet:** Don't you really remember, Jackie?

**Jackie:** (*feeling his head*) No, there are patches of my brain that are as dark as pitch, that don't remember a thing. The lights have been out in them since that damned County Sheriff brought his sword down on my head in Carmarthen town, in that hotel in Carmarthen town.

**Chislett:** You know why he did that, Jackie?

**Jackie:** Because he had a sword, because he was a County Sheriff, because I didn't duck when I saw the old fool coming at me.

**Chislett:** The room you were in in that hotel was a bedroom. You were there with the County Sheriff's daughter. You had run off with her. He chased you and found you there. He put two and two together and it added up to a clout on the head for you.

**Jackie:** And whole fields of the past melted away.

**Chislett:** Have you forgotten about the Moses business, Jackie?

**Jackie:** Moses? What's this now?

**Chislett:** It was the year before the County Sheriff business. We'd had a rough winter.

**All:** Oh! a rough, rough winter, Jackie.

**Chislett:** And you assembled us on the square. You spoke to us.

**All:** Your voice was a bell that morning, Jackie.

**Chislett:** And you said: I am Moses. I am not Jackie Rees, the Jumper, any more. Like a repentant snake, you said, I have sloughed off folly. For the first time in my life I am going to do something good and earnest.

**All:** Your eyes were big as moons when you said those things. We were wild and hungry and we believed you.

**Chislett:** And you said: I, Jackie Moses Rees, will lead you out of this place, out of this pain, away from this degradation. I have a good friend, you said, in North Pembrokeshire. He has a broad, deep valley, full of good grazing land, clear streams and rich soil. He is giving this valley to me. I will take you there. There will be room for you all. You will lead lives full of milk, honey and everlasting passion.

**All:** We could see this valley, Jackie. We could see the grazing, the streams, the richness, the milk, the passion, just from the way your mouth spoke them.

**Chislett:** We borrowed carts. It took all of half an hour to load them with our possessions. We followed you.

**Jackie:** You followed me?

**Chislett:** We made quite a procession. Mr Luxton and the justices and the policemen laughed as we passed the western boundaries of the town. You looked back as Ferncleft was just about to vanish from sight and you said: "You will never know the furnace-stink again, the killing glare of the fires."

(Jackie *looks at the faces around him with intense curiosity.*)

**Jackie:** This valley. What was it like?

**Chislett:** We never saw it, Jackie. We never got there. At Llanddarog, near Carmarthen, we ran into smallpox. A half of us died. A quarter of us were jailed for vagrancy. The rest came back here.

**Jackie:** Was I drunk?

**Chislett:** You were sober as a tree. It was early in the morning. All you'd had was a stoup of the Widow Evans' nettle beer which is, so to speak, a cure for drink.

**Jackie:** A man will say, when awake, the things he hears in sleep. People hear, people believe. No wonder I've spent so much time alone on the hilltops. That's the only safe place for me, by God. Tell me, what's brewing about here, except iron and Widow Evans' nettle beer?

**All:** Trouble.

**Jackie:** Of what colour?

**All:** Striped.

**Chislett:** We have a little union in the works. Sort of sick benefit thing. If you lose your wits we lend you a new set. If you're blown up, we help you to land. Simple charity. They'll smash that for a start. Your uncle, the reverend, says he saw the devil with a union card.

**Jackie:** He sees everything.

**All:** It was a vision he saw at Llandrindod Wells.

**Jackie:** Those waters. Kidneys wholly flushed supercharge the vision. (*To* Chislett) What else?

**Chislett:** Roofs will rise trying to keep up with the rent. So many evictions the men will be in the middle of the street asking what the hell happened to the sights and sounds they love. Luxton will

111

import new workers from Ireland and the north, specially stooped to cope with the new wage level. And they'll probably whip back a part of the old truck system. Your uncle says the old family spirit of love and trust in industry was really ruptured when we demanded payment in anything as cold as wages. So back'll come the old truck. You've heard about working for bread and getting a stone.

**Jackie:** Mm.

**Chislett:** Well, we get clinkers. Option, clink.

**Jackie:** They are really on form, on top form.

**All:** Speak out for us, Jackie. Sing out for freedom, boy.

(Jackie *looks around most craftily*.)

**Jackie:** Oh! no, I'm not going to speak. I'm not going to sing. Tonight I saw something in the eye of that uncle of mine that really put the chill on me. We're not joking any more, are we? Death is very clearly on the agenda. And something must have happened to me in that trip around the hills. People didn't seem to want me around any more and I didn't want to stay. When I used to sit with them around the fire at night and sing them my songs, I'd stop in the middle of a verse and say what the hell. I'd look around at the bare kitchen I was in and feel on my neck a draught from all the loose, rattling windows of the world, and I said to myself that there is nothing in life that is worth vocally more than a short moan. At the last farmhouse I stayed at, the farmer's daughter and I hit it off. She promised to join me on my palliasse one night. She did not come to me. And the palliasse was wet from a week's rain and a most considerable leak in the roof.

**Chislett:** Something detained her, Jackie. Her father found out or she read a pamphlet about honour or disease. No girl in her right senses would betray you, Jackie.

**Jackie:** I've had rheumatism ever since. My legs are slower. No, she wasn't detained. She didn't forget. I went to look for her. I found her. She was sharing the palliasse of the ploughboy. He was fifteen years younger than I. And he had a dry palliasse.

**Chislett:** You killed him?

**Jackie:** No, no. I'm telling you. Flames have gone down inside me. I felt no anger, no shame. Just a bit more draught as I stood there in my shift in the attic. I wished them well and borrowed some goose-grease from the ploughboy to rub my aching joints. And there was another farm before that. The man was jealous. He

112

slipped whitelead into my broth. He was too mean to buy the full dose and he didn't love his wife much anyway. It came nowhere near killing me but my bowels spelt out the entire alphabet.

**Chislett:** You're hungry and thirsty, Jackie. Two days of drinking, talking, dancing, and you'll be the same old Jackie.

**Jackie:** No, I'm going to make an offering to Mr Luxton and the Reverend Richie Resurrection Rees. The idle, seditious goat becomes the dedicated gelded toiler. I shall make amends for every slight I've ever offered the men of wealth and the sectaries. I shall offer myself for employment at the foundries at dawn tomorrow morning. And when I've done my twelve-hour stint, with the filth of labour still upon me, I shall present myself to my reverend uncle and swear upon his fattest Bible that from now on to the grave I shall be the most icily celibate creature this side of a monastery.

**Janet:** (*laughing*) No, no, no.

**Jackie:** Oh! yes, yes, yes. Even you, Janet, I am now seeing with new eyes. You are as remote as the moon. For the first time in my life I have no wish to touch you except as a brother: I will set new standards of loyalty to Mr Luxton and my days will be so lighted from within by selflessness that thousands now lost in defeat will once more find a way. I shall touch only the minimum of food and drink to keep passion flat on the kennel floor. The money I save will go weekly to any family named by you as more picturesque in its destitution than any other. I am going to rub the noses of Luxton and my uncle into the miracle of change, and even without wishing to, they will grow more reasonable in their dealings with you. Now, no more frivolity. To bed. I'll kip down with you, George, and no one will be stirring earlier than I tomorrow. And if you hear of any funerals going on, give me the wink. I'll be there, giving the final gloss to gloom and bringing tears to the boil.

**Chislett:** (*to his friends*) His uncle must have beaten him about the head with that black, stiff hat he wears for the big meetings.

**All:** Start laughing again, Jackie. You've fooled us long enough.

**Jackie Rees:** I don't want to laugh again. I can't wait to see myself abject, silent, tossed at the feet of those roaring destructive bastards who are giving the new black shape to life.

**Janet:** It's that wet palliasse that's affecting you, Jackie. Tomorrow I'll make you a pair of thick flannelette drawers that'll

113

drive the cold from your loins.

(Jackie *strikes a demure, penitential pose and lifts his eyes to heaven to signify that his virility has officially and forever crossed the Jordan.*)

**Jackie:** It'll be lovely not to be different,
It'll be lovely just to be cool,
Never again to say the wrong word,
To be a plain conformist fool.
And as the birds of freedom moult,
Haul down the emblems of revolt,
Pull the golden visions down,
Salute a shy and castrate clown.

**All:** One more Judas, one more Judas to plague us,
One more Judas, one more Judas to bear,
One more changeling, one more chiseller to fox us.
One more sack-cloth, one more sack-cloth to wear.

**Janet:** How do you think they'll be wearing the sack-cloth this spring?

**Women:** Short.

(*The furnace flares are crazily enlarged and intensified. They all turn round and look in terror at the new brilliance.*)

**Jackie:** What's this now?

**All:** (*quite happily*) Apocalypse!

**Jackie:** No. Apocalypse will be dark and ordinary. Tax-collectors, sergeants, preachers and lawyers; an unlighted lot.

(*Three men, in postures of revelation, appear at the top of the hillock.*)

**1st Man:** Luxton is raking out the furnaces. Every foundry for four valleys around will be stone cold by morning, and will stay cold until we meet Luxton's terms.

**2nd Man:** They've brought the army into Birchtown. There was a clash on Birchtown Square an hour back.

**Jackie:** Clash? What about?

**2nd Man:** Human rights and the allocation of Birchtown's four full-time harlots. The mayor read the Riot Act.

**Chislett:** He knows it by heart. It's the only steady reading the man's ever done.

**2nd Man:** The soldiers fired their guns. Two of ours are dead.

**Jackie:** As long as death is about somebody'll use it.

**Chislett:** There was no other way for you but this, Jackie.

**Jackie:** What do you mean? No other way?

**Chislett:** The cobbles of the road were laid down for you a long, long time ago.

**Jackie:** There is no road. From hour to hour we have the say: north or south.

**Chislett:** Tomorrow morning you were going to submit to bondage, forswear the sun and stand as suppliant at the smelting works of Ironhead Luxton.

**All:** The smelting works are cold.

**3rd Man:** In the white hillside mansion of Luxton, the County Sheriff and the colonel of militia are making plans for the defence of the realm, the future of iron and freedom from molestation of Luxton's three lovely daughters, Arianwen, Eirlys and Mona. With them is the Reverend Richie Resurrection Rees, and with him is a clutch of fellow divines. They are arranging the uprooting of impiety, the cauterization of unbelievers, and the banishment of lust to points north of Hudsons's Bay. From now on the footloose fornicant will need to be a bit of a trapper as well.

**Jackie:** That won't bother me. I've handled my last pelt.

**Chislett:** Tomorrow you were going into the presence of your uncle, the Reverend Richie Resurrection Rees. You were going to dust your hymnal, apologise to the nearest Bishop and give the Reverend Rees a souvenir package of regrets for all your infidel midnights. And the Reverend Rees will already be gathering the faggots for your hot and final redemption. That's about the only positive thing you can say about iron foundries. They took people's minds off heat as the best conceivable cure for heretics. You, Jackie, will be the last to burn. And the slowest. After that palliasse. You don't know what kind of a name you've made for yourself. Every time one of Luxton's foremen puts his boot into a loafer he says: "Who do you think you are, Jackie the Jumper?"

**Jackie:** I will do as I said. I have lived wantonly and unwisely. In a social way I have created much bewilderment by prescribing the witless anarchy of childhood as a valid way of life to the grave. In a sexual way I have made confusion as fixed an article of furniture in as many bedrooms as the wardrobe. There has been very little evil in this. Ever since I was able to see over a shawl I have never been able to see cold hands without wishing to warm them. I have never been able to see a stricken face without wishing to bring it joy. They had to tighten the shawl to stop me starting too soon on those astonishing capers. Also, I owe much to my uncle who had a matchless knowledge of every aphrodisiac herb that grows between Llantrisant and Llanpumpsaint.

**Chislett:** We'll gather a bagful for you tomorrow, Jackie.

**Janet:** We've worn you like a light, Jackie. Stop guttering.

**Chislett:** They'll reject you and destroy you, Jackie, if you go near them. But you won't. You road's laid down.

**Jackie:** Nothing is laid down; nothing is foretold. From moment to moment we can lay hands on life and scare it out of its trousers. Here, on the breast, you have a compass or a till. You have no till. You are free to choose direction.

(*The people turn slowly around and point in each direction of the compass. Each time they shake "No" with their heads, and when they finally face front again their fingers point to the ground.*)

**Chislett:** The compass says what it's always said, Jackie. We stay here.

**Jackie:** And so do I. My whole life has ripened to this one point.

**Old Man:** (*holding up his hands prophetically*) God be with you, Jackie boy. Go forward, boy. I see through the days to come. You'll be a martyr, Jackie. They want to hang somebody special. Let it be you, Jackie. You are martyr meat. Your corpse will shine like stars for us. The tears we'll shed for you will make us clean and strong. The three lovely daughters of Luxton will take pity on you as you wait to die. They will love you. It will be the death of the century.

**Jackie:** Do you know something? That isn't all nonsense. I will go to the Reverend Rees and Mr Luxton. I will say: You, uncle, you, Mr Luxton, are fools, heavy-weight fools. I am a fool. I have come to join you. We have a full hand. We have all won. Now, let's give folly a hundred years rest. Let's drop the mask of idiocy we feel obliged to wear for pride's sake. Let's give a respite to the starvers, burners and hangers.

**Chislett:** You're going to say all that to Luxton?

**Jackie:** Every word.

**Chislett:** Get your mouth very close to his ear. He had his skull-bones case-hardened in his father's first foundry. Was that right, Jackie? What you said about your memory going and all that?

**Jackie:** No. There's nothing I forget. (*He pats his head.*) Everything as fresh as dew, damn it. But it's nice to put it about that you might have a belt of darkness somewhere inside there.

It's nice to be able to turn an idiotic look at people when they come at you with questions sharpened to kill. I must practise my approach. I must let my jaw drop a little to reduce brightness or they might suspect me of some satirical motive. I must let my shoulders droop to suggest the acceptance of toil as the imperative truss of decency. (*His face and body become transformed as he enters his new role.*) I shall not wait until morning. I shall go up to the hillside. I shall demand entrance to the mansion of Luxton now, tonight. Assemble tomorrow at noon on the square. I shall be there with the man who hates us tonight. We shall see the embrace of peace, the kiss of restitution.

(*A thematic sound. A melody for brass based on the baritone harmony of the hymn 'Hail to the Lord's anointed.' The people hum it and the rhythm is fast, compulsive. Jackie leaves the stage. The people become more and more exalted as they watch him make his way.*)

**Chislett:** That whitelead may not have killed him. It certainly gave him a jolt. He's walking faster. (*The singing accelerates.*) He's breaking into a run. He can't get to Luxton and his uncle fast enough.

(*A man appeaers on the left.*)

**4th Man:** There's a warrant out for Jackie. They are charging him with organizing the riots that led to the deaths in Birchtown.

**Chislett:** Jackie's running.

**Janet:** He always ran to his pleasures.

**Chislett:** Where's the pleasure in this?

**Janet:** He'll know.

(*A great sound of galloping horses.*)

**All:** The militia. The mounted boys. Out for blood.

**Chislett:** Jackie's blood. He's fallen. He's down. They're all around him.

**All:** Come back, Jackie. Come back to us.

**Chislett:** They're putting chains on him.

**All:** Jackie the Jumper, in chains.

(*Their bodies droop as if they feel the weight of the imprisoning irons.*)

**Chislett:** They've put the chains on his hands, his feet. They are pushing him forward. He's fallen again.

**Janet:** How dare they do that to him!

**All:** How dare he do this to us! Our Jackie, the everlasting

vagrant, the singing boy, the tireless lover, a fettered fool. What'll
they do to him, George?
**Chislett:** *You* know. (*They all nod* "No, no".) No, you don't
know, do you? And your ignorance is the deepest grave on earth.

Curtain

# ACT TWO

*The dining-room of the Luxton home. At the head of the table is the ironmaster,* John 'Ironhead' Luxton, *a man of about fifty, intelligent, a little stooped and apprehensive. The other guests are* Rev Rees, *the* County Sheriff *and the* Colonel *of the County Militia, the last two in uniform and all radiant with assurance. The company is completed by Luxton's three daughters,* Mona, Arianwen, Eirlys. *On a small platform, right, there will be a modest type of harp.*

**Sheriff:** To crown that splendid feast, I have but one favour to ask. (Luxton *raises his hands in a 'The house is yours' sort of gesture.*) Some music from these lovely ladies.
**Rev Rees:** A balm for these unquiet times.
**Colonel:** (*who exhibits tone-deafness in his every gesture and inflection*) Indeed.
   (Mona *goes to the harp and plays a melody which will allow her sisters to engage in tender frills of counter-melody.* Luxton *and* Rees *gaze at them in almost besotted affection. The* Colonel's *fingers are heard strumming on the walnut of the table, and against the sides of his brandy glass. The* Colonel *gets up from the table and looks out through the curtain of the window. He does so furtively as if expecting a missile to be aimed at him through the glass. The* Sheriff *is much calmer, sitting back, even humming the shadow of a harmony with the music.*)
**Luxton:** Colonel, would you greatly mind heeding the music and stop putting me on edge?
**Colonel:** There are more stirring things abroad tonight than music, Mr Luxton. Down there, in that town, among those people, there is no thought of harmony and much thought of murder.
   (Mona *plucks a sardonic discord from her harp and grimaces at her sisters.*)
**Luxton:** What will they do?

119

**Colonel:** They follow a pattern.

**Sheriff:** They will start fires. They will set something alight. The hayrick of some poor farmer fellow or his cottage, or the drier sections of the court where we keep the records of debt.

**Colonel:** And by the light of that fire, every cretinous, disaffected cottager will crawl from every cleft of these hills to some central spot where they will demonstrate their wrath.

**Rev Rees:** I will do whatever lies within the word of God to calm them.

**Colonel:** In these situations God needs an ample crutch of executive aid. (*He looks out of the window again.*) They will start fires. They need warmth to give them confidence and leadership to make confidence into a weapon. But I give you this assurance. The fires will soon be put out, and whoever is the leader who emerges he will break all existing records for a run to the gibbet. (*He stares hard at* Richie Rees *who stares back at him without flinching.*) Even though the leader might be the kinsman of one we trust. We know where to look, we know where to go. And we have the only thing that is wisdom in these social affairs. Audacity, audacity, audacity.

(Mona *sweeps another great discord into the room.*)

**Colonel:** Did I upset you, my dears?

**Mona:** You upset my harp. I'm quite serene.

(*The* Colonel *sweeps the curtains back. A blaze rises to the sky.*)

**Sheriff:** We must go. (*He bows to the daughters, who have stopped playing and singing.*) Whenever my lips approach a cup of such enchantment you may be sure that some lout will dash it from my lips.

**Colonel:** Give us an hour or less and we'll have coolness back in business.

**Eirlys:** We'll see you to the door.

**Sheriff:** You are so good. Goodnight, gentlemen.

**Luxton** and **Rees:** Goodnight.

**Rev Rees:** God go with you.

**Luxton:** And don't make matters worse, gentlemen. Whatever you do, don't make matters worse. But they will, of course. Ironhead Luxton! These damned names stick and settle like ice over one. That was my grandfather, Ironhead. A loud and greedy idiot. He would have used his workers for fuel if wood had not been so reasonably cheap. The Luxton heads would have been getting softer since that day. (*He strokes his own head.*) Pap, sir, pap. The first Ironhead killed my father, his own son, with overwork, and he had me, at the age of ten, marching about his damned ovens learning to frown and bawl in the approved Ironhead way. I went cross-eyed and hoarse with the effort.

**Rev Rees:** There are men like Moses, Mr Luxton, who are meant to lead and rule. You are such a man, Mr Luxton.

**Luxton:** That Moses! He had nothing to deal with half so tricky as the market in iron, lining men and women up at a trough of regular work, the gymnastics of bread supply. Once he killed that overseer all he had to do was walk. And he was convinced that he was next to God. I walk next to you, Rees. And I'm not finding that a tonic.

**Rev Rees:** Anyone who aims his fist at improvidence and the foul-mouthed utterances of the equality-boys walks next to God.

**Luxton:** The going is rough, Rees, rough.

**Rev Rees:** Obviously. At every step we are tested.

**Luxton:** Did you know that I once got out of here, left here on the run?

**Rev Rees:** You might tell me, Mr Luxton, but I wouldn't believe you.

**Luxton:** I did. I wanted to be a painter. My eyes had been driven mad with the colour I had seen in the furnaces, in the faces of the people I saw streaming in and out of them.

**Rev Rees:** Colour, like love, can be a trap.

(Luxton *gives* Rees *a close look and it hints at the six or so mordant things that he would like to say.*)

**Luxton:** I went to Paris. I had the kind of gentle, demented manner that seemed to please the looser women. I did well. I painted gay, fleshy faces. Not fish, or trees, or seas, like some people. Just people laughing, people who were getting some clear charge out of life, people who'd never got up at dawn to rake clinker for me.

**Rev Rees:** Poor guides, gaiety and the flesh.

**Luxton:** They gave me a good enough light. I came away from France. Settled in London. My grandfather found me. He clobbered me with my easel. I was still cross-eyed with shock when I got back, and my first week at the furnaces was almost bearable because of the stupor I was in. You should arrange for more of that to be laid on, Mr Rees. Real stupor. I wanted to kill my grandfather. I considered it my moral, social duty to blow his greedy, stupid old head off.

**Rev Rees:** Oh no. This is some distemper, some nightmare you are acting out to fool me.

**Luxton:** No nightmare, Mr Rees. In a crumpled sort of way I am perfectly fit. Confused, but fit. I bought a gun. A cheap gun because my grandfather kept me short of money, and I think the sights must have been fixed by someone who was against violence. Several times I tried to shoot my grandfather when he was out in the fields with those damned ferrets of his. But I was no marksman and if I had kept up the attempt I would have wiped out the population faster than my grandfather was trying to do. So I surrendered. I opened my mind to the message of iron. I had my valet scrub my back with the laissez faire doctrine of the Manchester boys. I had a slight surgical adjustment to my nose which made it impossible for the smell of coke and hunger to dominate the odour of port and pheasant. My paintings went into the attic and until last night I hadn't set eyes on them.

**Rev Rees:** Burn them, Mr Luxton. Painting is a recognized wing of sensuality, and the people must not glimpse in you any vestige of flippancy. Not at this moment of challenge. They want, in their dark, quaking world, a message of absolute coherence and conviction.

(Luxton *flaps his arms helplessly with only a hint of anger, as if to say 'For Christ's sake, spare me that.'*)

**Luxton:** Coherence. A big thing.

**Rev Rees:** Within two days there will be utter peace again. Your tremors of doubt will have passed. You will see yourself as the rest of us see you. A man of unique social value and power; a man warmed by the love of all his working people, unaffected by the present blight of disbelief; a patron of science and a friend of the arts; and the father of three of the loveliest daughters in the realm whose wealth and beauty might well win them the hand of princes.

**Luxton:** You are truly God's trumpet, Mr Rees. After a session on you he must feel whacked. Now tell me, what have you got against that nephew of yours?

**Rev Rees:** I'd prefer not to speak of him.

**Luxton:** Half the time I'd prefer not to listen to you. But I do. So answer my question. Why make him so special a target?

**Rev Rees:** He is a man of moral character so loose that he has to turn back every five minutes to pick it up. He is a tramp, a defiler of holy matrimony and a subversive anarch. In the minds of many of his dupes he has replaced the image of God with the idol of a loaf.

**Luxton:** I know exactly how he feels. And I see the point of a lot of it. I tasted some of it myself once and the flavour was fine. Where is he now?

**Rev Rees:** Here. He had the insolence to return.

**Luxton:** And you want him destroyed.

**Rev Rees:** Destroyed? My dear Mr Luxton, my whole life speaks for the Gospel of Peace, for the unguent of love.

**Luxton:** Mr Rees, we are both mature men. If we are to make fools of words and ideas let us, at least, shake our clowns' caps at each other as we do so.

**Rev Rees:** I want my nephew warned. His life is a sty. I want it cleaned. But without violence. I want him to appear before the magistrates and to be told to desist from his mischief. It's an ethically directed bit of house-cleaning, no more.

**Luxton:** The first broom I heard of with a rope on it. I heard every word you said last night to the County Sheriff and the Colonel of the Militia. You thought I was dozing over my wine. I wasn't. You three had given me a pain in my head-bones. I was resting. You were striking blows for decency right, left and centre. You convinced them without any difficulty at all that your nephew should be hounded down and hung up. This fascinates me, Mr Rees. You want a part of what he is, has been. You want to inherit part of the vacuum that will be left when he dies.

**Rev Rees:** You need the doctor, Mr Luxton.

**Luxton:** We both do, Mr Rees. But he hasn't got the cure. (*Tears back the big damask curtains on the back window. There is a dying flare of light from a distant hillside.*) The last furnace. The smoke holes will be grey and silent tomorrow morning. These hills will cool off for the first time in eighty years. Some strange things will come out of the new coldness. If we could all be raked out from time to time that would be nice. (*Adopts a posture which is almost one of cowering self-defence.*) What are you people trying to get me into? Why didn't I let things go quickly and naturally to the devil, which is what they are meant to do? What a pack you are in with, Rees. The law-jugglers, the mountebank interpreters of God to man, the warriors who want a bit of cut-rate glory between the vast national butcheries.

(*Hooves and sounds of shouting men.*)

**Rev Rees:** The soldiers. The County Sheriff and the Colonel. You'll get a new strength from them.

**Luxton:** I don't want strength, new or old. You are not going to drag me along with this. According to the book this business of belting the hell out of those smelting helots should give me some sweetness of satisfaction. But all it does is plant the taste of death on my lips. The nerves of the tough boys wilt and a stammer like myself is thrown into these proceedings. I want to speak out loud the things my mind has been muttering in between the market booms and hunger riots. I don't want to go floating into time as the man who initiated three new types of deformity in undernourished children.

**Rev Rees:** A mere perverse bending of limbs. Some pre-sexual gambit.

**Luxton:** Those children would never have been capable of that, save with a couple of friends bolstering them up from the back. In a world almost totally unlit I shall confess to having created a little light. I'll go up to the attic. I'll get those pictures. I'll trundle them around those hovels. I'll show them the other side of my moon.

**Rev Rees:** Your pictures! They'd throw them in your face or use them as kindling.

**Luxton:** Good. Art is meant to spread warmth even if it means having one's canvases crackling in the grate. I'll get my paints. I'll use my ledger-books as palettes. I will write one great apology across the earth. Sorry! Sorry! This is the coke and clinker boy coming to heel. I will offer my own pelt as a girdle to mute the rattle of old iron in the body of our kind.

**Rev Rees:** We all stand under sentence of progress, Mr Luxton. Some of us wish it otherwise. At the heart of our belief is the Garden of Eden, a calm and smokeless bower. But we must artificially extend man's muscle if he is not to subsist on the same slender margin as the jackals.

**Luxton:** So be it. We must have iron. And we'll have iron. Tomorrow morning those furnaces will be lit again and I shall try to view the smelters as things of at least as much significance as the stuff they smelt.

**Rev Rees:** Do that and they'll tear you apart.

**Luxton:** I'm already torn apart. If I weren't I wouldn't have the feeling that I'm walking with the sort of boldness that normally lands a man in bedlam. And if any more bits of nobility come sailing in here to inspect my daughters for possible marriage, I'll slap them permanently on the night shift in front of the furnaces that are most likely to blow. I'd prefer to see them married to some shepherd who could speak to them without any cunning afterthought of gain, without flourish, without affectation. There's a lot to be said for that nephew of yours. What's his name?

**Rev Rees:** He is a wretch, a menace. If our morals are blue in the face watch for his fingers on the windpipe.

**Luxton:** Any man who follows, however imperfectly, the ideal of an unconditional freedom is not a wretch. He is a bird worth watching. What do the people call him?

**Rev Rees:** His name is the same as mine. Rees. Jackie Rees.

**Luxton:** What do the people call him?

**Rev Rees:** I have no idea. My work is preaching the word, laundering the urges of fallen man, presenting you men of enterprise to the labouring mass in a clearer Christian light, drying out the drunken, supplying a prop of pride to the chaste in their lonely trials.

**Luxton:** It's a big programme, Mr Rees.

**Rev Rees:** It fills my life. It keeps me too busy to have the time to catalogue the region's lechers.

**Luxton:** They call your nephew Jackie the Jumper. Why?

**Rev Rees:** He possibly has some twitch. I had a palsied uncle. The thing might be going through the family.

**Luxton:** They call him Jackie the Jumper because he doesn't settle in any one place, because he accepts no organized work. He stirs people's dreams into a hot broth with his gospel of a love and joy achievable here on this earth. Sexually he has prowled like a tireless tom over the roof of a nation's desire. He has me, with my foundries, and you, with your condemned-cell ethic, ticketed as a pair of tricky and undesirable monkeys.

**Rev Rees:** Which is why he must be thrust away.

**Luxton:** Which is why I must see him. This is a time when everyone must be heard. Heard and respected. Even when it outrages the hard crust of reason that forms around our self-interest. Respected.

**Rev Rees:** There are those whom it is treacherous and fatal to respect.

**Luxton:** Whatever the Colonel and his troop might say to the contrary, the only sweet and worthy death is to die in an effort to communicate.

(*Knock on door.*)

Here is the anti-communication squad.

(*Door opens. A flunkey appears and begins to make an announcement, but before he can produce his second word he is pushed forward by two large, gleaming men, the* Sheriff *and the* Colonel *done up in the most lavish and glittering cloaks available for cavalry officers of the period. The musical flavour of their entrance could be a fiercely fast version of the Welsh folk-song 'Hunting the Hare'.* Luxton *ducks behind a chair at the sight of them. He bends down as if trying to see what is at their feet.*)

**Luxton:** They haven't got their horses with them, thank God. Rees, I can take even when he's bouncing on a theme of Apocalypse. But these uniforms, they make a dwarf out of me.

(Sheriff *and the* Colonel *solemnly advance and shake* Luxton *by the hand.*)

**Luxton:** What's this for?

**Sheriff:** You are safer than you were twenty-four hours ago.

**Luxton:** Tell me about that.

**Sheriff:** Things came swiftly to a head and we chopped the head off. All we have to do now is wait for the blood to congeal and the patient will be well.

**Luxton:** What have you been doing?

**Colonel:** It might have been a little campaign, Mr Luxton, but it went perfectly. A mob gathered in the main square at Birchtown, five miles to the east of here. They meant mischief.

**Luxton:** The people in Birchtown always look as if they mean mischief. It's just the way they feel about Birchtown. They're harmless.

**Colonel:** Not that lot. They were going to storm the court-house and burn the debt-records, and then string up a couple of bailiffs as dessert. Then they were going to burn down two bake-houses as a protest against the dearer loaf, as if the wretched bakers had any say in the scarcity or abundance of wheat.

126

**Rev Rees:** How true, Colonel, how true. We are all between the thumb and finger of God. He exerts pressure or lets us breathe, as his love for us waxes and wanes. All of us, bakers, barons, buzzards, barnyard fowl. The thumb and the finger.

**Luxton:** You ought to pay a special tax on your metaphors, Reverend.

**Rev Rees:** One of those bakers is known to me. He is one of my precentors. He has a sweet, clear tenor voice. I trust they came to no harm.

**Colonel:** None at all. We rode our horses through them. They were adamant, sullen, calling for torches and telling the bakers to get ready for some really overdone crust.

**Rev Rees:** Anybody who launches that type of joke in a context of civic disorder wants watching.

**Sheriff:** Then Mr Benyon, the mayor, read the Riot Act.

**Rev Rees:** A splendid voice for proclamation, the mayor. At our prayer-meeting he is a supplicant of real quality. He calmed them, no doubt.

**Colonel:** They would not disperse. They treated the mayor to abuse. They charged us. I ordered a sabre charge. Two died.

**Luxton:** Whose two?

**Colonel:** Their two, obviously. We, Mr Luxton, are the County Militia.

**Sheriff:** They threw a burning brand into Mr Rees's church. It landed on a pew but it would not burn.

**Rev Rees:** A hint of miracle there.

**Luxton:** Miracle and the endemic dampness of wood throughout the region. What happened after you got your corpses?

**Colonel:** The rest fled.

**Sheriff:** If I get my guess you'll need a telescope to see a trouble-maker around here for the next ten years. And, of course, you know the furnaces were raked out this evening.

**Luxton:** I saw the light fade.

**Rev Rees:** Symbolic. This will cool the bowels of their wrath.

**Sheriff:** It will. Two or three weeks of hunger will bring their fever down.

(Luxton *walks around them, staring at them in bewilderment.*)

**Luxton:** You're all doctors, aren't you? Whenever life turns you see a taint of disease. You keep humanity so steadily on the hop no wonder the thing has a chronic hernia.

127

**Rev Rees:** Mr Luxton has been very depressed tonight. He even spoke of treating with these people, of restarting the furnaces tomorrow.

(*The* Colonel *and the* County Sheriff *take* Mr Luxton, *one at each arm, and walk him briskly around the stage.*)

**Colonel:** We are the dispellers of doubt, Mr Luxton. Doubt is squalid. We cannot afford it. Without our cool conviction of rightness life would liquesce.

**Sheriff:** The Colonel speaks for the Crown. I speak for property. Without those two pillars there can be no framework for order.

**Rev Rees:** Mr Luxton does not realize that without the few hints of discipline thrown out by theology, business and war, the masses would be a rabble of goats.

**Luxton:** Very sound axioms. We'll have them printed and pinned to the shrouds of those two cadavers on Birchtown Square.

**Colonel:** Do not sentimentalize, Mr Luxton. Had our sabres not seen those two fellows to the door they would have had their finish in a tavern brawl or an incontinent bed. It does no harm to give nature a little push if it will serve to teach better manners to the more sportive tenants of the sty. I cannot recognize as fully human anyone who does not see the instant truth of these propositions.

**Luxton:** I'm fully human. I see the pillars. I see the framework. I am for order, God help me. (*He breaks loose.*) Now put me down. That was a very smooth trip.

**Sheriff:** You are the last person to have any qualms in this crisis, Mr Luxton.

**Luxton:** Because I am an ironmaster?

**Sheriff:** No. As a father. Your daughters are jewels, all the better for being set in this dusky ground. In all the great houses from Maidenhead to Mold they are the toast.

**Colonel:** Eirlys!

**Sheriff:** Arianwen!

**Rev Rees:** Mona!

(*Their eyes are alight with enthusiasm and desire.* Luxton *watches them cautiously and as if with a bud of new understanding in his mind.*)

**Colonel:** We captured a man tonight. Same name as yourself, Reverend Rees.

**Rev Rees:** A major Welsh tribe, the Rees's. They are all over.

**Luxton:** It's his nephew, Jackie the Jumper Rees. A moral grasshopper. He gets a bonus from the clergy for serving as a walking text. The Reverend Rees shovels the clinker from around the neck of the species on Sunday, and the Jumper has them back in position on the Monday.

**Sheriff:** If I were you, Mr Luxton, I wouldn't talk about the man so flippantly.

**Luxton:** I'm sorry. I must have a touch of the moon. I had an attack of the quinsy right on top of listening to the Reverend Rees giving three sermons in one day. First I couldn't swallow. Then the world seemed to be having the same trouble. In what way exactly is he supposed to frighten me?

**Colonel:** Our best informants tell us that it was he who organized the rising in Birchtown. And I suppose you've heard that he serves as a kind of symbol of virility, an inter-shire stallion, seconded to the agitators during lulls at the County Stud.

(Rees *lifts up his hands in repudiation of his nephew's infamy.*)

**Luxton:** These reputations can be very spurious, Colonel. There is so much torpor in the field of sex that a stirring of a finger can sometimes look like a major assault. In the kingdom of the castrate the one-eyed man or whatever you'd call him is king.

**Sheriff:** You little know, Mr Luxton. This man has been heard to threaten that he will ravish each of your three daughters before these troubles are over. In view of the public, if possible, and executed with every flourish of virtuosity as part of a final programme of vengeance on behalf of the oppressed.

**Colonel:** And the unfulfilled. He mentioned those too.

**Luxton:** He would. It wasn't enough to have hunger, housing problems, the wish to vote, the urge to own. We've got to have this athletic lecher shooting his tongue out like a chameleon. Nothing will happen to my daughters. They are the clearest pool of coolness in this region. They sing, they sew, they talk in low voices. The flesh has cast no sort of shadow on them. They circle clear even of anything as raffish as gossip. Where's this man now?

**Colonel:** Until we are ready to move back to Birchtown he's being held in your stables.

**Luxton:** Is he safe?

**Colonel:** He's chained.

(Luxton *grimaces.*)

129

**Luxton:** Chained! Here! I'll go and talk to the girls to take the taste of this out of my mouth. I'll bring them in to meet you for a few minutes.

(Luxton *leaves.* Rees, *the* Colonel *and the* County Sheriff *move restlessly, watch each other cunningly as if, in this new situation, they are changing moment by moment, and are trying to determine what the changes consist of.* Luxton *returns with his three daughters. They have a demure radiance. Their dresses are white and have a theme of lace.* Rees, *the* Colonel *and* County Sheriff *are magnetized by them. The last two make a great whooping fuss of them, but* Rees, *in tribute to his own standing at God's side, hangs back, his eyes none the less lucent with desire.*)

**Luxton:** You have been saved from something by these gentlemen.

**Arianwen, Eirlys** and **Mona:** Oh! Please tell us what.

**Rev Rees:** We have restored purity to its prime place. Rough hands will not soil you.

**Sheriff:** Heads will bow in customary respect as you pass through the streets of Ferncleft.

**Colonel:** You might by this time have been fleeing from a burning house.

(*The* girls *pass their eyes from face to face. There is no gratitude in their expression, rather a kind of whimsical speculation.* Arianwen *and* Eirlys *take their place at the piano and begin playing some cool romance.*)

**Arianwen, Eirlys** and **Mona:**

> A shepherd sang to me through evenings cool
> But now I know that love's a fool,
> A minstrel offered me his love for crown
> But now I know that love's a clown.
> A soldier learned with nightingales to croon
> But now I know that love's a loon.
> A single maid on lonely bed
> Will know no harm if love be dead
> Let not my heart in disarray be wooed
> May my mind eschew all ardours rude,
> May my heart be cool, affections mild,
> All pure, serene and undefiled.

(*The men are nodding in cordial agreement but they hum, from*

130

*time to time, an urgent counter-melody which suggests that the Luxton girls might give serious thought to whooping it up a little.*)

**Colonel:** A splendid sentiment. But you mustn't carry this melancholy too far. Look outward, my dear ladies. Life is full of the most wonderful excitement. If I could only tell you the stupendous tingle I felt in my blood as we galloped tonight from Birchtown.

**Eirlys:** (*who emerges as the most articulate and resolute of the girls*) Horses depress me. So, in the main, do horsemen.

**Colonel:** You've been living in some mist of anxiety. I think you've done too many charity trips among the cottagers. And your father launched you on a raft of books. The mist will lift and you will see the horses in their true, good light. (*He edges amorously towards the* girls.) The horsemen too will fall into position.

**Sheriff:** I hope so. I sincerely hope so. I think it's a shame that you've never ridden with the County Hunt.

**Eirlys:** We're fully engaged, Sir George. And we tend to be a little on the side of the hunted. When we distribute our little gift parcels we slip two to the conformist poor and one to the fox.

**Colonel:** You should have set them an example, Mr Luxton. There is nothing inspires more respect in the serving hands than the sight of their natural leader mounted and soaring over hedges and gates.

**Luxton:** I tried it. The serving hands were rolling in the lanes at the sight of me soaring over gates and hedges with no horse beneath me. The touch of my buttocks on the horse's back, and the animal would have a passionate craving for the flat. Thirteen times I landed on my head; once on the fox. Frightened the thing to death, I can tell you.

**Colonel:** You communicated your fear to the horse and it panicked.

**Luxton:** Let's say we did a fair deal.

**Colonel:** And, Mr Luxton, you've done no good immersing your daughters in all those books.

**Sheriff:** Agreed. You have a library here as large as that in my college at Oxford. Quite excessive. What was the point of that?

**Luxton:** Literacy. You've heard of that thing. Shines well in certain types of shadow.

**Sheriff:** Demoralizing. Reduces a woman's fluency in the most vital functions. I'd allow my own daughters only the faintest drift of print. Invitations to the County Hunt Ball and then only in the largest print that would not wrinkle the surrounds of their lovely eyes.

**Arianwen:** We take nothing but fine print. (*The* girls *peer and grope comically.*) We are moles. Only last week we were reading an account of your estates, Sir George. Have you enclosed any good common land lately?

**Sheriff:** Not lately.

**Eirlys:** None left. What Columbus was to America your grandfather and father were to this county. You really moved in. How are the rabbits taking it?

**Sheriff:** They are not complaining. They appreciate my work against the foxes and they sustain a peerless army of poachers. What do you think of our young and lovely scholars, Mr Rees?

**Rev Rees:** I've never been a great believer in reading. At the seminary, the feel of a thick tome would make me feel a convict, and a long staring at print would set the temples of my head apart by the distance of a mile. Contemplation in fields and listening humbly to the talk of humble folk, those are the best doorway to the ministry. I have been astonished by some of the books I have found these young ladies reading. Quite beyond me, I'm glad to say. Voltaire and all those Frenchmen. Jealous, unhappy little men, griped by the most witless and agonizing doubt. There must always be one side of the mind in total darkness waiting for the final illumination.

**Eirlys:** You'll see to that, Mr Rees. You are the wick-snipper extraordinary.

**Rev Rees:** Irreligious doubts in the mothers of the future puts the whole race in jeopardy.

**Sheriff:** Agree with that. For children, fear of hell is part of the house-training process.

**Eirlys:** What if we don't want to join the mothers of the future?

**Rev Rees:** If my branch of the nonconformist church were not against crossing oneself, I would cross myself now.

**Eirlys:** Have you ever taken a good look at what happens to marriage and women down in those hovels? We know. We three good Samaritans have looked closer than any of you. Marriage is an antic so exacting it needs perfect soil even to keep breathing with moderate fluency. You provide it with what is strictly a stone patch. Without your permission, gentlemen, we intend to become the three old ladies of Ferncleft, last-ditch spinsters, perverse and inviolable virgins, as dedicated to excluding life as you are to breaking its legs.

**Colonel:** Mr Luxton, tell them not to be lunatic.

**Luxton:** I'm taking no sides. Where are the sides? My mind is shaking. If it falls you may push it back.

**Rev Rees:** You have, under God, a solemn duty to perform.

(*The* girls *take refuge behind the piano.*)

**Arianwen:** That was a real rattle of muskets, Reverend.

**Rev Rees:** It lies with you to found a dynasty that could give a new grace and dignity to our people.

**Arianwen:** I never thought to see you on the fertility flank.

**Sheriff:** Mr Rees is right. Now that the hand-workers are swelling with presumption after the vote, an unlimited supply of dainties and mansions after the style of our own, we simply have to out-breed them two to one.

**Eirlys:** What a gruesome thought. Here's a counter slogan. Liberty, equality, sterility.

**Arianwen:** We see the way clear. We are going to translate the works of Fanny Burney into Sanskrit and the sacred books of India into rhyming Welsh. We shall continue our works of charity. We shall seek out the paupers and sweeten their stretch with two bits of fresh fruit a year. We shall arrange an escape route for all women trapped into mortal compact with drunken and incorrigible louts.

**Sheriff:** These people have their own inscrutable brands of happiness. Often when they are at their most squalid they are at their most cosy.

**Arianwen:** That's a useful belief.

**Rev Rees:** There's no sight on earth as uplifting as that of serene faith in lives that are utterly doomed.

**Arianwen:** So you lay the doom on to keep the faith in fresh supply.

**Sheriff:** My dear young ladies. You play about with these ideas as if they were kittens. You have sport with them and you get some kind of fun from the notion that you are baiting us as reactionary idiots. But these idiots once removed from the sterilizing safety zones of studies and libraries have the mating and breeding power of termites. Some observe ants; others pity ants; others again have to crush ants because they realize that nature in the long run favours ants because they are cheaper to keep. Civilization is a protracted argument with nature.

**Arianwen:** You're right, Sir George, only termites won't make iron for Dadda, nor are they expelled from Mr Rees's chapel for fertility out of wedlock.

**Sheriff:** We shall show you the real face of this situation. We'll show you the bog of perfidy on which we've thrown up our flimsy cave-dwellings and the choicer type of creature who waits his hour of darkness and chaos to come out of the slime and put his teeth into your lovely necks. By the time we've finished the lesson you'll be rushing in ecstasy to embrace the good, cool bastions of marriage, money and dogma.

**Colonel:** We brought in one of the horrors tonight. A ripe example. Name of Rees, Jackie Rees. A nephew, unfortunately, of Mr Rees here. No fault of his, I'm sure. The man is a bone-idle womanizing pest. He has succeeded in putting work and chastity in the same category as flood and fire as nuisances.

**Eirlys:** Where is he now?

**Colonel:** In the stables.

**Eirlys:** What's he doing here?

**Sheriff:** Mr Luxton and I, as magistrates, will turn this room into an emergency court. We will commit him on charges of riot, murder and arson.

**Arianwen:** Bring him in. You'll need a public to see justice done.

**Luxton:** Girls, to your rooms, please. I want you to see no part of this.

**Mona:** Why not? We are the anemones you are supposed to be protecting. At least give us a good look at the blight.

**Luxton:** Girls, there is pollution in all this business. I want you to have no part of it. Go to your rooms.

**Eirlys:** Is this the man they call Jackie the Jumper?

**Sheriff:** That's the man.

**Arianwen:** Why the name? Does he resemble a frog?

**Sheriff:** The reference is not so innocent.

**Mona:** And he is the leader of all these troubles?

**Sheriff:** Whenever the people grow fractious and slow to work, the voice and the shadow of this man are never far away.

**Mona:** And after tonight there will be no more troubles?

134

**Sheriff:** His removal will cool the hotter heads and chasten the looser tongues.

**Mona:** So this is by way of being his last appearance?

**Sheriff:** He will appear briefly for his trial. I cannot see him as a public figure after that.

**Arianwen:** That settles it. We'll not budge until we've had a glimpse of the man.

(Luxton *makes a gesture of despair. He goes to a sideboard, pours and bolts a heavy slug of brandy and invites the others by gesture, to do the same. He is suddenly struck by a thought which clearly fills him with a thoughtful apprehension.*)

**Luxton:** Tell me, Sir George, I just saw behind the theory of this business. How many men have you got guarding us here?

**Colonel:** Six.

**Luxton:** Six? (*He makes a show of counting the people in the room.*) Less than one bodyguard per person. You don't make me feel very secure, Colonel.

**Colonel:** It was essential to let the bulk of the force continue into Birchtown. It's there you have the hardest fist of dissension.

**Luxton:** What about the people here in Ferncleft? They've seen the furnaces go out. They'll see the lights burning in my house. What if they turn ugly?

**Sheriff:** No fear. Ferncleft is a blessed town. The men are eunuchs and the women devotional weepers.

**Rev Rees:** A word from me would resolve any fit of temper on their part.

**Sheriff:** Rees is truly their pastor. Even their hair feels a little woolly.

**Colonel:** A large group of them cheered as we galloped through the square tonight.

**Arianwen:** There is a sect of people in that town that cheer at the sight of any horses. They believe horses are on to a good thing.

**Colonel:** The one or two who might have been fancying themselves as rebels gave up the ghost when they saw us hunting down the Jumper.

**Luxton:** So they'll not cry, nor stir nor molest us?

**Sheriff:** They are mice. They might nibble at the soft parts of the wainscoting, but apologetically.

**Rev Rees:** Tomorrow there will be a delegation of supplicants at your door asking no more than to live in a world where decisions will be made by God and you alone.

**Luxton:** When Rees gives me that kind of talk I feel a terrible draught. Bring in the Jumper. We'll commit him to the County gaol until the next Assizes. And if possible let's do the thing in mime. Legal phrases make my teeth ache.

(*Exit* Colonel. Luxton *returns to the brandy.* Rees *stares out of the window.* Sheriff *stares into a vast wall-mirror, pondering on himself. The girls return to the piano and resume their quiet playing and singing.*

*Then the door opens and* Jackie, *his hands shackled, is thrust in. He has two soldiers in attendance. For a moment he stands, head down, his whole attitude blazing with a taurine defiance. He becomes aware of the music, lifts his head and smiles at the girls.*)

**Jackie:** That's nice, the music. After those stables, that's very nice.

**Sheriff:** We didn't bring you here to listen to a concert.

**Luxton:** Stop playing. Now leave us. Please Arianwen. Lead the way.

(*As the girls leave the room,* Jackie, *with no trace of levity, gives them a short bow. When the door closes the two soldiers at* Jackie's *side give him another rough shove and he almost falls.*)

**Jackie:** (*pointing to his right hand*) There's a small bone there you still haven't broken. Take care of that or you won't get your bonus. (*One of the soldiers lifts his rifle.* Jackie *raises the chain that secures his hands.*) Now don't do anything that might rough up this splendid parlour. (*He turns to* Colonel.) You did well out there. A small army on horses against one man. You could be another Wellington.

**Colonel:** We achieved our limited objectives.

**Jackie:** And hunting me down like a fox was one of those?

**Colonel:** Obviously.

**Jackie:** Uncle, I see you there in the corner. Don't be shy. Come out and have a good look at me. What kind of a nightmare are you spinning now on the good old doom loom? Tell these people to stop their nonsense. Tell them who I am. Jackie Rees of no fixed abode, a tramp with a preference for lying down, unskilled, out of sympathy with smoke and metal, given, like a dog, to bursts of affection and, like a dog, guilty of no genuine sin. Tell these people to stop advertising their iron on me. There's been some mistake. I'll accept your apology, a meat pasty, a drop of ale and be on my way.

**Rev Rees:** John, my boy. On this occasion your best mood would be humility.

(Jackie *looks curiously at all the faces in the group.*)

**Jackie:** All right. I'm humble.

**Rev Rees:** Through all the years of your life you have walked darkly, in sin. Now the light is on. Look carefully about you.

**Jackie:** The view is terrible. What kind of clowning is this?

**Sheriff:** No clowning. We are cancelling your licence to be a pest, Rees. We've let you roam for too many years on a tether of loosely-lipped dissension. Now we are pulling in the rope for more practical use.

(Jackie *shrugs helplessly.*)

**Jackie:** No, I wouldn't argue with you. Anyone who can speak to another as if he were a goat cannot be argued with. You are amazing people. (*To* Sheriff) You have a glacier in each eye. (*To* Rees) You guide the wind of God's wrath. (*To* Luxton) But you are quiet inside. So you may be the one to watch.

**Luxton:** That's right. Watch me. We are both at ropes' ends, twitching.

**Jackie:** This talk of rope . . . You mean . . .

**Rev Rees:** I told you to go. But you lingered.

**Jackie:** What am I supposed to have done?

**Sheriff:** Conspiring against public order, murder.

**Rev Rees:** Blasphemy, carnality and sloth.

**Colonel:** Resisting arrest. Although I don't think we'll be needing that item.

**Jackie:** I don't think you will. Between you you've rigged up a dishful. Now I don't know what private dreams you are trying to gild here but stop using me as a paint-pot. Let me tell you again; I'm nobody. I have no wealth, no view-point, no hate, no particular love. I was ambling up here tonight to make my own particular peace. To tell my uncle that I have suspended all doubts I might have had about God and the goodness of His creation. That my passions have now the same heat and colour as old coke and women can now walk abroad without a visa from the County Sheriff. And to tell Mr Luxton that I now acknowledge the need to work. I see it as being as inevitable as death. I give in. I'll make iron. I'll make wealth enough to wipe away the last patch of penury. And if you want to give me time off to clear my head I'll go out into the countryside to find fresh recruits for the smokeholes. Now, please . . .

(*Smiles and lifts up his chained hands. The* County Sheriff, *the* Colonel *and* Rees *all shake their heads, No, no, no!* Luxton *watches them all in turn and reluctantly joins them in the headshaking.*)

**Rev Rees:** The people are confused and full of devilish impulses. A good, sudden, dramatic death will show them more clearly than any sermon of mine the need for a new gentleness.

**Sheriff:** Nothing restores social sanity more swiftly than a significant corpse dropped judiciously on heads made hot by dreaming.

**Jackie:** You wouldn't be such fools.

**Sheriff:** We are what we are because we are such fools. If by folly you mean the daring to choose our solution and the right ground from which to hurl it, you, Jackie the Jumper, are going to be hurled. When your neck is broken, lust, laziness and all doubts about the social contract will be dislocated as well. There will be no resistance, no hitch. Your friends might mutter something into their grimy mufflers, then shuffle back into their slum.

**Colonel:** We shall stand guard around the gallows to give you plenty of breathing space.

**Rev Rees:** I shall read the lesson from a specially made, resonant pulpit. What I shall have to say in the immediate wake at your death will make you a richer being dead than ever you were in life.

**Jackie:** I'd feel mean not to come along. I feel almost grateful. All this trouble . . . .

**Rev Rees:** And every shred of it woven by you. It's good to see you here, helpless, hurt, doomed.

**Jackie:** Uncle, I lose you, I really lose you. (*He moves hand to take in the others.*) These I understand. I can take it from them. Chaining and hanging are part of their games. I don't suppose they regard me with any more malice than they would the badger, otter, fox whose pelt they covet. But you. The words you've uttered. You've given pity a new lease. Your tongue has promoted tears enough to lubricate ten thousand dry and cracking hearts. In this business you should either be at my side or dumb somewhere in between.

**Rev Rees:** At your side! In this business, as you call it, I am the only one who perceives your full, true guilt. In your image the world would have assumed an animal crouch. Where I have tried

138

to make men upright and aware of the divine goodness, you have scurried like a stoat. I am what you might have been. My passions, too, were wild and clamant. I shouted them down. I tamed them. I clothed them with hints of divine grace and they learned to walk among the children of the earth, giving some succour, doing some good.

**Jackie:** A fulfilled man is always a pleasure to see.

**Rev Rees:** When I help them kill you, I shall be burying a part of me long dead, that might once have exposed me to danger and shame. In my pocket I have a list of one in ten of your transgressions.

**Jackie:** One in ten! Why the reticence?

**Rev Rees:** I grew tired of the research. A black business. I followed your trail of iniquity with loathing and devotion. There is no one better qualified to be your judge and sexton.

**Jackie:** Whatever men exchange carnality for, they're on to a bad deal.

(Luxton *shoots his head up.*)

**Luxton:** What was that?

**Colonel:** I hear nothing.

**Luxton:** You haven't kept your ears cocked as intensely as I. I hear something.

**Sheriff:** Your daughters singing from an upstairs room.

**Colonel:** My men talking in the courtyard.

**Luxton:** No. Many people marching and singing.

**Colonel:** I hear nothing.

**Luxton:** This is one of the advantages of living inside a really mature panic. One can follow life at a distance.

**Colonel:** I hear nothing.

**Jackie:** You wouldn't. Thunder couldn't get through to you.

**Luxton:** People singing and marching.

**Rev Rees:** I told them I would speak to them tonight. They are coming here to hear me. I'll address them from one of the windows.

**Luxton:** There is no piety in the mission of these people. Their mood is violence, and murder is their guide.

(*A distant sound of the 'Hail to the Lord's Anointed' on trumpets, soon joined by a chorus of voices. A sound of violent fighting outside. The two soldiers and the* Colonel *dive out of the room. For thirty seconds the fury of fighting continues. Then the doors of the room are flung open,* George Chislett, *armed, comes in at the head of a group of ironworkers.*)

**Sheriff:** We are ready to die, although I would have chosen cleaner agents.

**Jackie:** Oh no, Sheriff. You're a long way behind. We don't play that simple kind of marbles. Sheriff, you are going to be invited to grow up. And you, too, Uncle Resurrection. You are going to be invited to step from the realm of necessity into that of the imagination.

**Chislett:** Where to, Jackie? Birchtown?

**Jackie:** No. Away from Birchtown. Away from Ferncleft. To the 'Rising Lark', the loneliest tavern in the land. Two mountains away. For a few days, Sheriff, we are going to raise the banner of a friendly decency and free experiment. (Jackie *throws his head back in a delighted laugh.*) George, get these things off my hands. And you, Mr Luxton, get your daughters ready for the journey. And you, Uncle, make ready for your first true revival.

(*The trumpets make a new swoop of triumphant sound.* Jackie *moves swiftly from the room. The curtain falls as the others make to follow him.*)

Curtain

# ACT THREE

*The one and only bar-room of the 'Rising Lark' inn. In a corner is a*
*rough counter for the serving of drinks. On the benches are Jackie's*
*friends. They are singing a version of that brisk Sunday School*
*marching song, 'Awn ymlaen I'r Buddugoliaeth', a rattling old*
*rouser. From the outside is a noise of hammer on metal. The*
*hammering proceeds in rhythm with the singing. The baritone and*
*bass section is doing a sort of plom, plom harmony that suggests*
*marching.*

*An old, blind iron-worker,* Aaron Mead, *is sitting on one of the*
*centre benches. He is tapping out an accompaniment to the song with*
*his stick. On his face is a look of savage melancholy.*

**Aaron:** Jackie, what are those clowns doing in there with their
hammering?
**Jackie:** They've got a bit of a foundry going. They are making
pikes.
**Aaron:** What for?
**Jackie:** To fight with. We have no rifles, no cannon. So we are
making these pikes.
**Aaron:** Will they do any good?
**Jackie:** They are a gesture. I tried one out a few minutes ago. It
bent. We are aiming at a pike that will bend into the shape of a
question-mark, so that our enemies will get the idea that we are
querying the whole business of violence.
**Aaron:** When will they come? The soldiers.
**Jackie:** They've had some more trouble down in Birchtown. And
we've spread the news that this place is a fortress with deep
defences and a park of artillery. And the only thing we have here
that'll go pop is a bottle of Eli Scandrett's old ale. And if I know
Eli it'll be a reserved pop. But the lie will give the Commander of
Dragoons the feeling that he is on to something big, something
important. It'll make him happy as he deploys his forces to put
paid to us. And that's what we're here for. To make people
happy.

**Aaron:** All folly. Violence should flow from them to us. Our craftsmanship is spread too thin for us to have any joy or skill in killing. The function of the wise is to sit still with a look of pain and amazement on their faces. And people, looking at them, will grow worried, anxious. They will learn caution. And that is the nearest we will ever come to goodness. Caution.

**Chislett:** You mean we should have sat down and let them hang Jackie?

**Aaron:** Exactly. Ever since my eyes went in that furnace-blast I have had a vision. The vision of one of our own, killed for love of us. A gay, laughing one, to whom life means more than for the rest of us. Somebody in whom the dousing of light would have darkened the whole earth. Jackie, in a word. They would have hanged him in the County town. We would have asked for his body for burial in his home town. They couldn't have refused because we would have made our request as Christians and that's a word that makes people tender in their dealings with corpses. We'd have put his body on a farm-cart to strike the note of humility. We'd have followed it to its grave, over the ridges, through the fields, and on the way we'd have sung and wept. And with every tear our ingrained dirt would have grown less, would have been washed from the eyes of our minds. A tremendous funeral. Ten wonderful, educational miles. And your murderers, Jackie, would have been left in a colder day, full of shuddering, silent shame. And your spirit would have gone to provide one more flame for the dawn of a beckoning restitution.

**Jackie:** I'm glad you put that in about the dawn of restitution. It's always a tonic. I'm with you, Aaron. I can see it all. The grief and the pride. The mourners, the weepers. The ripening wisdom of the bereaved. The County Sheriff wringing his hands with remorse and promising a hundred pounds for a Jackie the Jumper memorial scholarship open to incipient missionaries. There's only one thing about your vision that I don't like. It's the way I'm looking, the quietness of me, on that farm-cart.

**Chislett:** Aaron, you're all right. You've been through the mill and most of us have done the trip with you. You've only got one fault and most of our people share it with you. You want your martyrs too cheaply. You want your heroes cut-rate. I want Jackie to live to be a hundred. And I want him to celebrate his hundredth birthday by chopping down a gibbet.

**Aaron:** Be hopeful, George. Be hopeful while you can. The Dragoons will come soon. They'll be in no hurry. They will carouse in Birchtown for a week or so, sharpening their appetites and laughing at your pikes. They will come. Some will die. There will be no gain in wisdom.

**Chislett:** Nothing is ever said, nothing is ever heard. We react like cats and dogs to kicks and blows. That's all.

**Aaron:** No; there are some who emerge, whose faces, voices, linger and glow in the dark. Like Jackie's might have been. Dead, they would have said of him, he loved his pint and his woman. Now in the cold and silence to which they sent him there's no supping or loving at all. People will learn more from that about the crime of deprivation than from a million pamphlets.

**Jackie:** I see the point of that, Aaron. But I don't want to be a knock to the printers. Let's make do with the pamphlets for a while longer.

**Aaron:** He'll play the fool here. He'll be choked in a skirmish. No dignity. Not the way they do it. Those soldiers marching with the judges, the tall court-room with its high echoing beams. That great black palaver about the place of execution.

**Jackie:** And my uncle reading the lesson.

**Aaron:** Oh! they stage the thing properly and no mistake. They are the only stage managers to trust. If we are going to have death, let's make a good long song of it.

**Jackie:** You've almost got me sold on this, Aaron.

**Aaron:** All you can do is run. Run. The lot of you. Keep running west until you come to water. Then swim. You'll find the same confused, hungry situation among the Irish as you have here. And you'll have to stay there and put down some proper root of understanding because the next patch of water is too broad for the dispossessed, unless they can afford a boat.

**Jackie:** You've got a fine set of roads fixed up for me, Aaron. Hanged, drowned or starved.

**Chislett:** Here's Iestyn Best, the messenger.

 (*Enter* Iestyn Best, *panting and bent double from the strain of belting across the plateau. He is given a drink and a series of encouraging pats that knock the last remaining puffs out of his body.*)

**Jackie:** Anything new, Iestyn?

**Iestyn:** Yes, and when these boyos stop lambasting the life out of my body I'll tell you. (*They recharge his glass and put him to sit* *down on a bench.*) I was in the Waggoner's Arms in Birchtown. Full of soldiers drinking and singing and taking the maidens off the list of protected game. They wanted a message taken to you. So the captain stood up and looked over the tap-room and he said: "Which of you local men might be serving as a spy for the disaffected artisans?" Nobody moved. Then he said, "For Jackie the Jumper and that lousy lot." And about eight of us stood up and said, "We're spies." We said this because we felt inferior in the presence of all those uniforms. The captain picked on me and he said, "Go and tell Jackie the Jumper that I have no wish to endanger the life of the County Sheriff, the Colonel of the Militia, Mr Luxton and his three daughters, Mr Rees, the pastor, or of my own men. So I shall post my Dragoons at intervals of ten feet around the base of the mountain on which he is supposedly defying us. And they will stay there until he, his hostages and partisans come down."

**Jackie:** Has he done that?

**Iestyn:** He's done it. I travelled right around the mountain. Every time you take a fresh breath you see a new Dragoon.

**Chislett:** So we have to stay here.

**Aaron:** Jackie doesn't. If the Dragoons were cheek to cheek he would get through them after dark. I've been out poaching with him. He's so quiet I lost him four times between the first salmon and the second.

**Jackie:** I'll stay here. For long, swift running I'm past my best. I have been, as you all know, a man busily depraved in all the ways he could afford. And that's bad on the wind. I might be able to sneak down the mountain and through the soldiers. But in the open country, with them on horses, they'd have me down like a sick wolf under the hour. I'll stay.

**Chislett:** I hope you mean that, Jackie. We're here because you are here. We don't want you bluffing us into making a great, last stand here, then giving us a friendly wink and slipping out for a free stroll, never to come back. Is it the thought of those Luxton girls that keeps you here?

**Jackie:** Who's ever thought of them? In this field many men tend to keep warm on other men's fuel. If my loins had kept up with the popular fancy in this particular, the London physicians would have had me pickled and exhibited as a freak before now. In any case, compared with the cow-girls and plough-girls who've warmed my way, those Luxton girls strike me as . . . waxen, under par. My flesh is austere, cold, ready for some act of passion that has nothing, nothing to do with one man, one woman. I haven't given them a thought.

(Janet, *who is in charge behind the bar, starts a sardonic, sensuous little jig to the following jingle.*)

**Janet:** There are people who'll say you're 'also ran',
    That love will run no more,
    But there's no such thing as a dried-up man
    Or a woman who's closed the door.
    Feed the fire at the heart of life,
    That's the law; I never broke it.
    Love's the fuel at the heart of life,
    And the man who complains of the bitter cold,
    All the fool's got to do is to stoke it.

**Aaron:** You should, Jackie, you should. Before you give yourself up, possess them, my boy, possess them. That'll feed the legend a treat. It'll add at least a couple more verses to the ballad I'm going to write about you. That's the most a man can hope for, to add a verse or two to the ballad that'll give free food and booze to a blind man as he goes from pub to pub.

**Jackie:** I'll see you right for material and rhymes, Aaron. This should be good for a verse. (*He raises his voice.*) Bring in our friends. (*The* County Sheriff, *the* Colonel *and the* Reverend Rees *come in. They have been divested of their uniforms and are now dressed in the rough jackets and breeches of the ironworkers.*) Now then Aaron, you cannot see this but it's really something for the pub concerts.

(Luxton *and his* daughters *come in.* Luxton, *his costume unchanged, is even more stooped and apprehensive than before. He moves to take up his position with the three other prisoners.* Jackie *says "Not you," and waves him to a chair, away from the others.* Janet, *behind the bar, studies the expression on* Jackie's *face and gives out with a rich little guffaw.*)

**Jackie:** Here are three men who cast a big shadow. They peeped at us over a wall. Genuinely talented and brave men who have made of their cleverness and courage the tools of a disinfectant aloofness. The sermon, the eviction, the sabre and some differences of dress have worked marvels for them. Now their uniforms are gone and up here there would seem to be little room

145

for their particular specialities.

(Janet *raises a glass to toast.*)

**Janet:** To particular specialities in any shape or form.

**Jackie:** They'll be here soon, the boys with the guns, the swords, the closed minds. While we wait let's let truth out on a tiny length of lead. We'll have a bit of a trial. No judge, and the only jury will be the feeling of what these people have done to us. And of what we've done to them, for they and we have been drawn unutterably out of shape.

**Sheriff:** Look, Rees. I have no objection to listening to you. Social position carries social responsibilities, and as a magistrate it is part of the cross I bear to have my ear-drums perforated from time to time by the perorations of half-baked Jacobins. But let's have it done in a place that smells a little less of stale ale and fresh human. And if you have made up your minds finally how you wish to hurt and humiliate us, hurry it up and have done with it. You may think your oppression, so-called, an infliction, but it is nothing to the tedium involved in making that oppression a good and sanitary concern.

**Voice:** Good point. He's very fluent, the Sheriff.

**Luxton:** I am prepared for any martyrdom you may devise for me.

**Jackie:** You've got a sort of compassion, Mr Luxton. That's martyrdom enough for one day. Just sit there and look thoughtful. Give the thing a philosophic gloss.

**Aaron:** That's the kind of big organ music I like to hear. Martyrdom, compassion. Words like loaves.

**Colonel:** I shall still see the moment when I run the lot of you down for good.

**Voice 2:** He really sees us as that, part of a hoof. He's a hell of a horseman, this boy.

**Colonel:** And if you wish to see an example of composure, kill me and see how a gentleman dies.

**Voice 3:** In the foundries we see men die with composure all the time. It's no novelty. It doesn't prove anything.

**Jackie:** We don't want to kill you. We don't want to martyr you. We don't want to molest you. We don't even want to take anything away from you because if we did the Government boys in London would take it away from us in two shakes of a dead attorney's quill. No, we plan to give you in fuller measure those

146

things which, in the past, have given you the greatest joy. Tell me, uncle, what have you most enjoyed doing?

**Rees:** Preaching.

**Jackie:** To what end?

**Rees:** To persuade and convert.

**Jackie:** Or to bewitch and seduce. You know you've based a lot of your life on the belief that you are so different a man from me. You've made yourself a fine, high platform, introducing God to his guests as rotundly as a good butler. Me you've depicted as a rampant and disgraceful stallion tramping the hills, vales and virginities of this land. But we're the same man working from different ends. I am the carnal boy with a post-coital urge to sermonize. You are the preacher who creates before him a vague cloud of generalized lust.

**Rees:** A lie.

**Jackie:** I've watched the faces of women after you have been pelting them with the hot words. Had it not been for two hours on a hard bench and six layers of thick clothing they would have put their cool piety in pawn for you, any place, any time. I envy you, uncle. You've had the real excitement, the real melting union. And always with pride and exaltation. No shame, no betraying weakness.

**Rees:** You dare to say that we are but shadows of each other. Go on, order me to a life of depravity and I would starve to death rather than yield one jot of the contempt I feel for your sort of squalor. Order me to silence and through the strength of my spirit alone I would, given time, chasten your brood off the earth.

**Jackie:** I would not have you depraved or silent, uncle. I would have you fulfilled. We are having one of the outhouses converted into a chapel. You will preach there. The place will be packed with your finest congregation. You can preach without cunning. You may expect no preferment from this performance. Nor yet disgrace. There will be maidens in your audience. They admire you. They will respond like harps to every plucking of your tongue.

**Rees:** I'll not see them. But I shall see my mission plain. I will preach as I have never preached before. Rage has given me a blistering simplicity.

**Aaron:** Give it to them, Reverend. I can't see you, but I feel that you are striding uphill to a great victory. Pour it over them.

Terror is the only guide of true authority. And aim some of the stuff at your nephew Jackie. Tell them to do the right thing by the progressive ideal and give the oppressors a real purgative field-day. To submit to cruelty and death, before a good audience, is the wiliest form of combat.

**Rees:** I'll not preach to him. I've had my last word with him. I'm after the conscience of mankind.

**Aaron:** And you'll find it, too, Reverend. The thing must be about somewhere.

**Jackie:** In an outhouse. Bare, no tall windows, no aids to piety like gloss on the benches or an organist in the loft, the lung of reverence, the breath of fear. There'll be no time limit. Indeed, it will be forbidden for you to shut up. Prophets have had their special potency to date because they have been given intervals in which to be silent and admired. But you'll keep on and on to an audience that's truly reached the end of the road, who can no longer be terrified or assuaged. Your rhetoric will be in as many tatters as their tympanum. And they'll see you for what you are, a bombastic clown, a destructive bore. And they will begin to laugh. And that laughter will be your grave, reverend uncle.

**Chislett:** (*shaking his head doubtfully*) He's going to be a hard boy to bury, Jackie. After two hours of him I'll be signalling the Dragoons to come and fetch me.

**Aaron:** He'll be a treat. By the time he's finished you'll have every sin you ever committed walking in front of you, big and slow like camels.

**Eirlys:** (*looking at* Rees *with a new interest and sympathy*) You will do well, Mr Rees. I'm sure you will. And I shall be listening.

**Rees:** Every note of rage and solace stands ready to be sounded.

**Aaron:** Every note of rage and solace. That's it. The cutting barb. The healing kiss. The cold slap, the hot stroke. Even without eyes there is delight.

(*Jackie's party could at this point go into a little jig based on a pelting adaptation of the hymn 'Through the night of doubt and sorrow' which proceeds to exactly the same rhythm as 'Every note of rage and solace'. The dancers' movements could match the ecstatic lurching of the blind* Aaron.)

**All:** More justice now, Jackie. More judgements, boy.

**Jackie:** Unto each man his most golden fancy.

(*He goes to stand in front of the* Sheriff *and the* Colonel. *They both stand stiffly to attention.* Aaron, *who is alongside* Jackie, *laughs delightedly.*)

**Aaron:** To hear a man's pride stiffen, that's a good sound. Be arrogant, Sheriff. Make Jackie wild. Make us all vindictive.

(Chislett *hands* Aaron *a stoup of ale.*)

**Chislett:** Try holding this between your teeth, Aaron. You are interrupting the court.

**Jackie:** What is your fancy, Sheriff?

**Sheriff:** To see you dangling and the rest of these scamps sweating.

**Aaron:** Death and toil. Both operate powerfully against mischief. Here's the boy for the tidy life.

**Chislett:** His fancy's land. God made the earth in seven days and this joker collared it in eight.

**Sheriff:** Land goes to him who treats it best.

**Jackie:** And you saw no wrong in the death from hunger of the people you evicted.

**Sheriff:** People who are capable of dying from hunger in *any* context are a gross nuisance. Nature flicks them off like midges.

**Aaron:** That's the thinking I love. Nature. Flick, flick, flick.

(*Performs elaborately the gesture of destroying with thumb and flicking finger imaginary insects in his clothes.*)

**Jackie:** Good. You've got death lined up like a co-operative bailiff. We'll give you land. We shall give you as much of this mountain top as you can dig to a depth of six feet. Six feet because that is the customary depth of a grave, and socially you've been something of a sexton. (*The* Sheriff *stares straight ahead.*) No protest? No demand for a soldier's death in preference to the degradation of work?

**Sheriff:** No. Your sentence is a wise one. I have always advocated the thorough turning over of soil as the mark of good husbandry.

**Mona:** Your hands will bleed.

**Sheriff:** And you will tend them, my dear.

**Mona:** I will indeed.

**Jackie:** (*addressing the* Colonel) And you are a fighting man, an extended man, an enlarged man. A sword and a horse are to you what the left arm and the right arm are to us. You've won many easy victories, Colonel, and that has given you a very odd opinion of yourself. Your brain has come to fit your saddle. You've hunted people down like vermin. That is a very unwise thing to

149

do because you and the vermin get to accept the truth of this situation. We mustn't coax people into being more stupid or corrupt than they would normally think of being. I'm sure you're a brave man, Colonel. At least I hope so because that's about your only virtue.

**Arianwen:** He'll give you proof.

**Chislett:** I thought those girls were supposed to be on our side.

**Jackie:** Pity . . . a crooked stream. And one's taste in victims changes. We were only truly loved when we were flat on the floor. Now, Colonel, we're giving you a chance to fight, to be brave. Let's talk about odds.

**Colonel:** Fix them.

**Jackie:** I wonder how many of these people you think you're worth? I suppose you could see a thousand of them dead by your hand and feel no alteration for the worse in your own person.

**Colonel:** Enemies of the King's peace are not people.

**Aaron:** (*laughing delightedly and going through once more his 'flick, flick, flick' routine*) There it is again. Flick, flick, flick. The midges brought to stillness by the fingers of the strong.

**Jackie:** The King is far from here and we've never known much peace. (*Points towards the yard of the inn.*) Out there, are four men. They are wrestlers. You will fight them one by one. Weapons: hands, feet, head, teeth. No sword, no horse. Up here on this mountain top we've established a kind of fundamental society. You can fight as ruthlessly and foully as you please. You can remain what you have set out to be, the Herod of the property-owners, the blood and guts boy.

**Arianwen:** Four against one! He's had no experience of your kind of mauling. What kind of justice is this?

**Jackie:** Slightly better than what he's shown to the gaggles of demonstrators against whom this man (*he points to the* Sheriff) has unleashed him.

**Arianwen:** He'll show you what courage is.

**Jackie:** Of course he will. That's his trade. And nobody'll be a jot the better for it. Now let the tasks begin.

(*They all leave the stage except* Jackie *and* Luxton. *They ask each other the same question simultaneously.*)

**Jackie** and **Luxton:** Aren't you going to watch?

**Jackie:** No. The judge never watches executions. Otherwise there wouldn't be any executions, would there?

(Jackie *pours a glass of wine for himself and* Luxton. *They sit facing each other across the long table, the posture of each of them suggesting that he is sitting on the lip of a familiar nightmare.* Jackie *rises from the table and opens a window on the left. The voice of* Rees *is heard, and the authority of eagles is in it.*)

**Rees:** Behind the granite cliffs of our indifference and treachery lie the green, warm fields of love. We must find them or die. We are rocks. We have lost the way to each other's hearts and until that way be found we betray every fragment of love and effort that went to our making.

(Jackie *closes the window.*)

**Jackie:** Good old Resurrection Rees. Game to the last. Do you know something, Mr Luxton?

**Luxton:** If I don't know, this is as good a time as any to find out.

**Jackie:** If even one heart had been genuinely touched each time the word 'love's' been mentioned, we'd have been out of the wood by now.

**Luxton:** Of love I know nothing. I have produced iron. I have produced children. And I am none the wiser. I am a speck of bewilderment. I have lived in storms and I've not known what the hell they've all been about.

(Jackie *opens a window on the right. The sound is heard of a man's grunted breath as he drives a spade into earth.*)

**Jackie:** The County Sheriff is shaking hands at last with earth that has no desire to be owned or used. (*The sound of a man's body landing heavily on the ground to the accompaniment of a cheer.*) The Colonel is finding that for shoulder muscles an iron-worker is the equal of a horse. (*Closes the window and he and* Luxton *are left once again in silence.*)

**Luxton:** You're a fool, Jumper.

**Jackie:** And you, Mr Luxton.

**Luxton** : Agreed. We both escaped. And we both came back.

**Jackie:** The old mole-run.

(*During all this there has been a formless sound from back of stage, the combined susurration of three audiences.*)

**Luxton:** You've been a nuisance, Jumper.

**Jackie:** That's my calling, Mr Luxton. Unskilled work in the main, but very enjoyable.

**Luxton:** It was not so bad when my daughters were as they were, full of contempt for men. It created a kind of coolness around me that might have seen me cosily to the grave. Kept me insulated from the iron and hunger nonsense. Now you've thrown them into the middle of all this fuss. They are stripping their fences down so fast you can hear it all over the county. You've excited them to tropical heights in a context stripped of all the old familiar dampers. If you could have been the boy who got the emotional bonus it wouldn't have been so bad. But you've got them fascinated by the virtues of three men whose confessed intention is to bore or frighten me to death. (*A third of the background sound drops into silence.* Luxton's *head shoots up as if he has noticed this.* Jackie *pays no attention. The second third of the sound falls still.*) You'll be left alone, you know.

**Jackie:** What's that?

**Luxton:** You'll be left alone. (*The last of the sound dies away.*) Did you know that? Did you know that the fall of evening might bring the fall of hope, that once they saw that little circus of vindication out there they might slink away and leave you alone?

**Jackie:** Oh! yes, yes. I knew that. Whenever you lead people against any citadel that's been whacking them over the head, it's just a trial run. Wanting to know how the legs will feel when they start in a new direction. And remember they've been whacked. They don't see too far, too clearly. Their legs are twisted and their feet are fearful. They have been made to stand in postures that are less than human.

**Luxton:** And you'll be left alone.

**Jackie:** Why not? Other people tear your arms out. But they are nourished on the memory of the man they dismembered. All the way along the road, the unburied dead trying to explain and warn. I've made two mistakes, Mr Luxton. One, never having looked hard enough for a woman who could dominate me, shape me, kill me.

**Luxton:** And the second?

**Jackie:** Having tried to interpret the dreams of people who didn't even know they were asleep. (*The laughter of* Aaron *is heard. He opens the door and leans on the jamb as if worn out by his spell of merriment.*) When this boy laughs, duck. What's up, Aaron?

**Aaron:** I'm out in the dark, Jackie, but I could walk the earth by the light of these fine, burning jests.

**Jackie:** Go on. Tell me. I've set jokes going. What made them jump?

(*The door is flung open. The whole crowd of workers flood in led by* Rees. *His eyes are blazing. His clothes are disarrayed. He laughs as he sees the pensive bitterness.* Luxton's first daughter *is at his side, radiant.*)

**Rees:** What made them jump? I did. I was tremendous. The sun and the moon swung from my every word. I was riding love to hounds. Then some heat, some intimations of climax flowed out to me from the listening people. I stopped talking. I held my hands out to the congregation. I started to cry. Then I said, "I will speak no more. I will stand here weeping until the core of flint in every human heart has been melted away."

**Jackie:** A fair tactic. Save on the words.

**Rees:** Oh! the shuddering of miracles. The walls of petrified restraint that are tumbling to nothing in my heart. Before this I was seeing only the heel of humanity, the fleeting heel of humanity. I am being liberated into the light as you are being lowered into the dark, Jackie. The light. And the first shaft had to be this. To ravish your little kingdom of confident licence, to inherit some part of your bold and laughing confidence. There is only one mistake, to operate on only one level. By the minute I am growing. See me now, my votaries around me in a tight cluster of caressive zeal. I timed this whole thing better than you did, Jackie. Shrink now and be still. Now, children, down into the valley, to the new freedom. (Rees *and his votaries tramp out singing one of the gayer hymns used before.*)

**Luxton:** You've started something, Jumper.

**Aaron:** He's finished something. Some of Rees's zealots knocked up a little gibbet for you, Jackie, before they left. Kind of keepsake.

**Jackie:** And the County Sheriff?

**Aaron:** He dug like a mole. A surprisingly good hand with the shovel. Your second daughter was at the side of the hole. Her body kept time with the spade.

**Luxton:** Bright girls, they were, my daughters. But the mind is a smudge, Jumper, no more.

**Aaron:** You must have heard his shout when his tool hit the metal.

**Jackie:** Metal? What's this now?

**Aaron:** You know there was once an abbey where this pub now stands.

153

**Jackie:** These holy ghosts are everywhere.

**Aaron:** A thousand years ago, the Danes or some other plundering pack came lurching this way. The monks dug a rough hole and buried their treasures before heading west. The County Sheriff found the very spot. He distributed the gold and silver pots among the people. They followed him and your second daughter back down to the valley.

**Jackie:** And the Colonel? Go on, tell me. The wrestlers had strokes.

**Aaron:** No. It seems the Colonel is an expert at some French type of wrestling in which the kneecap is driven with passionate force into the opponent's crotch. He had the four wrestlers writhing on the floor in as many minutes. And your third daughter was practically keeping them company, Mr Luxton. Do you hear that?

**Jackie:** I hear nothing.

**Aaron:** The soldiers are climbing the mountain. I can't see, but I know that their helmets, their horses, their lances are coming into view all round the skyline. They are spurring their horses into a gallop. They are coming for you, Jackie. (Jackie *flings the door open.*) Die well, Jackie. (Luxton *takes off his top coat and throws it to* Jackie, *who takes it.*) Die well, Jackie.

**Luxton:** Run hard, Jumper.

*Softly the hooves of many horses are heard. Softly, too, the choral theme of 'Hail to the Lord's Anointed'.* Jackie *smiles at* Luxton *and at* Aaron. *He slips Luxton's coat over his shoulder and walks out into the twilight.*

Curtain

# LOUD ORGANS

# Characters

Wffie Morgan — *Owner of the Cot Club*
Jim Bumford — *a stranger*
Nimrod Pym — *a former minister*
Bryn ⎫
Glyn ⎬ — *Rugby boys*
Wyn ⎭
Tiger Thomas ⎫
Pancho Powell ⎬ — *ex-boxers and now waiters*
Willie Rees ⎭
The Mighty Atom
1st Trustee
2nd Trustee
Mollie
Eirlys
Susie

# ACT ONE

*To left, a portion of street. Rest of stage is interior of Cot Club.
One of the windows is so shaped that it reminds you that the
building was formerly a chapel, though all the other churchly
fittings have been stripped away. A three-man jazz group is
installed on a corner dais.*

*Along the street comes* Jim Bumford. *He wears a distinctive
slouch hat of light yellow straw. He peers hard into the windows of
the dingy shops, mainly cafés with names like 'Krishna's Kaff',
'Orient Repose', 'Koh-i-Noor'. The people in the street gather
round him, without hostility but with a seeming wish to squeeze
him out of their world.*

*The combo starts strumming the 'Stranger's Theme'. The people in the street start singing the words and the song mounts into a great lament. In the street Mollie, Eirlys and Susie, and Tiger, Pancho and Willie whoop it up in a celebration number. They involve Jim, making it clear by their inquisitive eyes that they see him as a stranger. Jim and Mollie touch hands in a short sequence of the dance. Then the door on the right opens. Bryn, Glyn and Wyn appear and Bryn gives a great "Whooo!" of astonishment.*

*The song is interrupted as Wffie Morgan leaps into midstage from the top of the short flight of steps that leads to the back premises of the Club. As soon as Mollie hears his roared demand for silence and attention, she rushes away round to the back of the Club, Jim following. Wffie is a eupeptic meg of about thirty-five, clad in a suit of midnight blue serge meant to emphasize the impressive breadth of his body. There is a kind of lustful brightness about his face as if he is shortly going to bite himself a mouthful of the world's best flesh. There are prizefight overtones about him. He has a curious gesture of lifting his arms as if submitting to a search by a policeman and arrogantly confident that nothing will be found on him.*

*He laughs scornfully at the singers. When he speaks his accent has a South Wales base with a strong mid-Atlantic sheen. There are powerful hints of literacy in his expression and delivery. Wffie is managerial from his thick, waved hair to his splendid, Italian-style shoes.*

**Wffie:** That'll be enough Bute Street Blues for one night. (*To combo*) Get hep to something happier, kids. This shabby kingdom is going to get its first real coat of warm emulsion gloss. This is the first night of Wffie Morgan's new Cot Club. We'll lay the echo of the last hymn, won't we, boys?

(*The Combo plays the last five or six sonorous notes of some such grave, warming hymn as 'Rwy'n Weld y Bedd', then jumps on the echo of it with a convulsion of rattles on the drums and an erotic jangle on the strings.*)

Wffie Morgan is really going to bring the old broth to the bubble. A shrine for every fugitive from coldness between Cardiff and Cardigan, and some fine shivering samples we have, and all. For everybody who has blunted his teeth on a Gorsedd stone. For everyone trundled out of bed by fear of the flesh. For everyone with sore fingers after being taught the harp by parents who wanted to head him off from Satan's idle hands department. We've got the lot. (*He points to the Combo.*) The Bessemer Three, expelled from Margam by the Watch Committee for shaming the furnaces into a confession of chill. They are the boys who will remelt the slag of wasted lives and keep their thought low and thin. (*The combo break into a mopey shake of blues to which* Wffie *might sing some small, sardonic lyric.*) And waiters. No more manhandling of noggins from sloppy bars to floating tables. The Celt qualifies the really neat gill. Boys!

(Wffie's *three waiters appear. They are* Tiger Thomas *heavyweight,* Pancho Powell, *middleweight, and* Willie Rees, *lightweight. They are carrying new, shiny trays and snow-white towels. There should be no hint of caricature in their appearance. Their dinner-suits are well-made and they are rather handsome in a flattened, punchy kind of way.* Wffie *introduces them in the manner of that bouncy little man we have seen at the microphone in Madison Square Garden.*)

Tiger Thomas. Heavyweight contender. Best fighting weight twelve stone ten and a killer punch, but tonight at twelve stone because he doesn't want to kill anybody. Pancho Powell. Middleweight contender. Was touching the crown when he pulled out. Victim of a cut eye, a crooked referee and a wife who was a complete stranger to the whole idea of second gear. And now, Willie Rees, lightweight, the ballet-master of the feathers, the fastest twitching muscle of the Celtic fringe, the toughest little one of them all. Struck by lightning outside the gates of Aberbeeg cemetery. Burned all the way down one side. Then jumped up and shouted 'Foul!'

(*The three bow blandly.*)

**Wffie:** See that? Solid but suave. Courteous service and a sure guarantee against hooligans and the untidily lustful. (*He snatches one of the towels, flips it open and goes through a fanning routine in front of the three fighters as if helping them out of an inter-round fug.*) Our land's farewell to filth. Look at the gleam on this cloth. Makes snow look unshaven. But we won't be in bondage to whiteness. The only consistently clean thing in this pub will be the linen. Whatever the flesh demands, Wffie will provide. Girls!

(*From the same door come* Eirlys, Susie *and* Mollie. *All three are elegantly gowned. The first two are about thirty; they have a look of having slipped down a few drinks and are looking forward to an evening of serene triumph.* Mollie *is about twenty-two, a girl of crackling vitality. She is less easy in her attitude and stance. She looks around warily. She taps her foot and sings softly the love-theme being languorously swung by the combo. They break into the Venusberg song.*)

**Bryn:** (*Going to the harmonium*) In a world where love glows ghostly
Very dim and limping mostly
**All:** In a life where dreams are slain
Let the voice of love be plain
Through the silences of shame
Set the torch of love aflame
Through the silence and the blight
Set the torch of love alight.
**Wffie:** Love's been freezing long enough
Vote for Venus, do your stuff.
No loving lip without its kiss
No hunger left unsated
Just knock on the door of the old Cot Club
Let every wish be stated.
From each corner of the night
Let those who will be mated.
Let's make an end to frigid gloom
And the silences that freeze it —
Light up the lights, let the senses zoom
For joy, oh boy, we need it.
**Mollie:** In a life where dreams are slain
Let the voice of love be plain
**Eirlys:** Through the silences of shame
Set the torch of love aflame
**Susie:** Through the silences and the blight
Set the torch of love alight.
(*The* boxers *hand the* girls *a drink apiece and they propose a kind of toast*)
**Mollie:** No more whispers.
**Susie:** No more shadows.
**Eirlys:** No more cold.

**Wffie:** Not with you there won't be! The warm and willing welcome girls, the girls to take the last drift of snow from the last Welsh wrinkle, girls to serve an all-weather libido. All new to fleshly pleasure of the public kind, but all set to shatter the sexual equivalent of the four-minute mile. Shy and reserved until now, they are going to rise like three moons over this darkened land. Eirlys, from Ebbw Vale, crowned Banana Queen of Beauty by the combined fruiterers of the Western Valleys, also a soprano of the mezzo type for those admirers who want to keep in touch with our fine vocal tradition at all hours. Susie, Caerphilly's Vera Lynn. Would have made the top ratings if she hadn't had an over-excitable music-teacher. Kept time by rubbing his body against hers. Developed a dangerous vibrato. On certain notes made pieces fall from the top of the Castle keep. Told to shut up by the council, a muted, tone-deaf lot. Mollie, the finest model ever to strut her shape on the banks of the Taff or its darker tributary, the Epitaph.

**Mollie:** Pull the zipper, Wffie.

(*Loud knock on the door and in come* Bryn, Glyn *and* Wyn. *They are blazing hedonists, men of about the thirty-five mark, steel-workers and miners.*)

**Wffie:** The boys from Trecysgod!

**Bryn:** Damn, you've done it up nice, Wffie.

**Glyn:** You'll never beat THEM, Wffie. I've seen them. My mind is full of the faces of those women who sit around in courts prescribing cooling powders for the over-heated young. The temperance lodges will be gathering and whispering agendas of doom against their quarry-faces. They'll scribble their last cautionary text on the hardening underside of your drying scalp. When they get on to what you intend, they'll lash you to a brewery stack and scuttle you. And when they find out that you plan to start a ginger group on the looser urges, they'll add virgins to the export drive until you blow over.

(Jim Bumford, *still wearing his distinctive hat, has come in behind the rugby boys.*)

**Wyn:** The place is a treat, mind.

**Glyn:** Look at the girls.

**Bryn:** Good God, toffee apples.

**Wyn:** It's what we were promised in the Revival of 1904 but never got.

161

**Glyn:** (*to the boxers*) Boys, no referee would have dared count you out in that rig.

(Wyn *brings* Jim *forward. From the first instant* Wffie *views him with the most profound and bristling suspicion.*)

**Wffie:** Who is he?

**Wyn:** We were having a quiet noggin with him in the Bombay Bar. This is Wffie Morgan, Jim.

**Bryn:** We've had many a good Saturday with Wffie.

**Wyn:** Come down from Trecysgod for the Rugby, see, and stayed supping through the day with Wffie when he had the old bingo club in Benediction Terrace.

**Bryn:** Lovely. Big job finding someone with good sight who had seen the match, so that we could describe it in the club back home.

**Wyn:** Tricky thing, pleasure.

**Wffie:** (*to* Jim) What are you doing here?

**Glyn:** (*with a great lubricious glare at the* girls) What you think he's going to do here, Wffie? Knit?

(*The boys sit down,* Eirlys *and* Susie *with them.* Mollie *remains standing. She and* Jim *exchange cordial glances. Drinks are ordered and the boxers bring them in.* Wffie *is given a large Scotch which he downs with ferocious suddenness.* Mollie *and* Jim *take seats.* Wffie *continues to stare at* Jim *with militant distrust.*)

**Wffie:** You could be a nark. All my life I've had them underfoot. Narks. Beetles.

**Jim:** I'm no beetle, no nark.

**Bryn:** No, I can tell you're upright. (*He examines* Jim's *hand.*) And clean work, too.

**Wffie:** They are the really dirty sort. You'll see. What have you worked at? What's your tool?

**Jim:** The sad thought.

**Wffie:** Another slippery bastard.

**Wyn:** In London mostly, I expect.

**Jim:** Africa, America, I've covered as much ground as the Missionary League, but with less point.

**Mollie:** Get out your best eye-glass. We wear some fancy bits of darkness around here. We'll stand nice and still for you. (*She stands with mock demureness in front of him, hands held up in front of her.*)

**Jim:** It'll be a pleasure.

**Wffie:** What's your business?

**Jim:** Nothing fixed. Kind of research.

**Glyn:** Any research you do here will make you tired.

**Wyn:** We get research up at Trecysgod. Boys from the colleges, doing research. Questions, questions.

**Mollie:** When I was in trouble, the questions I got. I wish I could be as curious about other people as they've been about me. The way other people get weeds in the garden or a blockage in the chimney, I get questions. When I was a kid about seven I was up in the vestry pulpit for a quarterly meeting. There was a note of harvest in the place. The deacons were up to their necks in bloom. They were fidgety and started a fair drift of the old pollen. My sinuses were gaping. I was singing that little song, 'Twinkle, twinkle, little star, How I wonder what you are'.

**Wffie:** That's the approach. Ask them!

**Mollie:** I sneezed harder and harder. I almost put the star out. I was charged with impiety, second degree. The deacons had never heard of pollen.

**Jim:** I used to sing that song myself. 'Twinkle, twinkle, little star!'

**Wffie:** You would.

　　　(*The combo start up a kind of gentle waltz adaptation of 'Twinkle' in which all except* Wffie *join. Very briefly. Then* Mollie *begins incanting questions*)

**Mollie:** Do you eat less after you've had a row with the foreman?

**All the boys:** Not unless we ate the foreman.

**Mollie:** Why do you get black when you dig coal?

**All the boys:** Because we turned down the Coal Board's offer of dust-repellent flesh.

**Bryn:** Very kind, the Board.

**Mollie:** Why do you sweat when you tend a steel furnace?

**All the boys:** To make room for the beer. That's why ingots were born.

**Susie:** When do you least feel the urge?

**All the boys:** At longer funerals.

**Susie:** Do you prefer it on the mat on Sunday afternoon or in bed on Tuesday?

**All the boys:** We try to be impartial but we like it in the ferns on a fine Thursday.

**Susie:** Oh that smell of trampled fern.

**Glyn:** (*bending over and kissing her arm*) I likes a bit of trample.

**Eirlys:** How constant is love?

**All the boys:** Very shaky, love.

**Eirlys:** Do you go through life with one woman, one shape, in your mind?

**All the boys:** Many women, many shapes.

**Mollie:** Have your dreams ever caught up with the facts?

**All the boys:** No. Very easy to miss, dreams. Like buses.

**Mollie:** What are the facts?

**Bryn:** No idea.

**Glyn:** We've never had a clear view of the facts.

**Wyn:** If we see them coming, we duck.

**Jim:** Does the need to love grow less?

**All the boys:** No, it grows greater.

**Glyn:** And worse.

**Jim:** Does the dream and does the reality yawn apart until the strain is intolerable?

**Wyn:** Reality was never more ruptured.

**Bryn:** The dream was never more than a yawn.

**Glyn:** I've seen you on the home-screen, I fancy. Soap-flakes?

**Jim:** I've never consciously propagated suds.

**Wyffie:** Is that so now? (*He mimics* Jim's *rather suave way of speaking.*) You shake my faith in washing.

**Jim:** What are you looking for? (*They all look frankly puzzled. He addresses* the boxers.) What are you looking for?

**Tiger:** One last fight where the ref will be blind, benevolent, or my brother. One last fight with the magic somebody once told me was in these hands. Why do people say these things to other people?

**Willie:** One last fight and, win or lose, a line of willing girls queuing up outside to give me comfort.

**Bryn:** I thought I'd seen him on the home-screen. He's a truss salesman.

**Jim:** (*to* Bryn) What are you looking for? You have a face full of eyes.

**Bryn:** I want a place where there'll be no last bus to worry about and a wife who'll have forgotten what her last question was going to be.

**Jim:** (*to* Glyn) You?

**Glyn:** Same as him, but I've got a bike.

**Jim:** (*to* Wffie) I bet you've got something special looming up ahead.

**Wffie:** All I want is the scalp of the nosey codger who's using you as a guide dog.

(Jim *gestures his question to* Eirlys *and* Susie.)

**Susie:** We never ask for anything.

**Eirlys:** Risky, that.

**Susie:** You expose too many lights when you let a wish peep out.

**Eirlys:** We are girls who never want a fuss.

**Jim:** Try, though. Imagine I've come up with a loaded sleigh.

**Susie:** Two days that match.

**Eirlys:** A day that won't make yesterday look bent.

**Jim:** (*to* Mollie) And you?

**Mollie:** You tell me. You know.

**Jim:** I liked the look of the people. I wanted a rest, a bit of a talk. I've trailed around for years. You've heard of fish that circle the globe?

**Wffie:** Keep fish out of this. They keep moving because they are trying to shake off those things that people put on them — rings on the tail and so on. Keep this on a Labour Exchange level. We don't like people we can't put in a place like THAT. (*He makes a gesture that suggests ramming an identity-card into a pigeon-hole.*) You're from somebody. Everybody's got to be from something.

**Bryn:** (*in a mutter to* Wyn) He'll be from the insurance. Anybody who asks you what you want out of life is going to offer you a bonus for giving up the ghost. (*To* Jim) What are you, then?

**Jim:** I'm a writer.

**Bryn:** I was right. He's from the insurance. They're always writing, those boys.

**Wffie:** Don't answer any question from *him*. (*To* Jim) I've still got a feeling about you. These boys are from Trecysgod, a mouldering dump in the hills.

**Wyn:** Biggest rates-arrears in Britain on the council estate. Fifteen evictions last week.

**Bryn:** Told by the Borough Surveyor, Charlie Caustic, to

develop Eskimo crouch and go live in their new fridges.

**Wyn:** Corrupt council. Every time you pull the Mayor's chain you have a flushing sound.

**Bryn:** Wedlock doing poorly.

**Glyn:** No rapes — stamina down to zero.

**Wffie:** And these girls are *from* people who were a nuisance to them. Who are you from? Are you from the police? (*Jim gestures No.*) Are you from the Temperance League?

**Bryn:** A tremendous force for good. Dried us out after the greatest monsoon of ale since the Saxons stopped knocking it back to give full time to chasing the Celt. (*He brings his companions to their feet and leads them into one of those sweet little Band of Hope numbers:*)

**Boys:** A greater delight life never will bring
Than the touch of my lips on a crystalline spring.
Wine I renounce, and lust, its daughter
For the simple grace of a glass of water.
Oh, how much sweeter your days will taste
If you stay sober, clean and chaste.

**Glyn:** Big thing that, chaste.

**Wffie:** Are you from the League for The Re-elevation of Fallen Welsh Girls?

(*The boys start looking on the floor as if on the lookout for a few prostrate maids. The three girls stand up in a respectful salute.*)

**Glyn:** Engineering, the hope of the world.

**Wffie:** Are you from these parts?

**Jim:** I was.

**Wffie:** When did you leave?

**Jim:** Twenty-five years ago.

**Wffie:** Why?

**Jim:** Because the place was a mess.

**Wffie:** And now that you're back. What is it like?

**Jim:** A mess with a bit of money over it. (*He performs a delicate sprinkling gesture.*)

**Wffie:** A belly-acher. What are you?

**Jim:** A sort of watcher.

**Wffie:** Well, watch it, watcher. We'll be watching you, watcher.

**Wyn:** You'll see big changes, Jim. Wffie's the boy to follow.

**Bryn:** He'll have these centres of beauty and booze strung from one end of the land to the other.

**Jim:** I've heard about him. I've heard that the Welsh were going to shed their last frown. I came to see. A chain of Venusbergs right up the Celtic spine.

**Wffie:** That's it. We'll kick the last black truss into Cardigan Bay.

**Glyn:** Wffie will be the first winning bard to be crowned in bed.

*(The rugby boys hail this and go into a kind of scrum routine with marked sexual overtones. The girls join in. The boxers keep time by beating their trays. They go into a fast and catchy anthem of joy:)*


*THE RUGBY SONG*

Up and under, up and under
That's the thunder from the hills
Rugby outings are the answer
To the dark Satanic mills
If you talk to us of grief and such
We say grab the ball and kick for touch
In the face of the trampling foe
Take a dive and tackle low.

Fugitives from thought are we
Sons of heavy industry
Satisfied artisans, labour's cream
We've sold the pass on old dad's dream.
We've buried Hardie, banished Marx.
Give us the hedonistic larks
Car in garage, cash galore,
Was ever life like this before?

Better than a speech by Nye
Is the cry of Kelly's Eye
Kelly's Eye, Kelly's Eye.
Kelly knows. Kelly sees
We've won a wondrous social ease,
All thought vanquished, crises past
We're on the gravy train at last.

167

Fish and fish, to hell with chips,
Ten pints of best, twelve whisky nips,
Chicken suppers, trips to Spain,
No more conflict, park your brain.
For total peace inside your heads,
Take our cue and pot the Reds.
We've got everything we ever prized
In a Britain semi-socialised.
One tenth cultured, semi-free,
Fugitives from thought are we.
Dialectic, cease to tease us,
Slumps will come no more to freeze us.
So three cheers now for the Iron Men
Who'll bring us glory once again
At Twickenham, at Twickenham.
Hearts of steel and skulls of teak
Through them let modest Gwalia speak.
We may desert our ancient Muses
But let the Saxon count his bruises
At Twickenham, at Twickenham.
Up and under, up and under,
That's the thunder from the hills
Rugby outings are the answer
To the now hygienic mills.


(Mollie *and* Jim *have got into the scrum and seem to be
getting involved in an elementary embrace.* Wffie *circles around,
watching like a referee.*)
**Wffie:** I've got to watch the watcher. Always watch the watcher.
   (*The anthem ends.*)
**Bryn:** Lead on, Wffie. After we persuade the preachers to take
it easy, we've tended a little to lockjaw. But Wffie'll bring back
the old sweet sounds.
**Wffie:** You haven't seen it all yet. We've got a Bingo Hall to seat
two hundred at the back. They sit there for the whole evening
in a trance. There are big mirrors all around the walls. When
they stop getting misted up, we know they're dead. But watch
this.

(*Goes through the door top-right and returns followed by a man in a full suit of tails. He is about forty-five, handsome, grey-haired and preternaturally grave. When he speaks his voice has the quality of two organs.*)

**Wffie:** Ladies and gentlemen — Nimrod Pym!

**Glyn:** Who's he now, Wffie?

**Bryn:** He's an undertaker.

**Wyn:** Bingo, booze and burial, all under one roof.

**Wffie:** You thought I was doing something pretty fancy with waiters. This is the Head Waiter. You won't find Nimrod Pym carrying much around. If you shout to him for half a pint he'll give you a frosty stare and charge you for it. He's here to give tone and wisdom. He was once a waiter at the Copacabana, a valet to an earl and butler to a Cardinal.

(*The boys all line up to shake the hand of* Nimrod.)

**Bryn:** It's a pleasure to touch a hand that touched an earl.

**Wyn:** How was the Cardinal when you left him, Nimrod?

**Nimrod:** In high piety and gloomy about mankind.

**Wyn:** He would be.

**Glyn:** You don't look too bright about it yourself, Nimrod.

**Nimrod:** Over this winged collar and between these tails, gentlemen, I have seen much folly.

**Wffie:** A body-blow for the uncouth is Nimrod. No more disgraceful blots on the record of the Celt.

**Mollie:** Like those boys who went up to London for the rugby. For years just enough money for tea and buns at the Corner Café. Then a win on the Pools. Posh Café. Waiter comes up. "What will it be, gentlemen?" Far-back accent. Haughty. "Anything with chips," say these voters. "I," says the waiter, "am a wine-waiter." "All right then. Wine with chips." As Wffie says, a blot on the Celt.

(Mollie, Bryn *and* Jim *join in song, which* Wffie *concludes.*)


## WHAT A BLOTTED LOT THE CELTS ARE

What a blotted lot the Celts are
We let our sorrows rip
An organised anguish has swilled away

169

The starch from the once stiff upper lip
Oh Conscience of the Celt, speak plain,
Will ye no' come back again
From the graveyard of the slain?
Our longest songs extol the hosts
Of some of the world's most overworked ghosts:
The Celts betrayed, the Celt oppressed —
Groan a bit and sing the rest.
Plant an image in the young
Of burning city, buried tongue.
Split in language, knee-deep in oracles,
Politically lost and kicked in the coracles.
Rural ebb and brittle promises
For the harassed Macdonalds, Kellys and Thomases.
When Calvin and Knox had done with joy
It went off to the wars with the minstrel boy.
Our ears alert for that sobbing sound
Of villages emptied, valleys drowned,
**Wffie:** Just to keep water in the taps
Of those predatory English chaps.
**All:** The cheated Celt, the Celt oppressed —
Oh, let's give yesterday a rest.

**Jim:** Amen to that. (*To* Wffie) To the eraser of blots, the re-maker of whiteness.
**Bryn:** Survey-poll? You finding out how we're going to vote?
**Jim:** I've not yet met the government that was not more of a secret than the ballot.
**Wyn:** Encyclopaedias!
**Jim:** I've never peddled knowledge. Too modest. No. My trade is looking at people.
**Wffie:** That's a sinister calling if ever I heard one. Looking at people! What's the angle? Blackmail? Anthropology? Eye-tests?
**Jim:** I have been known on at least two occasions to help people to learn the truth about themselves.
**Wyn:** Oh! Sanitary inspector, I expect.
**Wffie:** God help us. For the truth about ourselves we build cupboards of three-ply. And you want to find it for us! Here's a boy who needs putting down.
**Mollie:** (*approaching* Jim *and patting him reassuringly on the*

*arm*) Let's air the cupboard for a change. Carry on with your research.

**Jim:** (*shaking* Wffie *by the hand*) I'm beginning to see the point. Since I came back here you are the most interesting thing. More interesting than the druids, more interesting than those coracles at Cenarth or the cockle industry at Penclawdd.

**Wffie:** I think so, too. Look carefully at this place. What did it use to be?

**Jim:** (*looking up at the tall, churchly window up top right*) Seeing windows that look as if they might be chapel-windows is an optical hazard of this part of the fringe.

**Wffie:** It was a chapel bulging with glum goodness and hot hymns.

**Wyn:** Bad luck, I say.

**Bryn:** Put your ear to a glass (*doing so*) and you hear 'Lead Kindly Light'.

**Wyn:** Like dancing on your mother's stomach.

**Glyn:** It's the wrong venue for a rhumba.

**Wffie:** It was empty, quiet as an old nest.

**Susie:** You should have let it be, Wffie.

**Wyn:** The chapels bred us. And even when the last coroner declares the last one dead, they'll still be dragging us back into their haunted churchyards.

**Mollie:** Have you ever been in one of those places, the quiet, noisy ones?

**Bryn:** Mossy beyond. In the place where I come from there is a graveyard. A fissure in the earth runs from one corner of it to the other, dividing the dead, making them feel more uneasy than they should even in that plight.

**Wyn:** Shame, that.

**Bryn:** The top soil gave a jump and there were those voters in the loam, disturbed. You'd think death would be a pretty smooth sort of tenancy.

**Wyn:** There's no smoothness, no security. Eviction is on every hand.

**Bryn:** It's too tricky. You settle down; you find a new companion in the silence. Then the earth splits and you've got nobody to talk to again.

**Wffie:** Rubbish. We'll make rivets of joy for the whole world's quaking surface. And a lick of paint for every fragment of a flaking past. And boy, how it flaked, all over us. All the echoes of timidity and terror in this place to be laid. And every time the past shows through there'll be Nimrod to sit in majesty upon it, while Tiger, Pancho and Willie rush up with a king-size drum of the best emulsion.

**Jim:** You'll run out of paint. Our people have adopted the deathwatch beetle as their domestic pet. Work as hard as you like and you won't find a single good foundation to build on. Our national leg is typically flexed to trip up delight. When you are really on top and crowing triumph, Wffie, then wham! the trap will go and down you come.

**Wffie:** Not Wffie Morgan. He picks up the bricks and the wall won't fall. I've heard the sort of talk we've just had from you a thousand times, watcher. The day after I made my offer to take the place over and make it a club, a half dozen crones surrounded me in the street. They had sung their first anthem between these walls, taken their first tumbling steps out of virginity against the back wall of the vestry after a hotted-up session of the Band of Hope.

**Mollie:** Don't knock the Band of Hope. Innocence may be retreating, but don't kick it on its way. There should always be the thought of something at the back of your mind that you did for nothing, that never did you any harm.

**Jim:** You're doomed, boy. Our shamans and double-dealers have spawned a cellarful of five-faced termites, each head competing with the other in the non-stop grub-stakes.

(*The boxers gape and* Jim *points quizzically at them.*)

**Wffie:** Wffie picks his bricks and the walls won't fall. (*He takes a sharp pull at his brandy.*) Take my boys, my stable. I put gold in their gloves. I studied boxing with the masters of the craft. I urged them to try out their most devastating punches on me. I gave them some of my best instructions when I was unconscious. We ran like hell over the hills. By the time we finished the whole dawn seemed to be sweating. I took the same bromides as they did to keep the urges moving at a cool creep. We were the frostiest foursome in Christendom for weeks before a fight.

(*The boxers all nod in solemn agreement.*)

**Tiger:** Wffie gave his life to us. He trained us even in his sleep.

**Glyn:** What's this now, Tiger? Did he have you running

around the bed or what?

**Pancho:** If we had an evil thought in our sleep that might reduce our fitness, he trained us to wake up, put our brows against a cold window and think about God and death, and so on.

**Jim:** All right. They're with you. (*He points to the* girls.) What about these?

(Wffie *and the* girls *burst out laughing.*)

**Wffie:** What did I say about them?

**Jim:** Shy and reserved until now. Strangers to passion in public.

**Bryn:** Three moons shortly to rise and supplement the street lighting.

**Glyn:** Rising moons!

**Wffie:** They're mine. All mine. (*He points at* Eirlys *and* Susie.) Good girls, my friend. But thieves. They did a duet of depravity around these streets that had half the police force grey around the helmet. Reserved, did I say? They were reserved for just as long as they were operating inside a tight shawl. They broke out of virginity as if it were a burning house.

**Eirlys:** We made an early start. We didn't think the day was going to last so long.

**Wyn:** Girls, we understand. (*He stands up rather stiffly and when he speaks it is in the manner of one addressing a public meeting.*) This is a social problem. It was explained to me by that well-known Fabian lecturer, Jehoidah Knight the Light, in the Cwmcysgod Institute. He was explaining to us the lines of the poet Blake: "The harlot's cry along the street/ Will be old England's winding-sheet." Poverty, said Jehoidah Knight, is a bigger tree than even Fabians have made it out to be, and harlotry is one of its branches. The original harlots were so poor they couldn't even afford to advertise. They had to go from street to street plying their socially necessary commodity.

**All:** Flesh! Flesh!

**Eirlys:** I never cried along any street. I just stood still and quiet. And I seemed to stand out like a lighted window.

**Susie:** I was like a sort of department store, from the start. I wanted a lot of people to be trying all the different parts of me.

**Jim:** (*to* Eirlys) You were never Caerphilly's Vera Lynn?

**Wffie:** Never heard her sing a note.

173

**Eirlys:** I did and all. When I was eight. I had a voice like a lark. Sweet, don't talk. Kept my father off the drink for a week and a half. When he heard me he would say, "I will stay dry and pure for the sake of the thrush." I won the junior solo championship in the vestry eisteddfod. A sixpenny bit in a pink satin bag. The song was 'Have Courage, My Girl, to Say No.' They got me to sing it again in the big meetings in Chapel. It was Easter. The tall windows were full of daffodils and the chapel was full of the sunlight.

(*The* rugby boys *cup their ears in their hands and seem to be listening to some distant song. Then the mood changes abruptly and the* girls *and the* rugby boys *go into this brisk little bit of instruction with* Mollie *putting the questions and the others roaring the replies*)

**Mollie:** When the winds of longing start to blow?
**All:** Have courage, my girl to say No, no, no!
**Mollie:** If his face is above you like a sunset glow?
**Wyn:** Have courage, my love, to say Blow, blow, blow.
**Mollie:** If he's pouting around like an untipped waiter?
**Bryn:** Concede a little point and murmur "Later".
**Mollie:** If he's frankly bewildered, why let him guess?
**Glyn:** Have courage, my girl, to say Yes, yes, yes.
**Mollie:** If he's nettled and apt to cancel his vow?
**Bryn:** Have the gumption, my girl, to say Now, now, now.
**Mollie:** To this thought of a life as white as snow?
**All:** Have the courage, my girl, to shout No, no, NO!
**Wyn:** The echoes of lost innocence are going off like cannon.
**Eirlys:** Then the sheen went out of my singing voice.
**Wyn:** Sung out. A negative and gloomy lyric, that 'Have Courage' number. Would take the gloss off a morally conscious budgie.
**Eirlys:** My father kept me singing it to keep his spirit strong against the drink. I led him down to the pub myself just to be able to shut up.
**Jim:** (*to* Susie) And you were never the Banana Queen of the United Chambers of Commerce of the Western Valleys?
**Susie:** The nearest I ever got to the banana trade when young was a job as a skivvy to the wife of a greengrocer in Tresychan. A contralto. Very loud. Believed in bare floor boards to give back echo. I had to polish them. Two stroke action. One flick of

174

the polisher for the floor, one for the greengrocer who was full of fruitjuice and kept coming at me from behind.
Say what you like about floozies and whores
Brother it's better than cleaning those floors.
Say what you like about sinning and Sodom
It's better than calling some silly bitch Modom
Say what you like about love for a fee
It's better than a spell of housemaid's knee.
By the time I finished that greengrocer was shining better than the floor. I know. I was practically one of the floorboards.
**Wyn:** Proposed: that we don't condemn. There is no innocence, no guilt. Things nudge you like an idiot and you go flat on your butt. In Cwmcysgod there was a magistrate . . .
**All:** "In Cwmcysgod there was a magistrate." The laugh-line of the month.
**Wyn:** There was a magistrate with a bushy beard and eyes like slate. Always reminded us of Moses. Talbot the Tablets, they called him, and he had a voice that could ground aircraft. I was up before him for abusing the freedom of the back-lane when I was coming home in grave need after a club outing. He looked at me as if I'd ravished the whole place and then made a poor offer for his hair. Proposed: that we do not condemn.
**The Others:** We do not condemn. Our nation's jaws are stiff with condemnation. The black cap of condemnation has darkened the brain beneath.
**Bryn:** The world's fallen women are part of the vengeance exacted by the world's broken-hearted mothers.
**Wyn:** In every laughing Lulu is the ghost of a grieving mam.
**Susie:** My mam died of a laughing fit on the Figure Eight in Barry. She was with the lodger, a joker. He came up with a joke as the Figure Eight came down. Cross current.
**Wyn:** We salute you, victims of inequality and lust.
**Glyn:** We ought to be doctored, the whole buzzing lot of us.
**Jim:** That's it. Take them away from Morgan. Start his little realm shaking.
**Bryn:** We've got a new button factory starting in Trecysgod. You could start again from scratch with a job at the lathe. We know a couple of defeated deacons who'd let you sing that song again, who'd load the Easter window with daffodils.
(Eirlys *and* Susie *go into a loud rhythmic laughter. The*

175

*tempo of this slows into the tempo and melody of* Mollie's *song which is quietly taken up by the combo.* Mollie *herself gets up and starts pacing around the stage as if she has suddenly become aware of the need for an exit.*)

**Eirlys** and **Susie:** A button factory!

**Jim:** Don't doubt the future of buttons. There will always be some people rooting for a thoroughly buttoned humanity.

**Wffie:** They are tied to me by tighter things than buttons. These two have gone into action like a pair of killer sharks. They'll get a man drunk and tired. Then they roll him and rob him. Always a duet. Their last job was an American sea-captain. If he had prosecuted, they'd have had six months each. But I set my boys on him and he shut up for international friendship's sake. If you got them a job in a button factory they'd invent the only brand of button meant to stay undone. And if Eirlys sang to a windowful of daffodils, they'd open the window of their own accord and walk out. Eirlys, if you're ever approached by a social reformer, have courage, my girl, to say No. God knows what he's after.

**Susie:** You can bank on us, Wffie. We're as much part of you as the legs of your trousers.

**Glyn:** That's cosy.

(Mollie *has gone to stand by a window that gives on to the dock.* Jim *goes to stand by her side. One can see from* Wffie's *look that he is madly in love with* Mollie *and he is prepared to go to any lengths of skullduggery to nip in the bud any affection she might feel for* Jim. Nimrod *returns from some mission and stands in the centre of the stage, a hub of grave, Buddhist calm for all the febrile ripples of the company.*)

**Jim:** (*to* Wffie *and nodding at* Mollie) And her? What about her?

(Wffie *just breathes savagely and does not reply.*

**Jim:** (*To* Mollie) What about you?

(*She leaves the window and comes up to* Nimrod.)

**Mollie:** Is it truth-time, Mr Pym?

**Nimrod:** It's never truth-time. Truth is a practice for dying.

(Bryn *and his friends lean forward to hear* Nimrod. *They look concerned.*)

Bryn: Hear that? We're not out of the wood yet.

**Wyn:** This is a land of simple stories.

**Jim:** (*to* Mollie) What's your simple story?

(Mollie *steps to centre stage, There is no reason why her statement should not be framed as a kind of mounting recitative, with the music swinging violently as the rhythms alternate between elegy and tirade.*)

**Mollie:** Before the court at thirteen and a half.

**Bryn:** That's rushing it.

**Mollie:** The three magistrates added up to two dim eyes and a ravelled sense of pity.

**Bryn:** Not always our best, the magistrates. The traffic is too one-way.

**Mollie:** In need of care and protection.

**Glyn:** Who isn't now, who isn't?

**Mollie:** That was my birthday. Hearing what I'd been up to was my real entrance.

**Bryn:** It should happen to us all.

**Mollie:** It happened just after my father . . . Shall I tell them about my father, Mr Pym?

**Nimrod:** Every father deserves an airing. And he never took up much room.

**Mollie:** It was just after my father'd been hit into the water of the dock by a swinging crane. He was standing there, thinking.

**The Boys:** It attracts trouble, that thinking.

**Mollie:** And the jib comes along. He was gentle. He read a lot of books with me.

**Wyn:** Books. Good things. We used to read books before we stumbled into the New Jerusalem of overtime and delight.

**Bryn:** Books are light, said Jehoidah Knight, the Fabian. But there comes a point when you don't want the light, when things are better, softer, kinder in the dark.

**Mollie:** He wanted me to be a missionary nurse in some part of Africa where he'd been happy when he was a merchant seaman.

**Wyn:** A shrewd choice. Africa will need nursing for a long, long time.

**Mollie:** My mother went off the rails.

**Bryn:** The miracle is how we get on them.

**Mollie:** She got picked up. Went inside. Slid off to London.

**Glyn:** Somebody is using a spray. It is guaranteed not to harm insects but it's playing hell with us.

177

(*In the next minute* Nimrod *becomes focal and grows in significance.*)

**Wffie:** (*to* Mollie) Who got you the job in the fish-shop when you left school?

**Nimrod:** (*very quietly*) Wffie.

**Wffie:** Who took your brother in when there was no one else to look after him?

**Nimrod:** (*more loudly*) Wffie.

**Wffie:** And who'll give your brother a job as third hand in my warehouse when he comes out of Borstal tomorrow?

**Nimrod:** Wffie.

**Mollie:** Who put me on the street when the fish-shop closed down?

**Nimrod, Susie, Eirlys:** Wffie.

(Wffie *spins round to threaten* Susie *and* Eirlys. Nimrod *throws his towel around* Wffie's *neck in the manner of a strangling scarf but is gently pulled away by the boxers.* Wffie *tears the towel out of* Nimrod's *hands.*)

**Wffie:** Before I enjoy the bonus of emotion, Pym, I fine you four bob for the abuse of a towel. (*He throws the towel furiously into the head-waiter's face.*) About you I wanted to shut up. I wanted you to be the one undisturbed cemetery. (*Circling viciously around* Nimrod *like a bijou Mephisto. His voice crackles with storms.*) I wasn't going to tell you a word about him. I've dressed him up as a kind of undertaker of the past. I dare him to tell you about it.

**Bryn:** Say something rich about truth again, Mr Pym.

**Wyn:** The truth. There's a thing now. That gloomy lecturer, Powell the Positivist, he used to tell us at the Institute: Truth is where the glands intersect, and Powell would tremble with a palsy of insight when he made those remarks. Truth is the spot where the glands intersect.

**Glyn:** But the glands jump about and the spot is never still.

(Nimrod *stands stock-still.*)

**Nimrod:** (*holding his white towel in front of him*) Truce.

**Jim:** Truce. With whom?

**Nimrod:** With all the days behind me.

(Nimrod *speaks slowly, plangently. While he speaks a group of old people appear in the street. Their movements at first are bewildered. They seem able to hear what* Nimrod *says and their*) *movements become more rhythmic and intelligible as the story proceeds; in not too specific a way they seem almost to be miming out what* Nimrod *describes.)*

Until the age of nineteen I was actively depraved. I was used as a moral warning in one hundred and five sermons. But at nineteen I got the call.

**Jim:** The call to what?

**Nimrod:** To God, who else? As a boy I had been a foot-runner. I won foot-races. Then the races were banned as encouraging nudity, flamboyance and the urge to wander. I went swiftly from village to village, making a quick harvest of delight. Then the call. I went to a remote, bleak village in the hills as the minister of the chapel. The men were harsh, the women stunned and loveless. I preached into their lives a gospel of beauty, light and joy.

**The Boys:** Good lines those, joy and that.

**Nimrod:** A clamorous and passionate challenge to the ethos of the three-ply serge in which they await death. I saw them as in a shroud and my fingers told me they had the power to tear those cerements away. The men rejected me as if I were an invader bent on their death. The women were kindled and inspired.

*(An illusion could be created here of* Nimrod *standing in a pulpit. There is the groundswell of some such Welsh hymn as 'O Iesu Mawr'. His gestures are the broad, magnificent ones of a topline preacher sweeping every last member of a congregation into his emotional maw.*

*The old women outside and the girls within nod their heads at* Nimrod's *last words, as if telling him they know exactly the way it was. As his story reaches its last phase they all begin to hum a gentle elegiac song.)*

**Nimrod:** The women came towards me. It was the first sound of gentleness they had heard in years. It was a siege of love. My life overflowed.

**Glyn:** Too much for one man, see. Nip out for a quick sortie, but never a siege. (Nimrod *is staring ahead and rubbing his face, as blank as one trying to recall his first impression of a bomb-shock. There are some fierce musical strokes, at which* Nimrod *winces as if being whipped.)* First came depletion. Then defeat. (*His voice rises as if in the perorative leap of a great sermon.*) Never try to do anything to repair ugliness over which men and women have laboured overlong. There are fashions in doom and they have AUTHORITY.

**Wyn:** True enough, boy. With us it was booze and the closing of the brain.

**Mollie:** With us it was love having no proper place to park.

(*She sings with* Nimrod)

> The dark is a park that we walk in
> The trees are the trees of regret
> And though we seem to smile as we're talking
> We cry with the need to forget.
> In the old dark park of remembrance
> The paths are in circles and long
> The stars and a touch of the fingers
> Are all that can guide us along
> To a place in the park where peace will grow
> Where the dark has a pattern we seem to know
> Where the trees won't tremble as they have long since
> Where mind falls silent and nerves won't wince
> Dog of a mind, lie down, lie down
> A truce to some carking frown
> And the bark of your night long talking
> For the past is a park in a haunted town
> The past is a park that we walk in
> The past, the long past, is a square that we dance in
> And the lights are tremendously gay
> The boring old dark of the park we were once in
> Has blown altogether away
> The rustling of trees
> That once made us freeze
> Now brings back the veins to full heat again
> On the Sunday School teas
> And the more pagan sprees
> Brought the lighting right back to the street again
> Now the situation's fluid
> We've shot the last Druid
> And the conscience of the Celt is taking meat again
> It's the end of the flight
> In a lightening night

In the arbour of roses
Not a greenfly in sight
Life's no longer a trap
We've discovered the map
The exits and entrances clearly told
No more slick, no more sad, no more lonely or old
And for all who require whole toilets of gold.

(*The first mood returns.*)

Yet, yet, yet,
The wind of regret.
The past is a park in the dark that we walk in.

**Jim:** (*quietly*) With me it was doors that were never there when I went back to find them again. All over the earth there is a tribe of door shifters.

**Wffie:** Doom, doom! You can put it on and off like a shirt. You can keep it like a dog. There's nothing outside as smart as what's inside.

**Nimrod:** They closed the chapel to me.

**Bryn:** Very quick on the key, those boys.

**Nimrod:** If I hadn't run out, I would have been carried out. I came down to this city.

(*His voice as he utters this last sentence will suggest authentically the descent from heaven to hell. A chord is sounded which strikes a frisson of dark suggestion around* Nimrod's *words. They wait for* Nimrod *to resume but he stands quite still, his head bowed and his white towel raised up as if to ward off the onrush of fierce, killing memories.*

Wffie *dances to the centre spot.*)

**Wffie:** He wanted to suffer, abase himself. He toted one of my fruit barrows about. I wanted to help him suffer. Whatever your hobby, Wffie Morgan will help you to lengthen the pitch. (*He turns to* Jim) That goes for you too, friend. Whatever your hobby, name it and I'll make it a nice slide down into the grave. (*He laughs and turns again to* Nimrod.) I loaded all the bad fruit onto him. He saw himself as the hub of all corruption and I laid on the props. He was known by the clients as greenfly. They didn't know whether to pay him in cash or spray. Half a dozen

181

times he was pelted. He enjoyed it. A man of sorrows. He hit the cider but he only hit the floor with a real bumpo when he added meths to the good old scrumpo. Wound up in a colony of addicts. Men and women. No holds barred. Under an old railway bridge. They called it Frankness House. A kind of sexual eisteddfod. They had a broken precentor from Cwmsnitch giving these maniacs the beat. And Nimrod Pym was the king of that crazy outpost. *I* rescued him. I put him in hospital. When they got him into the operating theatre they didn't know whether to treat him or use him to test the flatness of the table. He was halfway between a prize for hell and a filter for ICI. Now look at him. Bleached, respectable. *My* work.

**Nimrod:** (*raising his eye*) I am glad to be bleached. I am glad to be respectable. I thought there was an end of the road, a conscious stoppage, a dropping out of life. But there was only a curve, a bend in space. Let the fool persist in his folly and he will become wise.

**Bryn:** That's it. It's after you all the time, that old wisdom. Have you ever been followed about by an old dog you don't want in a night you never wanted to be in? That's wisdom.

**Nimrod:** Put out all eyes, all lights, and from the zone of blindness sprouts THE EYE.

**Wffie:** But you're safe now. You're all behind Wffie's shield. (*A cold wave of negation sweeps in from the street outside: NO! NO! NO!*) Tiger, Pancho, get those two baskets of fruit I've got in there for the first bingo winners. Dish the stuff out to those moaners. Lay on the sweetness. (*The two boxers nip briskly through door R and return with two huge hampers of fruit. As the old folk nibble at their jaffas and pippins* Wffie *calls out to them*) Even for you there will be renewal! (*They go into a great thumping frolic, a sort of Fruit and Love Anthem. All except* Jim *and* Mollie *go out into the street, leaping about to the cornucopia theme.* Jim *looks out at the scene with amused disbelief.*)

**Jim:** This place is a sort of nervous blink.

**Mollie:** Don't knock it. Where there's a blink there's promise. You don't believe in anything very much, do you? Not in oranges, renewal, anything.

**Jim:** I believe in the date, in death, the steady old fixtures.

(*He stares at* Nimrod *outside who, with Florentine grace, is kissing the hands of the old women who have been presented with*

*fruit. The women are as delighted by the sugared icing of the gesture as they are by the juice of the fruit.*)
Yes, I believe in the warmth that two particular people can bring to one particular moment.
**Mollie:** Any offers?
**Jim:** It depends on what you're prepared to take.
**Mollie:** No limits. I'm the heavy haulage section. Loaded dreams a speciality.
(Wffie *has returned to the doorway of the club. He has raised his right arm in a kind of dismissive benediction.*)
**Wffie:** Renewal! For us all, for you all.
**Mollie:** For renewal, cut-rates.
**Wffie:** And one day they won't be able to see us for gravy. Not through booze. Not from doing favours for every monkey who comes down from the valley with a tight collar and a broken hymnal. I'm going to find another Mighty Atom.
**Jim:** Who was he?
(*They all gasp with a mixture of astonishment and disgust.*)
**Boxers:** You've not heard of the Mighty Atom, Mr Bumford? Haven't you ever *listened*, Mr Bumford?
**Susie:** You gone through life deaf, Mr Bumford?
(Wffie *strikes an attitude of dreaming recollection as if trying to project some image of an age that was genuinely of gold.*)
**Wffie:** Alfie Childs, the Atom, the Mighty Atom. Small, lean like paper. Undernourished as a kid. And two new brands of rickets named after him. Mentioned in The Lancet and The Methodist Gazette. Arms no thicker than my wrists.
**Bryn:** Photographed side-view and front for that pamphlet, 'The Minimum Citizen'.
**Glyn:** He was hardly there, poor dab.
**Wyn:** Made the government think twice about austerity, that picture.
**Eirlys:** Could have cried to see him before Wffie put the food down him.
**Wffie:** But he could down an elephant.
**Mollie:** He spoke to me soft and he always had sweets.
**Susie:** When I was on the fruit stall and I had the banana boxes to move, Alfie the Atom would shift them around like corn-flakes.
**Rugby Boys:** Five times to London we travelled on the

183

Mighty Atom express to watch Alfie fight.

**Boxers:** Never lost. Never a muddy verdict depending on the eyesight of the ref. Just a stone-cold boy flat at his feet and Alfie bending over him like a nurse.

**Girls** and **Women Outside:** The tender boy, Alfie. Why do they never stay, the tender boys?

**Wffie:** Never felt pain. He would stand there patiently, a look on his face of wondering why the other bloke was so mad at him. Then something would flick him into life as if he was ashamed of being there under the light half-naked. He would coax the other boy's head in close. Then from no more than five or six inches, as if he wanted to save the bloke the embarrassment of a chilling draught, he would bang it home.

(*The* boxers *are miming the actions described by* Wffie. *Then they go into a routine of generalised fistic mayhem which might match the rhythm of the words of this song*)

**All:** He was the ghost with the hammer in each hand
Come to heal the spirit of our land
Now resin-boy for the heavenly strings
In the everlasting land.
He was the ghost with vengeance in each glove
Touched the faces of the vanquished with a kiss of love

**Bryn:** They need it too, the vanquished.

**All:** He brought pride to hearts and places
Where there'd been no pride before
And never once in his career
Did his buttocks touch the floor.

**Jim:** That's integrity.

**All:** He was the ghost with the hammer in each hand
But the ghost and the hammer
Have departed from the land
Bereft of pride, bereft of boast
Where are they now, the hammer and the ghost?

**Bryn:** No luck, even with phantoms, see?

**Old Women:** Gone like snow the meagre joys
Why can't they stay, the tender boys?

**Wffie:** He was daft about Mollie. He was the ONE boy who could have taken her from me.
**Eirlys:** He had a nice voice, Alfie. Uncanny in the upper register. Trained by Matthew Sewell the Sotto, the master of the head-voice in Meadow Prospect. We used to do a duet. 'Where is My Wandering Boy Tonight?' We used to sing it outside that pub, The Felicity, where all the old soaks go. And they'd come out crying.
**Mollie:** Overflowing.
**Old Women:** Where are the wandering boys tonight?
**Old Men:** Keeping a lookout for the people sent to fetch them back. A sly lot, the wandering boys.
**Jim:** What happened to him, this Atom? Did he die?
**Wffie:** Must have. He vanished.
**Susie:** One Friday night.
**Bryn:** We had booked seats on the Mighty Atom express for his fight on the following Monday night.
**Wyn:** Thirty-six hours overtime we worked to make the extra cash.
**Glyn:** We had the guard's van full of booze.
**Wyn:** Played hell with the chicken trade from Gloucester and exposed the toilet arrangements of British Railways.
**Boxers:** He was in the rankings. Two fights from the title.
**Wffie:** I ran with him that morning on the mountain road. I always ran with him. I was the fittest fruiterer in the fringe in those days. At that place where you can see all the mountains to the north he stopped and he said . . . (*stops and looks as if he is still trying to measure the true depth of that moment's mystery*) Alfie stopped and he said . . . He put his hand on my shoulder and he said, "Wffie, I don't want to fight no more, I want to stay up here. I don't want to get into a street, a sweat, a gym, a train or a ring again. I want to stay up here, Wffie, cool and not hitting anybody." But he came down with me.
**Susie:** That afternoon he helped me unload the bananas.
**Mollie:** That night he came with me to the Dressmaking class in the Tech. He loved needlework. He could have made dresses for queens.

185

**Eirlys:** Last thing that night we sang 'The Wandering Boy' outside The Felicity for the old soaked sad ones in the sawdust.

*(All sing the song together. The melody — it is one of the most beautiful Sankey and Moody hymns — has a rich eloquence. Every drop of banality is to be straightfacedly relished.)*

Oh where is my wandering boy tonight
The only love I met
Oh where is my vanished joy tonight
Why does he haunt me yet?
Oh bring the wandering boys once more
To the hearts they keep in pain
Guide them back and help restore
The lovers to their ghosts again.

**Eirlys:** *(alone)* Oh where is my wandering boy tonight,
The child of my tenderest care,
The boy who was once my joy and light . . .

*(breaks off as if the last line of the stanza escapes her. She repeats part of the third line)*

My joy and light . . .
My joy and light . . .

*(The others, except* Jim, *take up these words as little more than a breath on their lips and their heads turn as if they are all missing and seeking something as painfully tangible as torn flesh.)*

**Susie:** And in the morning he was gone.
**Jim:** Nobody can just vanish. The whole world is one great, organised eye. Nobody can vanish. Where did he go to?
**Wffie:** He vanished.
**Bryn:** Like Owain Glyndwr.
**Wyn:** No known grave and a vague promise to return.
**Jim:** The whole Welsh past is a vast doss-house of sleeping heroes waiting for the call.
**Boxers:** Wherever a man could search, Wffie searched.
**Pancho:** He was a nuisance. He stumbled on more people hiding than the police.

**Bryn:** We went up on the Mighty Atom express hoping he'd be there in the ring.

**Glyn:** On the way up we were too depressed to touch a drop.

**Wyn:** He wasn't there.

**Bryn:** No trace.

**Glyn:** On the way back we stayed in the guard's van with the drink.

**Wyn:** It was the saddest booze-up of the century.

**Wffie:** He hurt his head training. He'd never wear a headguard for training. He always sang when he fought. He said the headguard made his singing sound too important. That's not the sort of boy he was. He could have had a brainstorm.

**Nimrod:** When I was tapering off the scrumpo and meths he'd know when I was on the edge of the shakes and he'd walk and talk me through the dark.

**Mollie:** Wffie was like a madman. Every time he saw a pale, thin kid like Alfie, he'd whip him into the gym to see if he had any of the Atom's magic. A lot of small kids had a rough time. Wffie took most of the pleasure out of being underprivileged. If a kid was underweight, the recipe, if Wffie was about, was rouge on the face to look ruddy and four spare cardigans to look fat.

(*The* boxers *and* Wffie *go through the slow gestures of a long, desperate search.*)

**Susie:** He'll be back.

**Nimrod:** He didn't want to fight any more. He's hiding somewhere. One of these days I'll need him and he'll come.

**Old Women:** The boy is only wandering. He'll be back.

(Jim *looks around and begins to laugh.*)

**Jim:** (*to* Wffie) Boy, are you in a mud hut! Is the past going to split under you?

**Wffie:** (*enraged and shouting*) Nobody laughs at me! Wffie Morgan's no joke. (*To the* boxers) Get this bum, this nark, out of here.

(*The* boxers *take* Jim *gently by the arm.* Jim *turns round by the door and smiles back at* Mollie. *This puts a real white head on* Wffie's *rage.*)

Come back here and you'll be cut down! Nobody laughs at Wffie Morgan. Nobody smiles at his girl. Nobody doubts the light in Wffie's dreams.

(Jim *shakes himself free from the* boxers)

**Jim:** (*shouting*) There'll come a moment when life can't be bought off with a couple of Jaffas. The thing will come nosing around for real meat, prime meat. (*Loudly to* Wffie, *who doesn't seem to hear*) Yours. (*To* Mollie *who most emphatically does hear*) Or yours, maybe.

(*The* boxers *propel him forth. Revelry is unleashed.* Mollie *stares at the door. In between the verses of a whooping celebr̂ution number she speaks.*)

**Mollie:** Wffie, we are naked except for the couple of question marks. And that man knows the answers. And he's coming back with them, Wffie.

(Nimrod *is standing behind* Wffie. *He stares first at his towel, then at* Wffie's *neck.*)

**Wffie:** Question marks, is it? What questions are you asking? What are you asking him for?

**Mollie:** Something you'll never have, Wffie. He's heard the questions jingling and he'll be back.

**All:** (*preparing for a last celebration of music*) We'll all be back.

**Bryn:** We haven't been anywhere but we'll all be back.

**Nimrod:** Every day is a return from somewhere.

**Wyn:** Transport, the miracle of the age.

**Mollie:** Put your umbrellas up, kids. The answer-clouds are forming.

**Glyn:** Oh God, answers!

**Mollie:** We are all going to find out.

**Nimrod:** From all the darkened places strolls an eye.

**Glyn:** What's this now?

**Nimrod:** New sight grows from all the visions we've destroyed.

**Bryn:** We're playing the fool on a falling market.

**Wffie:** There is no dark. Old faiths, old pieties, old hopes are going up in flames all around us. We have abolished night.

**Bryn:** That's another knock to the old gasworks again. (*The lights dim.*) They heard.

(Mollie *dashes out.*)

Curtain

# ACT TWO

*The same scene. Empty stage. Effect of blinding sunlight. Steamer hooter. Up from the orchestral pit, wearing their festive hats, come the* boxers, *the* girls, Jim, Mollie. *The* boxers *savour the sunlight. Continental effect now. They collect some coloured umbrellas of the sort that go over little tables. As they line up for a celebratory march with the umbrellas open they sing 'The Steamer Song'. They march out on to the street and the light instantly goes. They proceed sadly up the street and around to the back entrance of the club.*

*The lyric is sung as if it were a game — the characters throwing each other lines.*

## THE STEAMER SONG

**All:** You'll wonder where the anguish went
When you turn your back on rain and rent.
The kids can eat the buffet bare with never resting jaws
And there's a heavenly suspension of the drinking laws
We wish God speed to every one of our immemorial devils
As we seek our ideal stupor on a dozen different levels
The ritual noggin partaken out of hours
The agenda is bliss, come scruples, come showers
Into the bin with our old sense of sin
And our bombazine and our serges
And a crown of golden flowers and a super vitamin
For our liberated urges.
Urges of the human mole
Where is the magnetic pole?
Lovers drifting to and fro
Here's the key — but where's the door?
Is this the place where love walks free?
Is this the ship, is this the sea?

189

No more rent like larks ascending
No more bailiffs apprehending
Showering writs and seizing chattels
Here's the end of all our battles
Here's the track through golden skies
To the silken beds of paradise.

There's posh!

**Pancho:** And they came right down on my hand and ate the biscuits. I was loaded with biscuits. They are as light as air, those gulls.

**Mollie:** As light as air. (*Makes a sweep of ecstasy.*) To be washed by that spray!

**Tiger:** And they're not afraid.

**Mollie:** And we're not afraid! What a gull can do, we can do. If I were a bird, by God, could *I* think of some targets; could *I* think of a few far lands.

**Glyn:** They're lucky, those gulls.

**Bryn:** A fine open-air job.

**Wyn:** And a fine cheap food policy.

**Glyn:** No time-table. No digestive system.

**Wyn:** Self-expression without malice.

**Bryn:** Birds are never really discourteous.

**Glyn:** They merely shrug their shoulders.

**Mollie:** And the softest-hearted trippers on God's earth to pamper them.

**Willie:** After the biscuits Pancho gave them this afternoon, those gulls are queueing at Weston-super-Mare for magnesia.

**Mollie:** (*to* Jim, *who has fallen moody and silent*) You've got a good line in silence. I hate people who seem to drop through the floor.

**Jim:** Sorry.

**Mollie:** Try not to do it. It gives me the creeps. Once I had a Probation Officer. A man. He had this habit. He had a nice voice. He would stare at me and go on and on about the need to give life a better shape. Then he would stop and just look.

**Jim:** Perhaps he was in love with you.

**Mollie:** In that office? Bare! Every draught in the business around your legs. One picture on the wall. A stern woman who had promoted healthy activities for restless girls to keep them in a chilled repose.

**Jim:** He could still have been in love with you. That sudden falling into silence and staring. That's a good sign.

**Mollie:** No, he told me about it. I reminded him of some exam he had failed, that had stopped him getting a really good job. What exam did you fail, Jim?

**Jim:** I passed the lot. Very bright with the books.

**Mollie:** You ever been rich?

**Jim:** Up and down.

**Mollie:** Been about much?

**Jim:** All over. I'm a great boy for getting ideas. I build them up. I sell them to somebody.

**Mollie:** (*looking somewhat blank*) Sell ideas? We don't do much of that about here. Fruit, love, stuff like that. But . . . ideas?

**Jim:** Oh, I've had some beauties. And just when they reach full height I forget exactly what the idea was and land on my ear.

**Mollie:** I do that. No ideas, mind. But I land on my ear too. Good position for looking at each other. What ideas have you had, Jim?

**Jim:** Once I was in Hollywood. They wanted me to write a film about the Incas, the sun-worshipping Indians. Their priests used to cut out the heart of living sacrifices with jasper knives.

**Mollie:** For grief's sake. The living heart. And that's blunt stuff, that jasper. Thank God we don't get much sun. I never saw that film. If it was made, I'd have seen it. Anything with a bit of gore, priests with knives and that, I'd have been there.

**Jim:** It was never made. The first morning the producer put me in an office. He opened a drawer. He took out a pencil about a yard long and said, "Mr Bumford, lay this pencil on them Incas. By tonight I want this pencil worn down to here . . . (*brings his two fingers to within about an inch of each other*) And could you make those living sacrifices kinda naked, and make the priests work with long jasper knives that don't weaken the view." Always somebody says something like that that puts out the light. Even as I was flexing my muscles to lift that pencil my mind had forsaken the Incas. The next day I sold another mogul the notion of a white girl sold into white slavery in Buenos Aires who became the mistress of a dictator.

**Mollie:** Why don't we hear about such openings?

**Jim:** Then I had a prodigious notion about agrarian revolt in

191

some such place as Kenya. Drums, rage, nocturnal horrors, the sort of thing we once knew in this place.

**Mollie:** Drums I like.

**Jim:** And when I was halfway through the first down-payment I heard about the fabulous frescoes of the Sahara.

**Mollie:** What are they, the Fabulous Frescoes? A troupe?

**Jim:** They are drawings on walls. I wandered about the Sahara like Moses. I had one guide who was against finding things on principle because it would whittle down the guide trade. I finished writing the book which explained why the frescoes were not there on the very day they were found.

**Mollie:** Incas, harlots, frescoes. Now what brings you here? You are a sort of confidence man, then?

**Jim:** I never even had confidence.

**Mollie:** Con-man, who are you conning now? Tell me that, Jim. Who are you conning now? I'm the finest fully licensed victim in the fringe and I'll want to know what hit me when the fuse begins to burn.

(*They sing together*)


THE ANTI-LOVE DUET

**Mollie:** The way's too dark, I've lost the sky,
**Jim:** My nerves are shot, my heart is dry.
**Mollie:** The fuel's set, just one more try,
I'm right and ready for the light.
**Both:** Each little phrase of loneliness
Falls round us quickly like the night.


(*Lead into*)


**Mollie:** How sweet was Fred? How swift was Joe
When stars and moon begin to glow?
Don't know. It happened long ago.
**Jim:** How keen was Kate? How kind was Nell
When night declared its golden spell?
The night once knew. The night won't tell.
**Mollie:** Where's Joe? Where's Cled? Where's Bill? Where's Fred?
The ghosts are silent, all things said.

192

**Jim:** Where's Peg? Where's Joan? Where's Meg? Where's Jane?
The ghosts will not come back again.

*(Reprise of verse between each of the following sections.)*

**Jim:** Who Joe?
**Mollie:** Nimble-fingered boy. Plumber. Left a small flood in every house. Got worn out carrying too many tools in his bag.

**Mollie:** Who Peg?
**Jim:** Daughter of a chip-shop merchant. Bad for love, the constant sight of chips.

**Jim:** Who Cled?
**Mollie:** He was a coalman. Stamina of an ox. Nice-looking boy but haunted by the smell of wet sacks.

**Mollie:** Who Joan?
**Jim:** The club warden found her in my tent when we were on a camping stint.
**Mollie:** What's love in a tent like?
**Jim:** Cramped. Very fundamental.

**Jim:** Who Bill?
**Mollie:** Bible student. He only came to me when he wanted to bring his righteousness to the boil.

**Mollie:** Who Meg?
**Jim:** That one left an ache.

**Mollie:** What did Meg have?
**Jim:** Practically nothing and virtually everything.

**Jim:** Who Fred?
**Mollie:** Fred was a tenor. He had a notion that love wasn't good for him musically. He'd get up in the middle of an embrace and practise scales.

**Mollie:** Who Jane?

193

**Jim:** Rich American. She had lived with so many writers she got a Good Housekeeping Award from the Nobel Prize Committee.

**Both:** We're each of us a team of ghosts
Of loves that didn't make the grade
That's struck the last unlucky match
Before the policies were paid.

**Mollie:** We're the out-of-luck kids.
**Jim:** M-m.
**Mollie:** How's your luck now?
**Jim:** I'm halfway across a private minefield. If I reach the other side, I'll give you a sign. Would you join me?

(Nimrod *comes in.*)

**Nimrod:** Where are the girls? Wffie'll be wanting them.
**Mollie:** They went off for a last drink with some friends they met on the boat. Some singing boys from Abersychan. They stood near the funnel to give themselves resonance and between the heat and the singing they wore themselves out. Where's Wffie?
**Nimrod:** Finishing off a bingo session with people who failed to get on the boat.
**Wffie:** (*his voice heard from the room behind*): Arise, O Sun, Twenty-one. Weep no more, Forty-four. Earth's your Heaven, Thirty-seven. Learn new tricks, Fifty-six. Cheat the State, Eighty-eight. Change your mate, Thirty-eight. What's yours is mine, Fifty-nine.
**Voice:** (*off*) House! House!
**Wffie:** (*off*) That's the lucky lady. Cashier, pay the lady.

(Wffie *comes swinging out into the room. The* rugby boys *are behind him. They are looking a bit bemused as if this is the first time they have seen bingo with perfectly clear eyes.*)

**Wyn:** They are very intent, very numb, Wffie. There are some of them in there, you could take a leg off and they wouldn't notice.
**Wffie:** (*not yet seeing* Mollie *and* Jim *who are standing up, right*): That's the game. Organised on a proper Babylonian scale by some sleepless genius like myself it could oust all such nuisances as systematic thought, remorse and God knows what else. King Bingo to the Queen of Carnal Delight. God, they sit so still with their little cards. (*He turns to the* boxers) Have you heard of Pavlov?

194

**Pancho:** Who did he manage?

**Willie:** He was a wrestler.

**Wffie:** He was a wizard, a whip-master of the nerves. Every time he rang a bell the government increased the dog licence. And did you hear some of the little catch-phrases. 'Cheat the State', 'Change your mate' and that? They'll loosen the old topsoil a bit. (*Turning, he catches sight of* Jim *and stiffens*) I though I told you . . .

**Mollie:** (*harshly*) Wffie, he came in here with me. And he'll go when I ask him to. No sooner.

**Wffie:** (*whose posture and expression show he is doing some fast, cunning thinking and deciding to play the matter smart*) Such loud tones! That boat trip must have done something to you.

**Mollie:** It was the fresh air. It nearly killed me.

**Wffie:** All right, then, if we are going to make a night of this, a lifetime of bliss in a single night, I've got to do some more thinking about the party-games. That's another key to the new life: games that will break down these damn barriers between people; games that will make them all look so daft they'll never go back to the old, stiff-necked solitudes.

**Bryn:** That's the way, Wffie. Daftness worn like chain-mail against all hurts. A week after I gave up hopeful thought about mankind, chap next door said: Bryn, what we want is an orgy. He said some people up the road had had an orgy. Drinking through the night. Cataracts of booze and lightnings of passion. Women blindfolded, approached by men in complete freedom. Men recognised by the women by touch and ardour. Half-past six in the morning, now. Knock on door. Milkman. Hullo, he says, you're getting a few laughs in there. Can I come in? No, says the bloke. You whizz off. You've been recognised three times already. See? Even at dawn and vending so chaste an article as milk, warmth is a need. But I decided to try my hand at the orgy business. Chance my arm, like. Strike a blow for the chuckling life. Paint the sky red. Lay fearless fingers on all the laughter and love under the sun.

**Wffie:** That's the agenda, boy. Fearless fingers, laughter and love. How did it go? Did the bomb go off? Did the joy whistle around the world? How did your orgy go?

**Bryn:** Backwards, if at all. Saved up three weeks for the drink. Sat around the kitchen, knocking it back, making suggestive remarks and laughing out loud, waiting for the miracle of wantonness to hit us. I think we laughed too loud. Must have chilled the tympanum. Our kitchen went cold, or we had the one wine merchant whose grapes grow in cellars. We sat looking at each other till one in the morning. Then we sang five hymns, shook hands and went home.

**Wffie:** You can't walk into Venusberg. Delight is a kind of cobra. And there's a kind of flute and a kind of tune that'll bring it nice and smiling out of its basket without wanting to bite you.

**Bryn:** Show me the flute, Wffie. I'm cobra-bites from head to toe.

**Wffie:** These games are the thing. Willie, fetch me those balloons from the cloakroom.

**Jim:** What's this, man? Balloons? We know about them. Skin and air. A parody of man.

**Mollie:** Give us enough and we float off, and there's a prize for finding us, or for the chap we land on. Is that it?

**Wffie:** No, that isn't it, Madam Know-all. That isn't it. (*He points at* Jim) Come to think of it, this particular game might be just the thing for you. Bring you down to our sort of earth and size, you know. Make you look the clown you probably are. Now watch.

(*Takes balloons from* Willie, *who has returned from the cloakroom with four of largish size, and gives one to* Jim, *one to* Nimrod *and one to* Bryn. *He is about to hand the fourth to* Pancho *but* Mollie *snatches it away. She smiles at* Jim.)

**Mollie:** Let's look daft together.

**Wffie:** Now put the balloon between your legs.

**Jim:** Where?

**Wffie:** Line up here and put the balloons between your legs.

**Bryn:** (*who is having some difficulty in getting his to stay put*) I've got the wrong shaped legs for this sort of thing. Too far apart, my legs. Spoiled me as a wrestler. Could never get a proper stranglehold on the other bloke. (*He gets the balloon into position*) Good God, I feel like the Graf Zeppelin. (*Shades his eyes and speaks with German accent*) Is that the Principality down there?

**Wffie:** Now the first one to do two laps of the room with the balloon in place gets a fish supper on the house.

(*They start their grotesque wobble. After a moment* Mollie *stops and laughs.*)

**Mollie:** (*to* Jim) Have we met before?

**Jim:** Not at quite this angle. Travel broadens.

**Wffie:** (*to* Bryn) How does it feel?

**Bryn:** All right, but not for long trips. One of my legs is saying something to the other, but I feel too buoyant to hear properly.

**Wffie:** (*to* Nimrod) And how about you? (Nimrod *is facing the audience, his mouth agape with the absurdity of his posture. He is exhibiting every known symptom of the bomb-blast.*) And what about you, Thunderguts, Voice from a Cloud, Revelation Bach?

**Nimrod:** In the days of my Philistinian dark, in Gaza, where light and love were mocked and put out, I dreamed that the dignity of man . . .

**Jim:** Speak up for that. Even like this, like a Corgi, I'm fond of that old thing, the dignity.

**Nimrod:** I dreamed that the dignity of man would be taken off the list of protected game and shot like a despised, distempered dog.

**Jim:** That could happen. (*To* Wffie) Have you got your gun licensed?

**Wffie:** I don't believe in licences. I live off my own private bat.

**Jim:** I bet you do. (*He turns to* Mollie *and relieves her delicately of her balloon.*) Might I restore you to your primal shape?

**Mollie:** That's the nicest thing anybody's ever said to me — while playing with balloons, anyway.

(Mollie *and* Jim *send their balloons floating into the street.* Nimrod *and* Bryn *solemnly untie the strings of their balloons and listen intently to the hiss of air escaping.*)

**Bryn:** Are you receiving us, Earth? This is our last message.

**Wffie:** I've got to be away from the club a bit tonight, so he won't get in my thatch. Pym, get in the back room and act as caller for the next bingo session. And for God's sake don't go tacking any bits of theology and Biblical reference to the calls. Keep it simple. That's what they want. A game that's as simple as death and a few bob in winnings to give them the illusion of life.

(Wffie *takes a long look around the bar as if making sure that everything is in working order. His last glance is at* Jim *and he gives a whimsical sort of a shrug. He leaves. The boxers slip on their white jackets but keep their carnival hats on too.* Nimrod *proceeds majestically into the bingo hall and the boxers follow him as gravely as Nubian slaves in the wake of a Pharaoh.*)

**Jim:** Wasn't that a nice afternoon?

**Mollie:** Lovely. Too short, though, too short. No one should ever go back where they came from.

(Mollie *walks distractedly round the stage. In the silence* Nimrod's *voice is heard from the bingo room.*)

**Nimrod:** Ration hate, Twenty-eight. Love in wine, Thirty-nine. Love's too late, Fifty-eight. Oh where's the road to Babylon, Thirty-one. Thirty-one! Who'll bring Jezebel together again, Three times ten, Three times ten! You'll meet more than one angel on the way back from heaven, Forty-seven, Forty-seven. When Sodom was burning, for excesses of glee, The gut of a whale was a shrewd place to be, But Jonah the prophet, he entered a plea, I know that it's safer, but what's there to see? Fifty-three! Fifty-three!

(*There is a pause and then frenzied voices are heard*)

**Voices:** (*off*) Go on! Go on!

**Nimrod:** (*quietly*) Who's alive?

**Voices:** The number! Give us the number!

**Nimrod:** (*raising his voice*) Who's alive?

**Voices:** The numbers, the numbers, the numbers, we've got no light without the numbers!

**Nimrod:** Then make fresh light, you crumby loons. Look at yourselves, you poor staring paralytics.

(*There is, but only for a moment, a terrible silence. Then there are noises that suggest a murderous rage among the bingo fans.*)

**Pancho:** (*off*) Buck up, Nimrod, boy. Don't upset them. (*Addresses the players*) Keep calm now. Here's your gripe-water. Here's your talc.

(*The* boxers *go into a frenetic list of numbers and there is a great choral "Oh!" of relief as the players sink back into their velvet mental shroud.*)

**Bryn:** (*savouring the silence with a kind of admiring trance*) Now there's a strange thing; how whole patches of life seem at times to go edging towards a willing grave. But we are not left at peace. The inspirers come. The wind of passion breathes over the round, suspended life. And we are left with only the craters of the moon.

**Mollie:** It's what I said. No one should ever come back to where they came from. I wish we could have gone down that Channel and away, away. I can't take much more of this. If you are going to wind up in a sty, life should give you the equipment to go with it. A tough hide and an interest in the price of pork. I put in for a

dumb heart and here's the thing asking a million whys. How did I get here? How did I never get away? If you are going to live daft days, the sort that keep you looking complaining or puzzled, then your mind should be de-barked, like they do to noisy dogs, or the same day they do those things to your tonsils. And another question, while we're on the round, noisy trip: Who are you, Jim?
**Jim:** Wffie'll tell you soon enough.
**Mollie:** Are you somebody bad?
**Jim:** Not sensationally so. Like the man in the Bible, I buried my talents, then forgot where the grave was or was too lazy to go back.
**Mollie:** All right. So now you're sniffing round the rubbish. Why pick on Wffie?
**Jim:** Because I'm drawing up a list of nightmares that haunt a sleeping society. I speak as a major sleeper. And I've got Wffie tabbed as one of the major nightmares.
**Mollie:** Another silly question. Probably brought on by watching all those white birds against the blue sky or the sinus trouble I get from the smell of wet fish. Could you love me?
**Jim:** I do.
**Mollie:** What exactly does that mean?
**Jim:** That I'd like to turn your life topsy-turvy.
**Mollie:** The way I spin, who'd tell topsy from turvy?
**Jim:** You can, I can. You don't want to be a Susie, an Eirlys. And with you Wffie'd make a real special job. Because he loves you too. Pimps in love are the top boys in the torture line.
**Mollie:** Would you be in that line too, Jim?
**Jim:** No, I'm in the first-aid branch. If you are trapped in a tunnel and you hear somebody pounding on the stonework, that's me. In a modest, glow-worm sort of way, I bring light.
**Mollie:** Bring it. Make it strong and keep it on. At least I'll be able to see you moving away.
**Jim:** I've got a friend. His father was a miner. He's in the clothes trade now. He's got a bug about face-lifting all the crumpled elements in our society, taking the last ounce of sloppiness and dross from the darker lives and swilling it away.
**Mollie:** Boy, what a sluice he'll need for that!

(*She sings*)

199

## LET'S FACE IT CHAPS

Oh, let's face it chaps,
There's a million gaps
In the citadel of beauty.
So, forward march
Through the victory march
To do our cleansing duty,

Bring a little grace
To each ravaged face
Some starch to each dropping body
And please restore
To the senile bore
The elfin charm of Noddy

Make a lighted room
Of the urban gloom
A bower of every slum street
Awake from sleep
The complacent creep
With a fine resounding drum-beat.

Pull up the screens
Round the fallen queens
With a courtesy grave and tender
Stitch back the wings
On the ruined kings
And robe them again in splendour

Guide the groping hands
Of over-active glands
Give us peace and reasonable scope
Arrange with the grid
To overheat the id
Make sizzling reality of hope

Tear off the tag
From the bag and the lag
Make everyone resurgent

From the stain and slime
Of trouble and time
With the great and last detergent

Let's face it, lads
Most mums and dads
Are lost in a thicket of worry
And worry kills
Like plague or chills
So hurry, boys, please hurry

We've grown so mean
Who'll take us clean
To the citadel of beauty
Down the magic lane
To the citadel of beauty.

**Jim:** My friend plans a chain of Paris gown-shops up and down the valleys. A fainting deacon given away with every plunging cleavage. He could find a sweet job for you in that outfit.

**Mollie:** (*becoming suddenly enthusiastic*) I think he could, too. I can see that. I can really see that. To give women a wider sky of grace, to make sure that never again will they be bent old women at forty. Up there, in those hillside streets behind all the rain and the rent and rubble is the ghost of a great, lost beauty. That's one bit of patching I'd like to do.

**Jim:** It could give your life a lovely new twist, a job like that.

**Mollie:** That's one bit of patching I'd really like to do. Patches enough to transform.

(*Her face is radiant with the dream. A sweet, languorous melody is heard. The whole stage darkens, but* Mollie *remains luminous. The street lightens.* Mollie *goes out into it. Down the street come two dim figures, a man and a woman, old, bent, ragged. They pass each other by with the indifference of death.* Mollie *dances round them. The movement of her hands suggests that she is trying to distil the essence of the music and pour it like a fairy-tale elixir. The two old people stop. They begin to be transformed. They straighten up. The illusion of rags gives way to an illusion of sleek elegance.*

*They embrace and dance. A pair of authentically young lovers drifts dancing down the street. They are stared at with daring desire by the transformed ancients, eager even now to extend the range of their potency. Each pairs off with a new partner and as soon as they feel the fresh arms around them the curve, the tatters and sadness of age return. The young ones flee and the ancients are left doing a little melancholy gavotte, staring at each other with a timid, tentative compassion. As the light returns and* Mollie *falls still, her expression is of some interest. First, a sort of rage at seeing on how short a tether magic operates; then a kind of amused satisfaction at having prophesied on how brittle a rainbow any dreams she and* Jim *might have are bound to rest. She looks around. Her face resumes its sadness. She throws her arms up and makes a derisive Ya-ya sort of sound.)*

**Mollie:** Odd job woman for a citadel of beauty. Talk like that should be left inside the heart. It's safer behind the mouth. It's bad to hear what your dreams have to say. They should be drowned like kittens you can't afford to keep.
**Bryn:** What's this now? Kittens? Drowned?
**Mollie:** I was talking about dreams.
**Bryn:** Oh, aye. Very difficult to keep housebound, cats and dreams.
**Glyn:** Guess who we met ten minutes ago.
**Jim:** Who?
**Bryn:** The trustees of the chapel that Nimrod once had. They were there, slouch hats very straight on their heads, sniffing around as if they were on the track of some old, old scent.
   *(There is a rumpus from the bingo hall. The three* boxers *come shooting forth.)*
**Mollie:** What's up now?
**Pancho:** Three or four tables in the far corner. They never win. We try to fix it for them, now and then, to make a phoney killing, but our fingers are clumsy with the tickets. And they are chaps who lost a good few quid on the last fights we had. And now, some nights they remember and want to pitch into us.
**Nimrod:** *(his voice heard from the bingo hall)* Peace, peace, you lightless dogs. You have made your terms with mental death. If you want to disturb the great kingdom of torpor, do it with amiability. Let us respect each other's obituaries, for God's sake.

202

No flapping of wet shrouds in the face of friends.

(*The* boxers *get drinks from the bar, sit down and begin a little sequence of dreaming.*)

**Willie:** There was a day I was so fast in the ring, do you know what was my biggest difficulty? The ref peering in close to see what I was up to. Slowed me down. Worried in case I connected with the peering ref. Did it once. Got me a bad name.

**Pancho:** There was a day . . . (*Bemused, he puts his hand to his head*) There was a day when all the lights, ALL the lights were on in here. Once I could see a thought, plain. I could walk behind it. Yes, I had thoughts. I still have them. But they are in a mist, in disguise or in hiding. Even when I see one and it beckons me to follow, I can't move. Oh, I was real punchy once. In a shop a till would go, and I would be in action. Flattened many a shop-keeper. Confused trade round Penygraig. I can tell you.

**Tiger:** There was a day. Everything was friendship. Everywhere was cheers. No people crowding around cursing and frowning like they do now. No kids coming around to try out some new punch on you when you're not looking. And never any need for booze because tomorrow always tasted all right.

**Pancho:** Alfie, the Mighty Atom, was right. He vanished.

**Willie:** That's what we should do, one day. Those people . . . (*He points at the bingo hall*) Those people are going to come awake. They won't have enough money for another stake. Wffie will have fixed it so that nobody wins. He'll have taught them to enjoy the slogans. Then they'll come awake.

**Pancho:** And they'll remember that this used to be a chapel and that Nimrod used to be a preacher. And they'll want to wash off the starved years with a real shower of Christian wrath. They'll want a sacrifice. And Nimrod and Willie and Tiger and me will wind up hanging from the beer pumps.

**Willie:** We should have gone like Alfie the Atom went, before the lights went dim and the sweetness sighed off.

(*The* boxers *put their heads together and join a sweet little lament*)

**Boxers:** There was a day when the air was wine
Not a fear in sight and the day was fine
Hope in abundance, no need for booze
Double breasted waistcoats and chamois-leather shoes
And a civilised ref who stopped counting at nine . . .

**Jim:** Nonsense, I have a friend . . .

**Mollie:** Another friend.

**Jim:** Another friend.

**Mollie:** You've got friends. Nobody can have as many friends as you and be normal.

**Jim:** He's planning a big holiday camp about twelve miles along the coast from here for people who don't want to go the whole holiday hog and have air that's absolutely fresh. He's got a mania about training the young in wholesome activities. Kind of penitence. He was the hub of an utterly corrupted Boy Scout group and he wants to make amends. He wants three physical instructors to guide the young campers toward the right kind of virtuous physical jerk. He'd jump at the chance of having you boys. Just imagine the gym there with pictures of you in your prime all round the walls. Just imagine it. The kids queuing up for your autographs again.

(*The* boxers *look imbecilically jubilant. Then their faces drop simultaneously with a kind of pitiable violence.*)

**Boxers:** We don't dare to leave Wffie.

**Bryn:** Oh, leave anybody, boy. Life's fissile.

**Mollie:** Wffie's got them brainwashed. On the subject of him they talk in a kind of shampoo.

**Glyn:** Suds everywhere.

**Wyn:** Used to taking the tattoo of commands that Wffie rattled at them as they sat on that little stool between the rounds.

**Jim:** You remember the last time you fought? The three of you on the bill?

**Wyn:** I can remember the headline now: 'Wales emerges as world force — The valley's fists of fate'.

**Mollie:** I made the knicks for them. White silk and I sewed their names on in letters of dark blue satin.

**Glyn:** On limbs chafed by childhood flannel, silk is a mocker.

**Boxers:** We remember, Mollie. The shiningest knicks that ever we wore.

**Pancho:** The silk will bring you luck, you said. You kissed the silk that spelled our names and you said, "This'll bring you luck."

**Wyn:** We followed you out of the train at Paddington.

**Glyn:** You walked down the platform with a real strut.

**Wyn:** We were glad for you.

**Bryn:** We wanted you to flatten the world.

**Wyn:** You were like bull-fighters marching into the ring.

**Glyn:** Like we saw them in that picture where Valentino falls in love and loses his footwork.

**Wyn:** Your walk was proud and marvellous and smooth.

*(The three* boxers *line up. The hold their towels as if they were tiny cloaks. They begin to march like the first rank of a caudrilla to the raucous sound of one of the popular Spanish marches.)*

**Willie:** And old Rufus Royle, our old second, stood just behind you shaking his head and saying that kissed knicks meant trouble.

**Glyn:** That's been known.

**Mollie:** Rufus knew. Rufus didn't know much but he was strong on knicks and kisses.

**Jim:** The three of you were knocked out in the space of an hour.

**Bryn:** I can see the headline: 'Celts rocked in actionful night'. You went down like corn. We wanted the referee searched in case he was shooting you.

**Wyn:** It was in and out. It was like a sequel to one of those old hunger marches. It was as if London wanted all the Welsh in one place, unconscious at the same moment.

**Glyn:** It was like the wrath of Moses falling upon us for all our sins of drinking and loving.

**Jim:** (*producing a newspaper cutting from his pocket*) This was what an American sports writer, Joe Springler, said about you . . .

**Pancho:** An American wrote about us?

**Jim:** Don't be too happy about it. This boy is strictly from the Sioux. (*He reads from the cutting*) "Three fighters on the bill, Celts called Thomas, Powell and Rees, turned their backs on every basic rule ever propounded on the subject of self-defence. The sight of them in the roped square suggested a new cowboy top-pop — 'Empty craniums in the old corral'. They were either pepped up on the same death wish, banner bearers for Dr Edith Summerskill, or converts to Ghandi. Their manager, Theophilus Wffie Morgan, who was at the ring-side, sounding off with more advice than Benjamin Franklyn, must be the supreme master of misdirection. Either that or he has taken out some meaty policies on the lives of these three gladiators. If the knockout can be said to give excitement and value to pugilism, then Theophilus Wffie Morgan should be given the prize as the game's top benefactor of this or any other year. If he had persuaded his fighters to swill their mouths with ether between rounds he would not have guided them more swiftly into a coma."

(*The three* boxers *shake their heads dumbly.* Jim *looks at them, in despair at their genial but impenetrable faces.*)

**Jim:** I'll set it to music later and it'll get through. Just hold your brains steady. Listen, Willie. A week after that fight Wffie bought his first fruit and vegetable business from the bets he laid against you. You were the first cauliflowers on his stall. (Nimrod *comes in from the bingo hall.*) That Wffie's made a tunnel for you all and he plans to be the only one to see the light. What about getting you out of it? Nimrod, Wffie's done his bit of first-aid on you. He's got you back to the crawling stage of convalescence. Now what about a full emancipated trot?

**Nimrod:** Oh no. My fall took me too near the bottom. My feet could never be at ease again on the surface I fell from.

**Jim:** Your feet are new, Nimrod, and surfaces are always changing.

**Nimrod:** No. I put too much talent into the muck-up I made. It was a big production, Mr Bumford, a first feature. I could never assemble the materials, never get the backing again. It was a fireworks night of folly that made night light and left a darkness of irremediable density. I could never again face the people who saw my disgrace.

**Mollie:** I bet they've been waiting ever since, tensed up for the next instalment.

**Nimrod:** No, no. Leave me here. What's wrong with tunnels? A single shout can bring yourself back loud on every echo and that's what it all amounts to anyway. To keep the voice that comes back to you from the dark, that's something. After some of the voices I've heard. And darkness is a sprouting soil. Leave me here. I took a gulp of death. Let the thing digest.

**Jim:** That's too simple. You are letting your life go at bargain rates. You put on an entertainment. Get paid. When a man takes the trouble to smash himself up it usually changes the people who see it for the better. The grief of others is a universal tonic. There should be a toll-gate at the portals of every broken heart because every splintered life serves to amuse or improve a thousand callous sons of bards who drop in to see what they can do to help

206

deepen the trouble.

**Bryn:** I bet he could even do something to help those chapel trustees, poor dabs. Something to set their old slouches on a slant, something to hang a fringe of hair on their sad old selves of slate.

**Glyn:** Let's go out and look for them.

**Wyn:** This is a big town and they are small trustees with tiny wishes. You'd need Elijah and Geiger both carrying counters to track them down.

**Bryn:** You, Mollie, do something with your mind or your voice to bring them in.

**Mollie:** (*cupping her mouth with her hands, moving slowly round and beginning to shout*) Hey there, trustees, grey moths, sad men! The light is on. Fly in, grey moths, sad men!

(*At that moment just the prim, grey slouches of the trustees appear around the corner of the street. Their gait, as they approach the club, suggests a griping timidity.*)

**Bryn:** A flag of truce is whitening the old black hat of self-denial.

**Mollie:** Come in, gentlemen.

(*The trustees enter. A mood of melodious conviviality is established. They sing the 'Oblivion Song'. It might swing between extremes of tempo, fast for the need for oblivion, slow for the inevitability of remembrance. The trustees to their utter amazement are whipped into a kind of mazurka by Susie and Eirlys.*)

OBLIVION SONG

**Trustees:** The good old mind would ache no more
If remembrance stopped at the night before
The itching past would no longer tease yer
If the National Health dished out amnesia

The little old griefs, love's old aroma
They could all do with a slice of coma
For an hour the mind can be dim and numb
With a slug of Scotch or a red hot rum
A roll on the mat with some awful crumb
And you think the bailiff will never come
Then the wind strikes an old, old note
And flicks the old drowned dreams afloat.

You glimpse the moon upon the sea
You find the wall where he stood by me
And flesh, in loneliness, recalls the heat
That brought its magic to a winter street
And flesh in tears recalls the thrills
Of wild love loping through childhood's hills
Cuddling up as the sun went down
Dodging the elders' bowlered frown
Cuddling down as the daylight burst
Still dreaming of bliss but knowing the worst.
You find the walk among the trees
Where the first little kiss brought the first unease
That brought my spirit to its knees
And made my life a long, long, crawl
That seems to have no end at all.

BUT the good old mind would ache no more
If remembrance stopped at the night before.

**Trustees:** Do you remember us, Mr Pym?
**Nimrod:** No. I'd like to, you understand, but I don't. I've put a lot of the past under darkness.
**First Trustee:** We're the new trustees of your old chapel. Elected last month.
**Second Trustee:** You must have read about it in the papers. Your successor was expelled for beating a drum up and down the main street to bring attention to God's grace.
**First Trustee:** It is a narrow street. It was a loud drum. God's grace was not much in evidence.
**Second Trustee:** The old trustees drove the man forth. We heard from Glyn and Bryn that you were here. We want you back, Mr Pym.
**Jim:** Will you let him have the drum?
**First Trustee:** No. We have subsidence and migraine, both sensitive to drum-beats. But we want him back.
**Nimrod:** Why?
**First Trustee:** You started a new thing among us, Mr Pym, whose end you didn't wait to see. You lifted an ice-cap. The strong-hearted began to feel. The flinty-faced began to smile. Through the night we could hear a tide of cramp rolling back.

Flesh creaked and undertakers wept as life stepped up to take its first decent bow since Calvin started planting ice-cubes.

**Second Trustee:** We searched for you, Mr Pym. We want you back. We want the full life, Mr Pym, but within the framework of modesty, of course.

**First Trustee:** We'd like a touch of warmth, Mr Pym, and a few bars of cordial music.

(Bryn *has gone to stand by the bass drum. He begins to give out a muffled beat.*)

**Wyn:** Drums between inclosing hills. Do you remember the summer of the carnivals, half a lifetime ago?

**First Trustee:** Recall them? Recall them! My eyes still blink from the strain of keeping them half-closed when I saw that band of harem-girls from Trecysgod. Hardly anything on but a suggestion of sand. Our first intimation as Congregationalists of the troubles that scourge the Mahometan Middle east.

**Bryn:** Too skimpy, those veils.

**Glyn:** And they were very weak on the musical side.

**Wyn:** They were tone-deaf with shame.

**Second Trustee:** They were led by a man on a camel borrowed from a bankrupt menagerie. One of the only two men in a band of women. He needed the camel, poor dab. He could hardly walk.

**First Trustee:** The other man was the bass-drummer. He could hardly reach the pig-skin with his drumstick.

**Wyn:** Great bodies of men marching through an everlasting summer. Dressed in costumes that had never been seen before, have never been seen since.

**Glyn:** A band dressed as Eskimos from a village where they had abandoned chips for blubber.

**Wyn:** A band dressed as pygmies from a village where the Celts were unusually squat.

**Bryn:** And all of us playing gazookas. (Bryn, Glyn *and* Wyn *take gazookas from their pockets and start playing 'Moonlight and Roses'.*) That was the theme song of our band, the Meadow Prospect Gondoliers. The place was subject to flooding, so we combined playing with rowing.

**Jim:** My father was the drum major of the Penygraig Grenadiers. Went so straight and stiff with all the saluting and marching he was never able to go back to his previous work which called for a lot of bending. Maddened himself with his antics with that pole.

Became sexually aggressive. And proud! Like a Pharaoh. He died ordering two York hams for his own funeral tea and a pyramid for his ceremonial rest.

(*While* Jim *is saying this, the* rugby boys *will have swung into some fitting grenadier-music on their gazookas and* Jim *will have done some of the actions, strutting and staff-throwing, suggested by his story.*)

**Bryn:** The throb of the drums in the sunlit mornings.

**Glyn:** Through all the valleys, drums and moving men.

**Mollie:** My mother marched in front of the Ynysmaerdy Toreadors. She was Carmen. Red shawl and swaying a treat. A red rose in her mouth. Ate her way through two rose gardens. Gave the Welsh urge its finest airing since the introduction of flannel. Had the deacons demanding that greenfly and blight be placed high on every agenda. She inflamed a pickle manufacturer who was a judge at one of the carnivals. He set her up in a love-nest down here. He wanted to have a red rose perpetually in her mouth. She developed a rash that goes with over-exposure to chlorophyl. He went back to his pickles and she ran out of the nest room.

**First Trustee:** What was your role in these carnivals, Mr Pym?

(Nimrod *shakes his head in a massive NO.*)

**Second Trustee:** You look a bit like that chap on the camel with the harem girls.

(Nimrod *repeats his gestures of negation.*)

**First Trustee:** We want that banging gaiety and noise back, Mr Pym. We want *you* back, Mr Pym.

(Nimrod *again shakes his head in agonised rejection.*)

**Mollie:** But they searched for you, Mr Pym. They searched for you. Like we searched for the Mighty Atom. Isn't that fine?

**Pancho:** The featherweight contender.

**Eirlys:** The wandering boy.

**Mollie:** I bet there's somebody searching for every single one of us. Isn't that fine?

**Nimrod:** No.

**Mollie:** Eyes getting nearer every day, getting more tender the nearer they get. Isn't that fine?

**Nimrod:** (*startled*) NO! Do you . . . do you know what happened to me?

**First Trustee:** We know. We've gone over the details of your

210

past with the same fine attention we gave to the chapel accounts. The faith needs men like you, Mr Pym.

**Second Trustee:** You've faced the lions, Mr Pym. You wear a sort of dark tooth-marks. Nice change from the old blank serge. With you we'll make the temple of a new saintliness.

**First Trustee:** When you preach, we'll have sin with us, like a tamed dog. And these girls . . .

**Wyn:** (*pointing to each as he mentioned her name*) Mollie, Susie, Eirlys.

**First Trustee:** Sweet singers. With these girls as gospel singers we could double the collections and give the gospels an extra glow that would help us buy the freehold of the chapel.

**Nimrod:** And from the zone of blindness sprouts the eye. (*He turns his head slowly round*) No. I see nothing more clearly now than I did before. (*He looks courteously at the* trustees) When the door opens there will be a great clang of daftness. You boys are not daft, neither do you clang. I shall fetch you all the drink of your fancy.

(*As* Nimrod *starts his journey to the bar,* Wffie *comes leaping into the club, his arms out and his body bent as if all set to launch some great pantomime of denunciation. The flaming of his eyes is mainly for* Jim. *The* trustees *are startled.*)

**First Trustee:** If sin of the less seemly sort is about to erupt, we must leave.

(*The* trustees *creep out sadly.*)

**Second Trustee:** (*turning at the door*) Even in the minds of men waiting for a world reborn there's still a place for a bit of caution.

(Wffie *points at* Jim *a finger that twitches with apocalyptic wrath.*)

**Wffie:** A talented boy, this one. I'm talented too. Expelled from the County School for selling fifty quid's worth of their books, but only about the subjects I loathed. The only matriculant of my time in the Approved School. When I told the Warden, 'I've matriculated', he sent me to the lavatory. Always speak clearly, I've learned that. But I'm not in the same class as this waldo. He wrote a book. So full of dirt it is called 'The Smallholding'. About a Welsh tycoon in London. Dairies, department stores, blocks of flats. Even tried to buy the Thames but the ghost of Evan Roberts, the Revivalist, frank and depressed for once, told him there was no future in water. And he swung like a trapeze artist between beer and sex. Every time he finished a long randy, he'd found a missionary college to cool off. Bumford here wrote the book about him. A real dirty book. Serialised in a popular Sunday paper but they switched back to simple rape after the second instalment.

**Bryn:** Boast back. Say something to make Wffie feel *little*.

**Jim:** (*a trifle gropingly*) It was a good book. It would have done something to swill a little of the dirt and shame of us all, all us people who grew up like fungus in the chapel gloom. All the things that have prevented us from growing into a proper song, the rustle of serge and censure, and hymnals that put a silence on our dreams. It was a disgraceful book. It was banned. But it had an edge of rage about it that would have sliced away a lot of our abasement.

**Wffie:** I'll do that twice as well without putting pen to paper. What can you *know*? What can you *say* to us?

**Mollie:** (*savagely*) That's it. What can you *know*?

**Susie** and **Eirlys:** Yes, what can you *say* to us?

**Bryn:** Always we were waiting for Moses to come down from the mountain.

**Glyn:** With the tablets, with the truth. Do you want a hand with them, Mr Bumford?

**Wffie:** Are you still in touch with the truth, watcher? You wait. He'll go plop and fade away. He's not in our orbit at all.

**Jim:** Oh yes, I belong to your root. From the start I've breathed your air. I know my version of the score. For years I've been as scagged and scuffed as the rest of you. I stand on the same shore, waiting for salvation. My father was the caretaker of the chapel.

**Bryn:** Honourable trade, caretaker.

**Wffie:** I bet the chapel got away from him.

**Jim:** No, it was one of the less mobile sects. He was a mean, timid, defeated man. I don't know what he was paid but we had so little to eat the mice shook their heads at us as we passed. He served me up as a kind of scapegoat to the wrath of the sidesmen and elders. If there was any disturbance among the kids in the gallery they would not look for the real area of guilt. They would lead me forth. I can hear the rustle of their thick, sombre suits even now and feel their great calloused clouting hands on my face.

**Bryn:** Very exciting to a man living without love, lashing out at the young.

**Jim:** And my father with the best he could do in the way of a smile, urging them on to cleanse me of insolence. He died of a surfeit after winning two pounds of baked meats for a prize poem denouncing lechery and fattening foods. I was adopted by one of my teachers.

**Wffie:** Local boy makes good.

**Jim:** He changed my accent. With him I learned to write and travel. He converted one half of me to the new good life. But the other half was anchored to the stupid past. I never lost the quake in my bowels. Time and again with fame and total transformation in my grasp, the old terror would call round and choke me. But now I'd like to see you destroyed, Wffie. Because you like to see people shorter and meaner than they really need to be. You want to aggravate the inward quake that's bitched up ninety-nine per cent of us.

**Wffie:** He was invited to Hollywood but they couldn't find the right sort of culvert for him to work in. He almost starved. The tycoon whistled him back. The tycoon is dying. He wants to do something to protect and preserve the chapel innocence of his childhood. So he hires Bumford to do an exposure of us to sweeten his dusk and make monkeys out of us. Oh, he'd whip us all into a pretty picture. (*To the* boxers) He'd work you stumble-bums into the joke of the year. (*To* Eirlys *and* Susie) And he'd wire you two into a sweet bouquet. He's been makng offers, hasn't he? He's been running up the curtain on fancy dreams, hasn't he? Come on, tell me now. He came here with a box full of draws. What were they now?

(*As his finger swings questioningly round they reply in flattish tones as if they are already appalled by the suspicion that* Jim *might be no more than a demented liar.*)

**Pancho:** Holiday camp for us. Physical instuctors. Wholesome activities. He said you sold our last fight.

**Susie:** Marriage to decent, hard-working men.

**Eirlys:** Gospel singers in a redecorated temple. They were the trustees you saw here.

**Mollie:** A throne in the fashion trade in the valleys. Give back beauty to graceless lives.

**Wffie:** (*delighted, prancing up to* Nimrod) And you, and you? This is going to be the richest of the lot. (Nimrod *remains still and utterly silent.*) But later you'll tell. Because telling for you is the last, lovely liqueur. (*To* Mollie) He'd have loved telling the tycoon about you. A throne on the rag-trade in townships that couldn't tell a sari from a sack, where they take as much trouble being immunised against beauty as against bubonic. Take your head out of the ether, Mollie. The gutter here fits you like a glove. In the long run a cosy gutter's a fair accommodation. Leave here and if you didn't die of frost-bite you'd be rejected and hounded so fast you'd be back here screaming in a week, asking me to tape the bits of your heart together. If Mr Bumford wants you, let him take you. You're in the window. You've got your tag. You're not too dear. Wffie's against inflation. He doesn't have to shoot you all this bull to get you into the horizontal.

**Glyn:** Make Wffie feel little again, Mr Bumford.

**Jim:** All our lives we've specialised in producing people who make a mess of other people's talents. We have been ruled by two types of pest. One that saw everything from the view-point of heaven and denied every vestige of grace. The other is you, Wffie, and all those who see everything from the viewpoint of the gutter. The only gutter is the cowardice that makes us tolerate those who think we belong there. Give us time, Wffie, and we'll flush you away. (*To* Mollie, Susie *and* Eirlys) We had a vision of freedom. The light gave out. We didn't have enough knowledge, enough simple fitness in the tanks to keep the vision clear. This man grew out of the darkness. The earth is full of roads of escape from what we are. I hope to God this isn't nonsense. (*He turns to the* rugby boys) Is this nonsense?

**Bryn, Glyn** and **Wyn:** No notion.

**Bryn:** But keep it up, Mr Bumford. Torment Wffie.

**Glyn:** Set his mind prowling.

**Wyn:** Set his thoughts glowing in the dark.

**Wffie:** (*laughing*) Watch them glow. I love my dark. It fits, it hides. It's fine when you know that you yourself, joyfully, put out the lights. Could never afford it, really, the light. Tender eyes, tough desires.

**Bryn:** Good combination, that. Isn't there anywhere else to go then, Wffie, except where the first pointing finger said we should?

**Wffie:** Of course there are roads, of course there are escapes. (*To* Susie *and* Eirlys) The chapel trustees have plenty of respectable earth for the growing of clean, new lives — and after a fortnight you'd be planting the trustees in it. Gospel singers? And I know

214

what you'd be doing between the verses. You'd be working your way through the diaconate, then through the tenors and baritones in the gallery. Either you'd be put down by the County Health Committee or torn apart by a mob of militant Calvinists.

**The Girls:** Have courage, my boy, to say No.

**Wffie:** And by God it's 'No' they'd say. That's what most of the boyos on this earth most like saying. They see a bit of warmth, a bit of joy, and they're not happy until they've covered it over with the ash of NO, NO, NO.

**Jim:** And you. You'd cover it over with something worse than ash. Before, we were crouched. You'd have us prostrate. You are the ultimate rat, Wffie. You are the real agent of indignity and death. We have been deformed by a lack of confidence and worldiness. The men who led us made us tidy fools, restricted, wasted lives, but, by God, laundered well and buttoned up to the neck. You, Wffie, would make us degraded fools. Between the strangling net of respectability our elders wove for us, spotting girls pregnant out of wedlock as we now spot birds, between them and the sort of squalor you peddle here, there is some wise, joyful medium.

**Wffie:** Rubbish. Extremities are the only guarantee against collapse. We support our arches on fanatical assertions of vice or virtue. I know. I've been under a few fallen arches. (*To the* boxers) So I sold you down the river? Let me tell you I couldn't have sold you up a river or down, not even if there were a famine on and men were potatoes. Your reflexes have been following guide-dogs since you were born. Even now you've got to take two tries at your trousers when you dress of a morning. I only let you wear boxing gloves to keep you in trim for the waiting lark. If Mr Bumford gets you taken on as organisers of wholesome activities for the young, we are going to see the biggest generation of cripples since they patented rickets. Wffie's the only friend you'll ever know. Wffie's the only sky you'll ever be safe under. And Alfie Childs, my little Alfie, the Mighty Atom, a bigger miracle than Wilde, has to vanish off the face of the earth, and you pin-headed oxen have to survive. Who puts the poison in the broth? (*To* Nimrod) And even you caught a glimpse of the sun. You feel you could look the world boldly in the eye again. You feel you could walk up the steps of a pulpit again, Nimrod? They want a full account of what went on in that Meths school under the bridge, and you will give it to them.

**Pancho:** You should not do that to Mr Pym, Wffie.

**Wffie:** I'll do that and worse. I'll provide this damned peeping Jim with so much dirt, they'll ban his next book before his pen hits the paper. You want to know things, don't you, Mr Bumford? All right, find out what your master thinks of you now. Go on, watcher, ring him up.

(Wffie *is wearing the grin of a honeymooning wolf.* Jim *has lost every bit of his assurance. He looks stricken and fearful.* Mollie *smiles at him and points to a telephone in niche near door to bingo-room.*)

**Mollie:** (*as* Jim *stands still, fascinated by the menace in* Wffie's *voice*) Go on, ring. Don't mind him. He's been standing in the wind. His tiles are falling.

**Glyn:** Go on, ring.

**Wyn:** Never be afraid of thrusting your arm out into the world.

**Bryn:** The worst that can happen is that you won't get it back.

**Mollie:** What's the matter with you? Move, man!

**Jim:** My feet won't budge. The mine-field, remember?

**Mollie:** He's no bomb. (*She points at* Wffie) He's just a liar, like you. Whatever you hit each other with, it won't be true. Go on, phone. You may hear the one thing that may make some sense out of all these lies. Go on. You'll hear the word that'll push you in the last, the right direction.

**Bryn:** Go on, Jim. Don't be afraid.

**Wyn:** You know more than Wffie, and knowledge will win the world.

**Glyn:** My old dad said that, though he was dull as a bat most of the time.

**The Boxers:** You can eat him, Jim.

**Wffie:** (*handing* Mollie *a slip of paper*) This is the number. Get it.

(Mollie *goes to the phone.*)

**Wyn:** He'll hear the voice of the great man on the telephone, shouting his hallelujah news.

**Glyn:** Re-birth will be rampant.

**Bryn:** Rivers of gold and joy will flow through every kitchen.

**Mollie:** (*returning to* Jim's *side*) I've got your number. Get off this raft and into safety.

**Jim:** (*with miraculous fresh strength*) I think you're right, Wffie. Prepare to be eaten. I feel some final bit of luck filtering into my finger-tips. We're going to show ignorance and vulgarity the door. (*He goes to the phone.*)

**Bryn:** That's the programme. There won't be much left, but it'll be a big reform.

**Wyn:** The television adverts will take over from the facts.

**Bryn:** The brain resting on a bed of chocolate creams.

**Glyn:** Doubt going down for the third time in a sea of suds.

(Jim *looks as if a bullet has shot out of the phone's ear-piece.*)

**Rugby Boys:** Hullo!!

**Bryn:** We're back to form.

**Wyn:** We've come to the end of the opium.

**Glyn:** The chimney's coming through the roof.

**Jim:** He's dead. The tycoon is dead.

**Wyn:** What from, then?

**Jim:** He was knocked down by a taxi in St James's Square.

**Wffie:** I wished him to die. My club licence includes witchery. And what's more, I've got a brother with a taxi in St James's Square. You can never have too many brothers.

**Jim:** (*softly, pathetically*) He was going to set me up. He would have set you all up.

**Mollie:** To be in and out of people's dreams, that's bed-hopping. Why don't you take up pigeons?

**Bryn:** The worst thing out for flat feet.

**Wffie:** Now, Nimrod, get that white towel back over your arm and restore the headstone of hopeless repentance to your brow. And you, (*to the* boxers) bounce this snooper out of here so hard he'll tamp against the arch at Chepstow.

**Nimrod:** (*picking up his towel and throwing it down*) I'm going, Wffie.

**Wffie:** You dare not.

**Mollie:** What's to stop him? What's to stop any of us?

**Wffie:** He killed a man. And not just any man. He killed Alfie Childs, the Mighty Atom, the loveliest boy that ever breathed.

**Nimrod:** Me? Kill Alfie? What is this now?

**Wffie:** It was when you were tapering off. He tried to help you. You hit him with a bottle.

**Mollie:** Are you lying, Wffie?

**Wffie:** Who is he to care? Where is Alfie Childs to care?

**Nimrod:** He's somewhere. Somewhere in that night, Alfie Childs is stirring.

**Bryn:** Alfie's still about.

**Nimrod:** (*grimly*) I shall find him. I condemn you, Wffie Morgan, and in the night through which I shall walk, I shall arrange for your certain destruction.

(Wffie *goes for* Nimrod, *but the* boxers *intercept him and with a slow and perfect rhythm they proceed to belt the lights out of him, passing him from one to the other, dealing him every foul, forbidden punch in the game, to the back of his neck, the kidneys, the whole paralysing lot.*)

**Boxers:** After that last fight, Wffie, we read a book — we found what we should have done. This, Wffie, and this, and this.

**Mollie:** (*regarding the prostrate* Wffie) And again we have made a call. Someone will give an answer.

(*Reprise of the theme of 'The Wandering Boy'. The light in the street becomes intense. Into the street come the* old women. *They are walking backwards, staring, as if they have just seen a great portent. They stop and at that instant a seraphic figure appears in the street. It is* Alfie Childs.)

**Mollie:** It's Alfie!

**Bryn:** It's the Atom!

**Glyn:** The same weight.

**Susie:** The same smile.

(*The* boxers *put the semi-conscious* Wffie *to rest on a chair at the table.* Pancho *takes a large 'Reserved' ticket and puts it out in front of* Wffie. *They all escort* Alfie *into the club. He takes* Mollie *by the hand and goes to the table at which* Wffie *is just barely managing to keep off the floor.*)

**Mollie:** Where have you been, then?

**Alfie:** I have been up in the hills, the far hills.

**Wyn:** Fighting?

**Alfie:** Dear me, no violence. I have been the tea-boy to a group of monks. We are trying to build a monastery, as an alternative to light industry.

**Wyn:** Well, well. Monks!

**Alfie:** It's nice to see Wffie quiet. He should always be quiet like this. Let's take him back to the mountains and the quiet people. They need a challenge, someone to badger their silence. He's the one.

**Wffie:** (*opening one eye*) Oh, God. Ghosts now.

**Alfie:** It's quiet there, Mollie. The sins and the fidgets will fall from Wffie like old leaves. It's time for Wffie to be quiet.

**Bryn:** Why are you back then, Alfie?

**Alfie:** Two weeks leave from the Settlement's Missionary tour and collecting funds for the quiet people. There's not much profit in purity. How are your funds?

**Bryn:** Very frail, boy, very frail. But keep up the good work. There's a big future for quietness.

(*They walk out into the street.* Mollie *is propelling* Alfie *in a quite decisive way.*)

**Mollie:** Wffie? Quiet?

(*She shakes her head. The combo begins whatever is the most evocative piece of music, whatever best suggests that she, to the very end of her compassionate days, will never cease to create, lose and re-create all the dreams of the world.*)

**Mollie:** Alfie!

**Alfie:** Yes, Mollie?

**Mollie:** Keep walking, Alfie. Before he sets eyes on you. Never come back. Wherever you've been, never come back.


(Alfie *walks away up the street.* Nimrod, Susie, Eirlys, *the* boxers *and the* rugby boys *all follow him, suggesting some sort of exultant, religious procession. He points them back to the club. As he vanishes, the balance of light between street and club is restored to the club.*

Wffie *is still in his chair, not aware of very much.* Nimrod *and the* boxers *do a balletic routine around* Wffie, *flicking him back to life with their towels.* Susie *puts one of the comic straw hats on his head.* Mollie *offers* Jim *another of the hats and eyes him quizzically. He just lifts it in salute and leaves.* Mollie *goes to the window and hums or sings 'Mollie's Song'. She stands at the window and moves her body as she sees* Jim *disappear. Then she jumps fiercely around and there is a short passionate snatch of the 'Bounce' theme with which the play opens.*)

Curtain

219

# Appendices

## Introduction to The Keep

Some families burst apart like bombs and never again achieve unity. Others grow circular, deep like old ponds. The family in this play, the Mortons, are like that. They are intelligent, fairly gifted people, yet all, except one, conscious that they are creating for themselves a sort of velvet tomb.

The play is a May-day parade of our more twitching neuroses. The Mortons move dimly behind a veil of sardonic anguish. Their laughter is of a savage suddenness that makes the ghosts of their old dreams spin around like shot goats.

I am myself genuinely puzzled to know how distinctively South Welsh these people are. I believe that our community, between mammoth explosions, a unique range of apocalyptic terrors, a severely trussed sensuality, an almost pathological concern with education and self-improvement, has taken on some fascinating bruises. Our traumas have the dental reach of leopards and we have a way of standing stock still and taking it when they come around for a more exhaustive nibble.

The father, Ben, is a survival of the days when our preachers, as well as our disasters, seemed to be powered by methane. In a society rachitic down to the last toe with every sort of insecurity, assurance was found in sermons of a length and sonority that reduced the collective tympanum to the quality of beaten brass. My own father used to say that he was religiously revived three times in the course of a single winter, but, he would add, that was a very cold winter. Ben, in the far past, has made a brief escape from this bondage into a pasture of sensual liberty. But self-lacerating piety is a rough but fascinating wine. Its kind of rhetoric is irreplaceable, and once a man has filled his mind with it, its echoes will hound him into and beyond the grave.

Our lives are largely attempts to lay the ghosts of massive embarrassments. Ben is the embodiment of that proposition. He has emerged from a past whose main achievement was to shatter the vessel meant for the reception of joy. One can hear the broken pieces rattling about inside Ben, but if he were to find all the fragments again and a blue-print of the original design he would not have the slightest idea of how to go about the job of salvage. Freeze a set of human fingers just once and they will never again be able to fondle the lump of living with any sense of purpose. The one lesson of our patiently laboured idiocy is that it is easier to make than to reclaim a fool.

The lives of all the Morton children are spoiled, but none on the same classically bleak plane as Ben's. The brothers, Russell, a teacher, and Wallace, a doctor, typify the strange malaise that attends the too fanatical development of talent as a social tactic. The whole of my own boyhood saw a vast cult of hatred directed against such brutalizing antics as pit-labour. The Grammar Schools were seen as escape shafts out of the tunnels of the proletariat, and high literacy was the North Star that was to guide us finally out of the night. Contempt and kicks awaited the boy who failed to make the 11-plus grade or who faltered in his march to the University. The mark of Cain was on the boy who, through mental slowness or indolence, slipped into the penumbra of shop work or the authentic shadow of the mine. Book-learning was to be the key to the New Jerusalem, and the average earnest miner saw heaven not so much in terms of release for himself from scars, hazards and petty pay, but a tidy collar and clean hands for his sons. My father carried this kind of faith so far that he forbade us to engage in any useful manual activity that might have led us into the ranks of the artisans. This induced an inertia on the physical side of our existence which more than once put the immediate future of our household in jeopardy. If a tap dripped, my father would never be in any danger of being driven mad by the drip. He would get us to recite a clutch of Latin declensions and he would be happy. We were outstripping the gentry. We were going to be real toffs. We would not have to shuffle through dawns of contempt in stinking clothes to drive a hard heading in a deep hole. We would be laundered, respected, carrying the promise of an adequate pension before us like the Holy Grail.

The dream was, of course, better than the realization. Scholarship can become a natural part of one's fabric only when there is a sense of joyous ease among one's elders, the feeling that knowledge is its own delight. Most of our education, organized on the same lines of relaxed ease as a gaol-break, was tedious toil, conducted often in bedrooms ill-equipped for study, with means of lighting that would have depressed an owl. When economies had to be made and there was no oil for the lamp, we went out and read the larger print by the light of the fuller moons, disquieting lovers around and about who were not on to the ways of the studious.

In all the sages of my South Welsh generation I detect an air of something fungoid, a suggestion that the serenity and gaiety which should be the first fruits of prolonged education have been completely left in our contemporary miscarriage of social intentions. Russell and Wallace are botched jobs of this order. They waver uncertainly between the idealism of the pioneers who hoisted them from the ranks of the morlocks and the genial banality and hedonism of the man who has put his mind out with the cat.

Alvin and Oswald are two bits of scar tissue in the con-vulsions of a society still as unable to adjust swift technological change to the need for social fairness as it is to accept that war is no longer an extension of diplomacy but merely an extension of ash and the simpler sort of *pompes funèbres*, expressed thus only because French used to be the favoured idiom of the old graveyard diplomacy. Alvin works in a small tinplate-works shortly to be devoured by a neighbouring, automated plant. Oswald works in an unimportant railway station which has become one of the most expendable out-posts of British transport. Oswald stands propped up in his ticket office holding up his tickets with the same sort of abandon as those dead *légionnaires* holding up their bayonets in the last scene of 'Beau Geste'. Oswald is a recessive. As soon as he finds the ghost, he will promptly give it up. Alvin, on the other hand, is a latent Luddite. His mind is a resonant canyon full of echoing cries from the Syndicalist age of Eugene Debs, Tom Mann and Arthur Cook, who saw a universal trade-union card as the door to paradise, and the idea of strike-action as the most significant evolutionary leap since the first ape tried to straighten his back.

The themes of waste and voluntary self-destruction obsess the great bulk of verbal art. In every human situation, however passionate the mouth's dedication to freedom and compassion, somebody is being put upon, spoiled, wasted. In this play it is the only Morton daughter, Miriam. She is the intelligent donkey, a walking reflex to the fact that her brothers become cold and hungry. She is the sardonic counter-melody to the wanton ways of male superiority. Miriam is a part of the knife that is being honed to deathly sharpness in the shadow by women everywhere for men everywhere who have had the unspeakable nerve to regard an utter frustration as the proper portion of the female.

The last brother, Con, is the archetypal pest of this and all other ages. He is the ungentle shepherd, the manipulator, who regards no other life as complete if his nose is not in it. Where most other Welshmen find a fairly cosy tomb in a conjunction of work, sex, singing and ale, Con's nerves cry out for a more sinister sublimation. The people around him he sees, not as people, but as wires which, conjoined with proper cunning, will provide just the right light and warmth that will bring Con to his full growth and puissance. Con is a pain in the neck, and if your neck doesn't feel it yet, be sure that Con will be getting in touch with you.

And then, of course, there is Mam. We do not see her in this play. She is a lustrous portrait on the wall of the Morton's parlour. Yet such a woman throbs and booms through a vast area of our South Welsh life. Creative, handsome, very often a contralto with the vocal impact of a herd of Jerseys, she will become the magnetic core of her home, exercising a pull upon her brood which will keep one side of their being vibrant and joyful. The other side, denied free communion with the rough and inconsiderate world without, will slide into the most terrible atrophy and regret. But from the outside the citadel seems firm and well.

Then of a sudden the stones of the keep begin to crumble. At the same moment, Wallace, Russell, Alvin and Oswald all feel a crazy desire to make an assertion, to give their pallid dreams an airing, to see Con flat on his Machiavellian back. They want to raise their fists and smash a hole in the old, venerable roof and have their first clear view of the sky above. Can their fists reach that high? Is the sky really there? Are their fists really there? So we come to the seminal question in all human affairs. Who is fooling whom?

# After the Chip Shop: Introduction to Jackie the Jumper

After years of writing rather quiet philosophic novels featuring no weapon deadlier than the blunter type of chip-shop fork, I had a fancy to write something gusty and rollicking, festooned with swords, horses, gibbets and mayhem in all its stock sizes. In 'Jackie the Jumper' I've broadened the social scope of my fiction. My preoccupation with proletarian characters is no longer so acute. I've pulled in people from the top levels of the bourgeoisie. The chip-shop is way, way behind.

The transition was a natural one. A life-long addiction to grand opera made it inevitable that one day I would move away from my wry chronicles of the brighter among our under-privileged. In a social ambience so emphatically tainted with lunacy as that of a mining area moving into dereliction, I took even the dottiest libretto in my stride. The plots of the early and middle Verdi in which probability stands in the centre of the stage, bow-legged and gaping, I accepted as prosaic reality. As a member of the Band of Hope junior operatic group I once played in 'Trovatore'. After years of being harassed into primness and piety by the zealots of the diaconate addressing me in Welsh, a language I did not understand, I found no difficulty in accepting that a vengeful gypsy, whose mother has been burned at the stake by a Duke, should not only wish to burn the Duke's child but actually burned her own child in error. A predilection for violence, ashes and serious mistakes overlay my entire culture.

Years later I was the tutor of a cultural group in an Educational Settlement. We were pursuing a course called 'The European Mind', which covered everything from the amoeba to the burning tip at Dinas, Rhondda, a well-known local nuisance

224

except to the chillier type of voter who wanted to be set alight by the floating embers. One evening we got on to the subject of Verdi's 'Force of Destiny', an opera in which coincidences go off like cosmic gongs. I gave the group an analysis of this work so excessively cogent it still has some of them confused. It is an epic of revenge, and seeing the world at that time as a pretty malignant parish, I had cordial feelings about revenge and I could treat with Don Alvaro and the sons of the Marquis of Calatrava as rationally as if they were fellow lodge-members. As for the heroine, Leonora, living as a hermit in that solitary grotto in the high sierra, I knew dozens of female neighbours who, psychologically, were doing just that.

At about just the same period I did service as an unpaid stage manager to a company that was frightening the wits out of audiences in the local Welfare Hall with performances of such works as 'The Dumb Man from Manchester' and 'The Crimes of Stephen Hawkes'. (Hawkes was a man who had the strength to break people's backs as others do matches and he used it.) And of course, 'Sweeney Todd'. Besides stage management and seeing that the barber's chair really tilted clients into the pieshop, I also appeared as a passing stranger who leers through the window, a kind of omen of the doom that was surely on the way. The producer was a sucker for omens and he kept me pretty busy, passing and leering. He even had me enlarge the window so that the audience could get the full flavour of what, in those days, was a savagely saturnine and disturbing face.

So, with that background, it was inevitable that I should edge my way back to melodrama, but melodrama invested with a kind of verbal dignity and a range of ideas that would have stood Todd, the demon, on his ear and reaching for the brush to stop my mouth with lather.

When I started casting about for the theme that later became 'Jackie the Jumper' I considered the possibility of a Spanish theme. This was the old early-Verdi-trauma and the baked-gypsy-motif still kicking around for laughs. I gave a thought to the revolt of the 'comuneros' in 1520, an incident in which Carlos Quinto suppressed insurrection and did a brisk undertaking job on Spanish democracy for centuries to come, and left the cadaver of a stifled radical on every tree from Cadiz to Segovia.

But my mind came back to the place where it abidingly

belongs, South Wales. I wanted a play that would paint the full face of sensuality, rebellion and revivalism. In South Wales these three phenomena have played second fiddle only to the Rugby Union, which is a distillation of all three. I wanted a theme that would illustrate this curious see-saw of passivity and defiance in human life. Why some stir it up and others allow the scum of conformity and defeat to form into a mortal pall above their heads. The urge to exult and couple at odds with the compulsive wish to geld and part. Dionysus beating the living lights out of St Paul and the other way about.

The valleys where I grew up were the classic arena of this duel. Political turbulence and a fiercely flowering libido singed the minds and the fern-beds of the zone. Time and again one would have the feeling that disgust and love had reached a climactic tumescence that would have life bursting its breeches in no time at all. Often, leaving the chapel after an interminable sermon and six rousing hymns, one would have an ache for carnal relief in some shape or form that would have bleached the deacons' bowlers if they had truly known how perverse are the tides of piety in the minds of the younger sectaries. Then in answer would come a wave of evangelism, chastening the peccant, fettering the id and spreading caution in all directions. And I, whether the cause was earthly insurrection or heavenly salvation, was always one of the leading banner-bearers. My bardic name was ambivalence.

For the story of 'Jackie the Jumper', the facts are loosely set in the context of the early Chartist movement. The Merthyr Riots, to be exact.(A South Walian carries his tally of riots around as proudly as a Tahitian would his necklace of shark's teeth.) Involved in them, by the same kind of tricky double-devotions that have been my own plague, is Jackie the Jumper. Facing him is his uncle, Richie 'Resurrection' Rees, a thundering divine. And between them the early struggles of a society tormented and besmirched by the eruption of the great iron-furnaces and the descent of the great puritanical vetoes.

226

# Notes

## The Keep

p.25   *The Cast List.* Readers may wonder about the degree of autobiographical inspiration behind this play. The author was the youngest of twelve children, of whom the first four were daughters and the next eight sons. Thomas's mother died in 1919 when he was six; the three eldest girls had left or were about to leave home, and the running of the rest of the family was taken on by the fourth girl, then aged 17. His memories of growing up therefore were essentially of a rather irresponsible and improvident father, a gang of brothers, a sister who sacrificed her own chances to look after her brothers, and a mother who vanished when he was very young. Like Russell, the author himself had written a novel in the 1930s, though this was unpublished until fifty years later and after his death; like the other brothers in the play, Thomas's brothers were intelligent, argumentative and of disparate talents: one became a local government health officer, two were teachers, several had excellent voices and one sang in opera at Covent Garden, and so on. But unlike the Mortons, the Thomas family fragmented quite early, and the young daughter who accepted the duty of replacing the mother was able in the mid-1930s to marry her sweetheart and go away to create her own family.

p.25   *Constantine.* A good choice of name for this ambitious and devious power-wielding second brother; he recalls on the one hand a great Roman Emperor while the shortened form of his name (commonly used) on the other hand evokes the wheeling-dealing confidence trickster.

p.26   *degree.* Constantine would have been working over a period of years for an external degree of London University's extension scheme, an early forerunner of the kind of system developed for the Open University in the 1970s.

p.26   *woolsack.* The large wool-stuffed cushion on which the Lord Chancellor sits in the House of Lords.

p.26   *magnesia.* A standard old-fashioned remedy for indigestion, as in 'Milk of Magnesia', frequently invoked by Thomas as a cure for both physical and mental dyspepsia.

p.26   *soup kitchen.* Places where the children of those made needy and indigent by unemployment were fed. Thomas retained particularly bitter memories of the 1921 Miners' Strike, when he and his brother Eddie were sent by their sister for food to a soup kitchen established in a chapel a hundred yards down the road.

p.27   *Constitutional Club.* Every valleys town had its club where men of different persuasions could meet to relax, discuss the times and drink at more reasonable prices than in the pubs; some wore specific political colours, while others declared themselves emphatically Non-Political, Constitutional or something such.

p.27 *Russell's novel.* In 1936-7 Gwyn Thomas wrote a novel in which Victor Gollancz was sufficiently interested to summon the young author to London to see him. Nothing came of it; Thomas reported that he had been too shy to go up the steps to Gollancz's office in Henrietta Street and had fled back to Paddington and South Wales. Gollancz entered the novel in a prize competition for a novel about unemployment, but when it failed to win he dropped it. The novel, *Sorrow for thy Sons*, was eventually rediscovered and published in 1984 in a version edited by Dai Smith.

p.28 *Belmont.* The setting for this play is a town called Belmont, which occurs also in many of Thomas's short stories written for *Punch*; there seems no reason to identify it as anything other than Porth, the Rhondda township closest to his home village of Cymmer. Anyone attempting to draw a map of the world of Gwyn Thomas's imaginations would no doubt be wise to start with an outline map of the Rhondda, Pontypridd and the Vale of Glamorgan as they are; difficulties soon arise however when one tries to say with any confidence that 'Windy Way' is Cymmer, 'Birchtown' is Pontypridd, 'Ferncleft' is Barry or whatever, for apparent clues sometimes contradict each other and in any case the real world was no more than a starting point for the author in his creation of a fictional one (see comments on location of *Jackie the Jumper* later), just as his real family was no more than a starting point for the imaginative development of possibilities that *The Keep* embodies.

p.28 *brewers' yeast.* Like magnesia, a standard recipe, in this case for enervation.

p.29 *Prospero.* Thomas's nomenclature is often perceived as a thing of joy by his admirers; his strange and alluring effects are normally achieved by giving a character a name in which one element is recognisably ordinary and Welsh, the other exotic, perhaps English, conversely mythical Welsh plus ordinary, even bathetic, English, creating a pleasing compound. Caradoc Slee in this play is a good example. Thomas also loved the Welsh habit of adding to a name a witty or rhyming or otherwise apposite qualifier: Jones the Milk at its simplest; Erasmus John the Going Gone (local auctioneer) at its most developed. In this example the fictional grandfather Morton has a first name from Shakespeare's *The Tempest* (with all its associations of magical grandeur) and a qualifier from legal jargon, *sine die* meaning that a matter is adjourned indefinitely (literally 'without day'), suggesting a man who is a true temporiser, a Fabian in fact.

p.29 *Moab.* A name for one of the many chapels in the area: Thomas drew attention to "the explosion of stone" which had taken place where every successful businessman seemed to endow yet another chapel to increase his own importance and sphere of influence. Brought up in chapel, Thomas became very suspicious of all religious belief and often wrote of the secular implications of the power gained by the faithful in the valley communities. Thomas was immensely interested in and disturbed by the proliferation of sects in the valleys, and frequently writes very satirically about some of their stranger manifestations; he frequently also takes an interest in the coincidence of religious and sexual enthusiasm, as several references in the plays in this volume demonstrate.

p.30   *Alderman*. A senior councillor, and a person of much local influence; the rank and appellation were abandoned in the late 1950s, so that a 1966 radio play by Gwyn Thomas called *The Alderman* had to have its title changed to *Testimonials* when it was adapted for the stage in 1979.

p.30   *Omdurman Row*. Thomas's predilection for exotic names was based on realities; many Rhondda streets are named for places in the Crimea or other noted sites of war, and Thomas's use of names for people or places such as Kitchener Bowen, Fashoda Terrace and so on will not necessarily seem odd to many readers.

p.30   *convenience*. Thomas sometimes made references to the large and prominent public toilets in Porth Square; he told a tale of how he had there overheard himself being discussed as a Red spy.

p.30   *Sinai*. The mountain where in *Exodus* Moses received the Ten Commandments; symbol of greatest reachable height of achievement.

p.30   *chips*. For Thomas the fundamental luxury for the indigent valley dweller.

p.30   *potatoes and the Celt*. Recalls the Irish potato famines of the nineteenth century and the consequent westward emigrations of myriads of Celts.

p.31   *Burnham Committee*. The body set up to determine teachers' pay, now replaced by a system more closely related to the government's notions.

p.31   *Thomas Malthus*. Victorian economist and prophet who warned about the consequences of over-breeding and population increases.

p.32   *Granch*. Short for Grandfather, sometimes Gran'cher'.

p.32   *divining rod*. Forked stick used to find water by sensitives.

p.33   *methane*. Gas most commonly responsible for explosions underground in the coal mining industry,

p.33   *at least five chapels*. Thomas constantly drew attention to the unnecessary proliferation of chapels throughout the valleys. *cf* note on *Moab* above.

p.33   *Frederick the Great*. Militarist emperor of Prussia.

p.34   *'send me back to January'*. i.e. 'Cool me down again, return me to winter'. Thomas regularly associated religious enthusiasm with sexual excitement, especially in many references to the Revivals of 1904 (which he had not seen) and 1921 (which he had). The idea of part of the theme of *Jackie the Jumper* and comes out especially in the portrait of Rev Resurrection Rees. *cf* note on *Moab* above.

p.35 *the 'flu epidemic*. In 1919, as if the desolation of the Great War had not been sufficient, a new influenza virus swept Europe, causing much loss of life.

p.36 *Wilksbarre, in America*. Thomas's father had been born in the United States, his father having emigrated there along with many of his compatriots in the late nineteenth century in search of work and a new life. It was part of a pattern of a great deal of Welsh migration from (and subsequent return to) the south Wales valleys.

p.36 *unidentified bodies*. An early hint that Mam did not die in the accident but took the opportunity to vanish and be reborn without responsibility to her large family at home in Wales. It is an interesting twist on the cliché of the 'Welsh mam'.

p.37 *shinto*. Japanese (hence exotic) religion demanding extremes of reverence.

p.37 *that book you wrote way back in the thirties*. See note above about Thomas's youthful novel written in 1937 (note to p.27).

p.40 *Bannerman Club*. See note on clubs (note for p.27). The clubs were a standard rendezvous for the people in Thomas's stories and plays; in his Belmont stories (of which *The Keep* is one) Thomas has his business or professional characters meet at the Bannerman Club, presumably named with reference back to the Liberal Prime Minister of 1905-8, Sir Henry Campbell-Bannerman.

p.40 *Trevethick medal*. Named after Richard Trevethick, (usually spelled Trevithick) the Cornish engineer who invented the steam locomotive, his first practical success being at Merthyr Tydfil in 1804.

p.41 *Caradoc Slee*. A notable example of Thomas's ploys in nomenclature (see also Vulcan Philpott, Milo Ashton, Cadmon Moore in this play, and note to p.29 above).

p.41 *sfumatura effects*. This evidently refers to an effect in choral music, but the word appears to be of Thomas's invention, perhaps on an analogy with 'coloratura' with 'sforzando' in mind.

p.43 *Caerphilly Castle*. A specially notable ruin because of the leaning tower, reputedly exploded from the vertical by Cromwell in an attempt to destroy it completely.

p.44 *Birchtown*. Seems to bear the same relationship to 'Belmont' as Pontypridd does to Porth, i.e. a larger market town some four or five miles away.

p.45 *Ruskin College*. A college for working men and women, founded in 1899. Not actually part of the university of Oxford, it had close links with it and is traditionally the place for working people, particularly concerned with the trade unions.

p.45 *best duet since Il Trovatore*. Thomas's good memories of youth in the valleys included much music, not only male voice choirs and church music but also opera as mounted by local operatic societies; he adored the great Italian operas and played recordings of the most affecting and powerful arias, duets and quartets late into the night. See too his essay 'explaining' some of the characteristics of 'Jackie the Jumper', printed as an appendix in this edition of the plays.

p.46 *Mrs Loomer-Barkway*. The first part of her name as well as Alvin's worries about her power offer a hint about the likely development of the plot which comes from Ben's "I think she fancies our Con."

p.46 *'Jesus wants me for a deflator'*. Ironic twist on the well-known Sunday school hymn, Jesus wants me for a sunbeam'.

p.48 *When next I sing . . . in Moab*. Although the play is not autobiographical, it is interesting to note the number of ways in which Thomas used precise correspondences with his own family: his sisters all had good voices, as his mother had done, and Nan (who brought him up when the mother died) was frustrated in a promising singing career by the need to attend to the wants of her family.

p.50 *Abersychan*. One of the very few genuine place-names Thomas uses. I wonder whether it's because it appeared to him as bizarre as a made-up name, or because the town was in the news as the birthplace of rising political star, Roy Jenkins.

p.50 *nationalization*. The nationalisation of the railway system, turning all the old romantic regional names like the Great Western Railway, the London Midlands and Scotland Railway and so on into one great amorphous thing called British Railways, was still a relatively recent memory when the play was written.

p.51 *Inkerman Place*. Another example of the strangely exotic nomenclature of the valley towns; Thomas may have made this one up, but there probably really is an Inkerman Place there somewhere.

p.51 *Temperance Song*. Thomas's memories of himself as a nine-year-old being a robust singer of temperance songs such as 'Have Courage, My Boy, To Say No' frequently recur in his autobiographical writing; see also the treatment of this theme in *Loud Organs*.

p.53 *Prometheus*. Prometheus in Greek legend brought fire from the gods to man; his punishment was to be chained on Mount Caucasus where an eagle gnawed at his liver which was daily renewed.

p.53 *before he hits the box*, i.e. the coffin.

p.54 *South Africa*. Although the philosophy and practice of *apartheid* were disapproved of, this was in the days before the world had come to its present determination to isolate South Africa until the system is changed.

p.55   *to burst apart out of their own mousetraps.* It was from this phrase that the German translator of the play found a title under which it could be presented for its extremely successful run in Hamburg: *Traüme in der Mausefälle (Dreams in the Mousetrap)*.

p.61   *rickets.* Typically the disease caused by malnutrition among working-class children in Britain in the 1920s and 30s; the bones were pitifully underdeveloped and bent.

p.62   *The County Keep.* The County Gaol, so called by Thomas in many of his stories; it seems to be more a Thomas family idiom than a local usage, but it foregrounds neatly the two almost opposed meanings of 'Keep', place of refuge, defence and safety at the heart of the castle, or place where one is kept willy-nilly, i.e. prison.

p.63   *Town Square and the toilets.* Porth's town square used to have a large and obtrusive block of public conveniences right in the middle of it. (See note to p.30; this is the second reference in the play).

p.64   *lobechtomy.* Apparently a coining by the author on an analogy with appendechtomy (removal of the appendix). Attempts at surgical control of behaviour by lobotomy, seen by the layman as removal of a frontal lobe of the brain, are among those gruesome kinds of science that fascinated Thomas. It was common for him to refer to the brain as 'the lobes' and to invent images having to do with the lobes to account for behavioural peculiarities.

p.64   *burbs.* Perhaps more commonly rendered as 'burp' — a continuation of the flatulence metaphor.

p.64   *I'd sooner be trepanned.* To have one's skull operated on — a reference back to the lobechtomy idea.

p.67   *Mrs Loomer-Barkway gave that house to the County Council.* A similar idea occurs in *The Thinker and the Thrush,* where Wedlake Roper seeks to establish his power and influence by buying Flaxton Hall and giving it to a charity which will run it as a convalescent home for silicotics. The idea, of course, falls through, just as this one does.

p.68   *Trecysgod.* This township occurs in *Gazooka* and *Loud Organs* among other Thomas writings; the name may use the Welsh word cysgod, 'a shade, shadow' and be translated as 'Place of Shadows', though some may detect in it the force of the English words 'cuss God' and see it as a rather more blasphemous invention. Some internal references in the stories where the name appears suggest the actual placec so represented may be Trealaw, a characterless village a little further up the Rhondda Fawr.

p.68   *subsidence.* Thomas's constant theme and metaphor was of subsidence, the feature common to valley life where ground under which mining has taken place may begin a long slow collapse into the space beneath. Thomas's Gwyn Jones Lecture was entitled 'The Subsidence Factor'.

p.71 *'Your mind has been on the chilly side since you went over to the rationalists'*. A feature of life in the Libraries and Institutes which constituted for Thomas one of the most admirable phenomena of working-class communities was the anti-sectarian feeling and socialist philosophical basis of much of the discussion. There would have been a local Rationalist Society, and the members would discuss such works as *The Martyrdom of Man* and The Riddle of the Universe. One of his favourite characters in the stories, Milton Nicholas, was of this ilk, and when the play 'Gazooka' was first broadcast it was Thomas himself who played the part.

p.78 *The Spanish 'flu*. The strain of influenza virus which further devastated the people of Europe in the wake of the 1st World War.

p.79 *The Black Meadow*. The local graveyard is commonly so called in Thomas's work.

p.82 *Williams Pantycelyn*. There are so many Williamses in Welsh history that the important ones are often known by the addition to the surname of the name of their place of birth or work. William Williams was a great Welsh hymn writer and Romantic poet.

p.86 *panel patients*. Before the National Health Service patients would register with a doctor to be 'on his panel' and often part or all of the doctor's fees would be paid by a works scheme to which the patient contributed regularly.

p.89 *a dab like Caradoc Slee*. 'Dab' or 'poor dab' is common in south Welsh; what is odd for Thomas is that he normally spells the word as 'daub', perhaps on an analogy with the mere drop of paint that suggests.

p.94 *Ivor Novello*. The Cardiff-born composer of songs and musicals. Ivor Novello Davies, had recently died after a hugely successful career in the world of entertainment.

p.95 *The Buffs. The Hearts of Oak, the bloody lot*. In his ironic compilation of a guest list for his abortive banquet. Ben names all those of local pelf and influence, including the semi-masonic societies here named (The Buffs being a shortened form of The Buffaloes and having no relationship to the famous military regiment).

## *Jackie the Jumper*

*Setting*. In 1831 the general grievances of a depressed working class flared into a brief rebellion in Merthyr Tydfil. After a clash workers and soldiers fired on each other, with more than twenty deaths. When order was finally regained, a show trial condemned a lad called Dick Lewis (Dic Penderyn) to death, and he became the first martyr of the Welsh working class. (See *Oxford Companion to Welsh Literature*, ed. Meic Stephens, for a fuller account.) In *All Things Betray Thee* (1949), Thomas published an imaginative novel based on these events; *Jackie the Jumper* is a return to a theme which obsessed the author.

p.100 '*Oh what a lovely flavour of hell it has*'. The theme of puritanism *versus* libido is introduced with little delay.

p.101 *Reverend Richie 'Resurrection' Rees*. Thomas's nomenclature is sometimes inspired, as here. The alliterating R's and the force of the appellation 'Resurrection' are superb.

p.101 *John Ironhead Luxton*. On page 120 Thomas makes Luxton meditate on the reverberations of his own name. It is an English name (the figure on whom the character is based was William Crawshay), and the peculiar tension between the implication of 'Ironhead' taken literally and the actual sensitivity and bewilderment of the man resemble the presentation of the character of Richard Penbury in *All Things Betray Thee*. Thomas's sympathy for the apparent villain is marked.

p.101 *cured the deacons of the screws*. 'The screws' is a common expression for 'rheumatics' in the Rhondda Valley; it must have been a powerful sermon that would cure the deacons of rheumatism.

p.102 *Ferncleft* See comments on Thomas's local place-names above (note to p.28); Ferncleft is the location for the events of the novel *Now Lead Us Home*, where it is placed three miles from the sea but seems to be a valley town.

p.103 *Teify*. The Teify flows through Cardigan in west Wales, where Thomas lived and worked as a teacher in 1940-2.

p.103 *tickets in the next whale* i.e. with Jonah, who sought to escape the Lord's instruction to preach in the great wasteland of Nineveh.

p.103 '*Aderyn Pur*'. Famous old Welsh folk song; the title means 'The pure bird'.

p.105 *Venusberg*. In German legend, a magic land of pleasure where Venus reigns; Anthony Powell used it as an ironic title for an early satirical novel and Thomas frequently uses the term (usually with some irony) as shorthand for a life-style given over to pleasure. It appears for instance in *Loud Organs* as a term for the pleasure palace Wffie Morgan is trying to create in his former chapel in Cardiff Docks.

p.105 *Mithraism*. A pagan cult developed in Persia similar in some ways to early Christianity, which it rivalled; but little is known about how the worship of Mithras was practised because it is wrapped in 'the Eleusinian mysteries'; the god was god of the sun, and one element in his worship involved young men and perhaps girls in jumping over charging bulls.

p.105 *Towey*. The river which flows through Carmarthen in west Wales' on its banks was a theological training college.

p.112 *the old truck system*. Workers were controlled under this system by being paid not in money but in tokens only redeemable at the company stores.

p.114 *Birchtown*. Normally taken to be Pontypridd in Thomas's work. As in *All Things Betray Thee*, where Merthyr Tydfil became Moonlea, Thomas avoids placing the events of the play exactly in time and place, seeking greater universality for his art.

p.114 *The mayor read the Riot Act*. This was one of the most provocative actions in the Merthyr riots of 1831.

p.114 *Two of ours are dead*. As mentioned above, the true toll of death and injury was considerably greater than this at Merthyr, but Thomas is writing a fable, not history.

p.132 *You are the wick-snapper extraordinary*. One who snaps the wicks turns down the lights, and metaphorically (like Othello's "Put out the light, and then put out the light") Eirlys perceives that Rees will employ death as a means to an end if necessary.


# Loud Organs

p.167 *Hardie*. Keir Hardie, first Socialist MP.

p.167 *Marx*. Karl Marx, writer of *Capital*, the Socialist's handbook.

p.167 *Nye*. Aneurin (Nye) Bevan, Minister of Health in the Labour Government that constructed the National Health Service, and a key figure in the history of the Labour movement. Thomas was fascinated by him, and wrote two plays based on his perception of the man (see Introduction).

p.167 *Kelly's Eye*. One of the coded calls in Bingo, signifying the number 1.

p.172 *Boxing*. Boxing, from championship levels down to the fairground boxing booth where champions of the future hoped to make a start, was a very important sport to the men (and some of the women) of Thomas's time. In his story 'Hugo My Friend' (in *Selected Short Stories*) there is a very funny account of an unwilling recruit to the fairground ring. The south Wales area produced in its time several boxers whose names still vivify the imagination: Tommy Farr, against whom Gwyn Thomas's brother Walter is said to have squared up once to help settle a political debate; Jimmy Wilde, Jim Driscoll, Howard Winstone, and Johnny Owen, for instance.

p.183 *The Mighty Atom*. The almost absent hero of this play. The Mighty Atom, takes his sobriquet from the featherweight, Jimmy Wilde, with whom he is compared (see note to p.172).

p.205 *caudrilla*. Spanish term connected with bull-fighting; it refers to the phalanx of four attendants who introduce the Toreador.

235

p.205 *Dr Edith Summerskill*. A member of the Labour Government of the time (Minister of Education); a very devoted opponent of boxing as a sport.

p.205 *Gandhi*. The renowned pacifist rebel who attained virtual sainthood; Dr Summerskill is placed in good company.

p.205 *Benjamin Franklyn*. American statesman, inventor, writer, controversialist and epitome of home-made goodness.

p.207 *slouches of the trustees*. The slouch hat was the nearest thing one saw in Britain to the type of hat traditionally worn by American gangsters; Thomas often wore one himself, seeing himself in his mind's eye ironically as a Chicago mobster.

p.209 *since Calvin began planting ice-cubes*. John Calvin was the puritanical French reformer whose tenets had an enormous influence on the development of Protestantism; a fundamentalist, he treated lapses with exemplary strictness. Thomas's image of the man planting ice-cubes to damage the possibilities of joy in human life is typical.

p.209 *band of harem-girls from Trecysgod*. Readers wishing to know more about these harem-girls should read 'Gazooka' and *A Few Selected Exits*, where Thomas's magical memories of the strike-torn summer of 1926 find their best expression.

p.211 *the ghost of Evan Roberts the Revivalist*. A final reference (in this book) to the celebrated preacher who came out of the west in the great revival of 1904 and made the hearts of his congregation — especially the women — burn with sexual as well as religious enthusiasm. The theme is memorably developed in a short story, 'Revivalism and the Falling Larks', in *A Welsh Eye*.

## *Appendix*

p.219 Gwyn Thomas, 'Introduction' to *The Keep*.

p.224 Gwyn Thomas, 'After the Chip-Shop', introduction to *Jackie the Jumper* in *Plays of the Year 26*, pp.213-216.